"One of the most historic cottages in the heart of Glen Lochay - - - (and) a labour of love to delve into the lives of those who lived there from the present day all the way back to the Stone Age."
The Oban Times

"A very well-written account of Scottish history that takes a wonderfully unique angle - - - with a conversational style and personal touch, charming, and full of Scottish humour."
CreateSpace

"Sheds light on centuries of Scottish life."
The Stirling Observer

"A jolly mix of imagination and historical fact. - - - I enjoyed the swashbuckling style."
Professor Christopher Smout CBE
Emeritus Professor of Scottish History, St Andrews University

"A delightful mixture of reminiscence, history and humour."
Royal College of Physicians & Surgeons

"I have just finished reading this wonderful book. I loved the fact, the "fiction", the humour and most of all the style in which it is written. I know for certain that I will place it on the shelf for a while and then pick it up and read it all over again."
Killin Heritage Society

D0271147

About the author

Professor Waddell is a Scot, born and bred, who lives in Glasgow.

He had a long and distinguished career as an orthopaedic surgeon, medical scientist and world authority on low back pain. His textbook *The Back Pain Revolution* is a classic. He also co-authored a series of educational booklets for patients, the most successful of which, *The Back Book,* has been translated into 25 languages with two million copies printed worldwide.

Since he retired, he has turned his research and writing skills to the story of his Perthshire cottage. And had a lot of fun.

HIGHLAND ROOTS

The real story behind one Highland cottage

GORDON WADDELL

Dalgirdy Publishing

Dalgirdy Publishing
Published in the UK in 2013 by Dalgirdy Publishing
Glen Lochay, Killin, Perthshire, FK21 8UA

First published in the USA in 2013 by CreateSpace and KDP
on Amazon and Kindle

Gordon Waddell asserts the moral right to
be identified as the author of this work.

Cover painting: Glen Lochay
Copyright © 2013 Sandra Waddell

A CIP catalogue record for this book
is available from the British Library.

ISBN: 978-0-9576839-0-7

Printed and bound by Bell & Bain Ltd, Glasgow

For my grandchildren
Heather, Niamh, Ewan, Marco, Lucia and Anna

CONTENTS

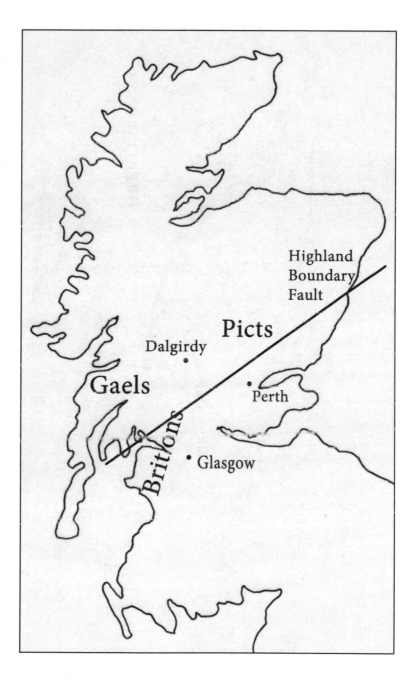

Highland
Boundary
Fault

Picts

Dalgirdy

Gaels

Perth

Britons

Glasgow

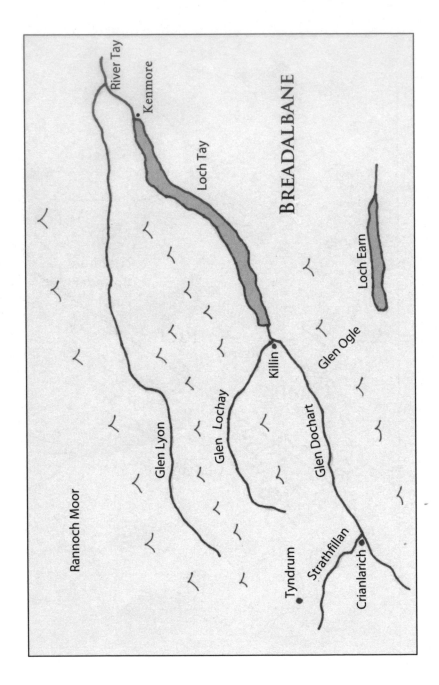

BREADALBANE

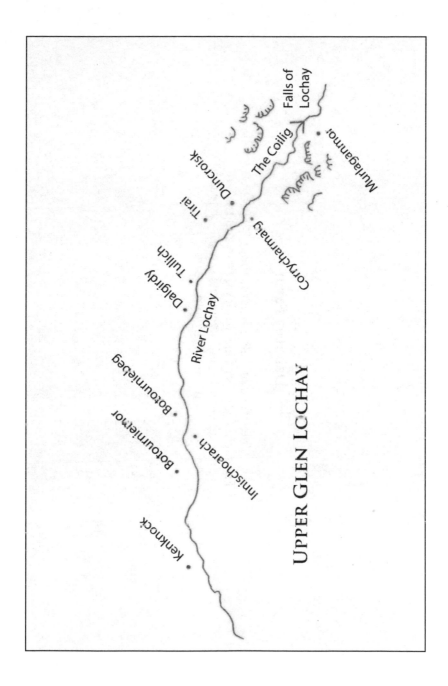

Upper Glen Lochay

Falls of Lochay
The Coilig
Muilagannmor
Duncroisk
Tiral
Corrycharmaig
Tullich
Dalgirdy
River Lochay
Botouniebeg
Innischoarach
Botouniemor
Kenknock

Dalgirdy Farm

The infield of Dalgirdy farm about 1780.
The main features of the medieval farm and the late
eighteenth century Improvements can still be made
out on the ground today.

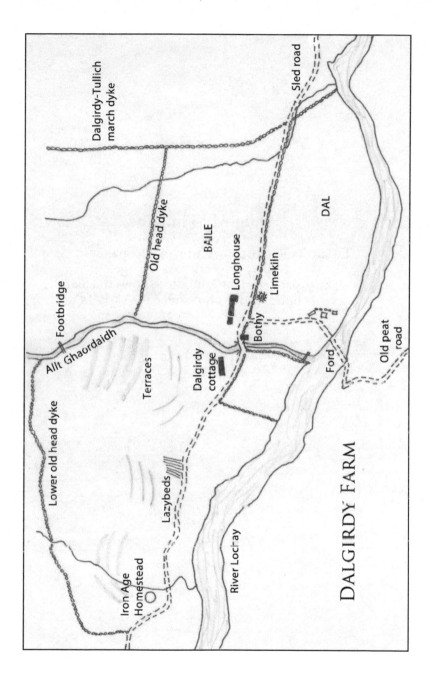

DALGIRDY FARM

Sled road

Dalgirdy-Tullich march dyke

Old head dyke

Footbridge

Allt Ghaordaidh

Terraces

Lower old head dyke

Lazybeds

Iron Age Homestead

River Lochay

DAL

BAILE

Longhouse

Limekiln

Bothy

Dalgirdy cottage

Ford

Old peat road

Dalgirdy Timeline

The left-hand line shows human occupancy of Glen
Lochay since the last Ice Age.
The expanded right-hand line shows the main
events in Dalgirdy's story since the early 1450s.

2000AD			
		1982	Holiday home
1350AD	Great Plague		
1314AD	Wars of Independence	1960	Hydro Scheme
c700AD	Christianity	1933	Last inhabitants Dalgirdy
82-3AD	First Roman invasion		
+/ 250	Iron Age Homestead Dalgirdy	1888	Longhouse fell vacant
		1870s	Bridge bothy fell vacant
		1825	Dalgirdy incorporated into Tullich Farm
		1780s	Dalgirdy cottage built
	Cup & ring	1776-97	McVeans. Improvement
2500BC	marks Duncroisk		
		c1743	1st school Glen Lochay
2900BC	Stone axe factory Craig na Caillich	1732	Sled road Glen Lochay
		1707	Union of Parliaments
4000BC	Neolithic long cairn Kenknock	1681	1st Earl of Breadalbane
		1644	Raid of Montrose
		1638	Covenanters Roll
		1610-20	1st school Killin
5500BC	Hunter gatherers Ben Lawers		
		1560	Reformation
		1540-50	Start of detailed records of Dalgirdy
		1513	Battle of Flodden
	End of last	1476	1st record of Dalgirdy
8300BC	Ice Age	1450s	Lairds of Glenorchy

PROLOGUE

Killin glistened in the summer sun, far below, as we came round the shoulder of Meall nan Tarmachan on the new Hydro road.

The village nestled beneath the hills at the head of Loch Tay, strung out from the Falls of Dochart to the Bridge of Lochay. It was a typical Highland village of its time. Solid stone houses and slate roofs blended into the landscape. The last thatched cottages had not long gone. It had three church buildings to keep the religious sects apart. There was a school, a doctor, shops to meet everyday needs, an old-fashioned smithy and a new-fangled garage. A market with pens for cattle and sheep lay next to the railhead of the short branch line from the Callander to Oban railway. Hotels waited hopefully for the day-trippers who came by the trainload from Glasgow. And after they left, the village settled down to the quiet of the night when, if you were lucky, you might see the aurora borealis.

We had spent a week hiking from Killiekrankie, camping on the way. By Loch Tummel and Schiehallion and Glen Lyon we had come, by hill tracks through the pass beneath Ben Lawers. Young and fit and striding forth.

Killin was journey's end.

But Killin was also a beginning, for my love was waiting for me in Killin. These were the days when students could get summer work and earn spending money for the year ahead and Sandra had a job in one of the local hotels. We have fond memories of Killin that summer, where we did our courting and our romance blossomed.

Fifty years ago, when Meall nan Tarmachan really was the hill of the ptarmigan before hordes of hillwalkers chased them all away. Just after the Hydro Electric scheme, Scotland's first large-scale renewable energy, had raped the land and the scars were fresh. A lifetime ago and it seems like yesterday, when the world and we were young and fresh from a passing summer shower. And Killin was lodged forever in our hearts.

It snowed at Easter 1963.

I remember it well, because we tried to take a party of Scouts hillwalking. We had it all planned – routes, campsites, menu, supplies, the lot. But when we tumbled out of the train in Killin that Friday evening it all fell apart. The best-laid plans of mice and men are always the first casualties of contact with the enemy. The ground was covered in six inches of wet slush and the snow fell thick, unexpected, not in the forecast!

A quick rethink and we set off up Glen Lochay to look for some kind of shelter. We trudged five miles up the glen and the snow got deeper while we got wetter and colder. The night was black and full of gloom and the glen seemed empty of human habitation. Late at night, just as we were giving up hope, we came to the faint lights of a farm in the trees above the road. We knocked on the door like lost souls in the storm and, to our relief, the farmer took pity on us.

We spent the night in his barn and it seemed like a palace. Mr Macaskill gave us a lamp and spread out bales of hay and straw. We hung our wet clothes round the walls. Mrs Macaskill made large farmhouse pots of tea to warm the chill from our bones and we cooked sausages and beans on our stoves. We warmed up in our sleeping bags, while the wind howled outside like a dervish frustrated at losing its prey. Soon only our snores rivalled the gale outside.

If you have never slept in a barn you probably do not realize just how *alive* it is. Soon after midnight the farm dogs remembered we were there and decided to show us how well they could bark. At four o'clock in the morning, still pitch dark, the peace was shattered by an early-rising cockerel that could not tell the time. Some poor sleepless soul counted 116 cockcrows before morning. A sheep in the pen next door spent the night pulling our hay through the wall and munching it in a most unmannerly way. And hay contains a remarkable number of bugs and beetles of every kind. It is testament to youthful slumber that most of us had a good night's sleep.

Next morning the wind still blew and the snow was turning to sleet. We were not equipped to camp in such conditions, so Mr Macaskill suggested we might use a nearby cottage and kindly drove down to Killin in his Land Rover to get the key from the Factor. We only had to tramp a quarter of a mile up the glen but that was enough to convince us of the wisdom of his advice.

The cottage was tiny and old and deserted, sitting all alone and forlorn on the hillside. The walls were three feet thick. The roof was thatched, built on tree trunks and covered in corrugated iron. The ceiling was simply boards across the rafters, with a space about three feet high below the thatch. But it was dry and snug and you could not even hear the wind outside.

There were two small rooms. One had an open fireplace and Mr Macaskill brought kindling and coal and soon had a fire blazing merrily. We cleared and swept out the rooms, but the 'loft' had an inch of dirt from the thatch so three boys had to strip to their underwear and wear hankies over their faces to brush it out. Then they had to wash in the freezing burn beside the cottage. Others went out in the rain to get water from the burn and gather fallen wood for the fire. We had a great day settling in, cooking and eating, and talking late around the fire. Twenty-three of us slept like sardines in the cottage that night but it seemed the height of luxury.

Monday morning we had to leave and walk down to Killin to get the train home. We were warm and dry and rested, even if not very clean. The sun shone and Glen Lochay seemed a different place. Gone was the cold and wet and misery of Friday night. Now it was a bright and cheerful place with snow-capped peaks against a deep blue sky and spring bursting out in all its splendour.

That was the first time I saw Dalgirdy and I never guessed what an important part it would play in my life.

Twenty years passed while I completed my training and we

settled back in Glasgow. We had to live in the city for my job but yearned for an escape to the country. To get it both ways, the answer was to keep the town house with all the advantages of city life and also get a small holiday home in the country.

We drew a circle of two hours' drive from home. Anything further would be too far to travel for a short weekend. Because we lived on the north side of Glasgow, it had always been easier to go north. We did not rule out the south but it had less appeal. There were some beautiful spots down the Clyde where we might also have had a small boat, but we had never sailed and there was less access to the mountains we loved. Worse, these places relied on ferries. Winter timetables, bad weather or missing the last ferry on a Sunday evening could be problems.

We spent several months exploring, up country tracks and into hidden corners. We found plenty of possibilities. There were many houses on the market but we could not afford them, and most were in villages rather than true 'country life'. There were empty buildings in various states of decay scattered across the countryside but they were not for sale. Most landowners were very protective. Some day, perhaps, someone in the family might find a use for that one. And anyway, they really did not want strangers on their estates.

Eventually, one day, we came to Dalgirdy. We had not planned it but perhaps subconsciously this was what we had been looking for all along. It was ideal. It was about one-and-a-half hours' drive with a good road right to the door. It was out in the country but only five miles from the village. Glen Lochay was a dead end so there was no through traffic and the road was quiet. The situation was magnificent. The cottage was perched on the open hillside with a burn down its side, the River Lochay and its wooded slopes in front, and surrounded by a panorama of hills. It was solidly built on a rise, well drained, and bone-dry. It was, just, large enough for a family but small enough to make renovation a practical proposition.

Best of all, we were not strangers. The landowner knew who we were and we had previous dealings with him, so negotiations were surprisingly quick and easy. There was still the natural hesitation about any outsider gaining a foothold on the estate, so they would not sell, at least not now. But we soon agreed a twenty-one year lease at a peppercorn rent – £1 a year. The condition was that we would be responsible for any repairs and renovation.

Dalgirdy was ours! But we did not know what we had let ourselves in for.

Lazing in front of the cottage on a summer evening with a glass of wine. It is early June, the sun is high, the evenings long and the midges have not started biting yet. Warm, relaxed and peaceful. Watching the hills go by. What a wonderful time and place to be alive.

But it was not always like this. What was it like to live in Dalgirdy before it was renovated? Go further back. Can you imagine scraping a living from this land before the agricultural 'Improvements' of the eighteenth century? How did people live and raise a family here before there were any roads or schools or health care? When Picts clashed with Gaels? Or when the Romans came?

What was history really like for the ordinary people who had to live through it?

And what would they think of our lives now? What would they make of driving up from Glasgow on a Friday evening after work? Of heat and light at the flick of a switch, water from a tap, an inside toilet, staying in touch by iPhone? Never mind the variety of food from the supermarket or a glass of wine from Spain or California or Australia.

It makes you wonder - - -

1. DALGIRDY

The meadow at the foot of the noisy burn

Today, Dalgirdy is a cottage, but it was once much more.

Old buildings are like human fossils. Even their empty shells can tell us a lot about the people who lived there. But they were not built one day and fossilized the next, so they do not tell us about a single point in time. Old buildings have a history of their own. Over the years, in fits and starts, people repair and improve, adapt and enlarge them to suit changing needs. Old buildings are shifting anchors on the sands of time.

Dalgirdy today has all that you expect of a modern house. It is clean and dry, warm and bright, with light flooding in from windows in the back roof. It has hot and cold running water, a modern kitchen, a toilet and a shower. All it lacks is television and the Internet, and that is by choice. But even now, it is not quite what it was when we re-built it thirty years ago. We have had to re-design the roof windows to deal with leaks. We have replaced the old fireplace with a wood-burning stove, which is more efficient, uses less fuel and gives more heat. It also sends the smoke up the chimney instead of into the room, which keeps the place cleaner and means less painting. At first we had gas for cooking, hot water and lighting, but now we have the electricity. We left the old gas pipes in the walls and some day a future builder will find them and wonder what they were. We have upgraded the kitchen and bathroom. So even in thirty years the building has changed, like a living organism.

And thirty years is but a blink in the eye of time.

When you come up the glen and over the bridge and see the cottage, you know immediately that it is **old**. It is low and squat, deep-rooted in the hillside. The walls are thick and uneven because they are built of rough uncut stone lifted from the land. The front of the building rests on an outcrop of rock that appears in the corner of the room inside. There is a narrow front door flanked by two small, old-fashioned windows. There is a shed on each end and a woodpile at the back, because country life is a working life. The chimney is smoking and the reek of wood and peat smoke greets you as you approach. Once smelt, never forgotten. There are sheep grazing on the grass around and a collie lies on the doorstep, head resting on her paws, keeping a watchful eye on them. The cottage feels part of the landscape in a way no modern building ever can. There are hints of 'back to Nature' and The Good Life. It is classic *grannie's Hielan hame,* straight out of a film set.

The cottage was built about 1780, which makes it a rare example of the transition period in Highland rural housing. The only other house like this in the glen is Moirlanich longhouse and that is now a National Trust for Scotland museum. Before that, ordinary people built their own crude shacks from the materials to hand, but these are now all gone and only ruins remain. Into the nineteenth century, professional builders built neat houses of cut stone with slate roofs and many of these country cottages are still lived in today.

In 1780 this was a good, modern building for a prosperous tenant farmer. But it soon slid down the social scale as building standards and expectations rose. By 1825 the farmer was in the large, two-storied farmhouse down the road where his successor still lives today. Dalgirdy then became a house for farm labourers, shepherds and estate workers. The last family lived there from the 1870s to 1922 and brought up six children in two rooms. After that, shepherds came and went on short-term contracts. By 1933 the cottage was vacant and it was never a permanent home again.

But Dalgirdy is much older than the present cottage.

On the other side of the burn are the ruins of four small, crude houses from the eighteenth century. Only crumbling dry-stone walls remain, two to six feet high. One is now incorporated into a sheepfold. Old maps and the Census show one inhabited until the 1870s and another until 1888.

When you look more carefully, you find other traces of human activity. There are faint outlines of smaller, older buildings, though it is difficult to tell if these were houses. There are small enclosures. There are remains of ancient tracks, footbridges across the burn, and a ford across the river.

Dalgirdy was a *baile,* what in other parts of Scotland would be called a clachan or fermtoun. At one time there were probably half-a-dozen houses and twenty to thirty people lived here. A *baile* was a Highland township where a small farming community lived and worked the land.

If you climb up the opposite hillside you get an eagle's eye view of Dalgirdy. The cottage is a tiny white dot at the foot of the mountain. There is a small field in front, enclosed by a drystone dyke. There is a larger field of rich fertile ground on the other side of the burn, below the old *baile.* Beyond that a march-dyke runs three-quarters of a mile up the hillside, with another march-dyke about half a mile further up the glen. These are old farm boundaries, marking out a section of the lower slopes of the hill. Within that area on the hillside above the cottage are faint traces of medieval farming.

Dalgirdy was a farm.

The first written record of Dalgirdy is in the Exchequer Roll of 1476, which was an account of rent and other income from lands belonging to the Crown.[1] The Register of the Privy Seal of Scotland in 1541 gives more detail.

The yearly malis of our soverane ladies landis within the bounds of Bradalbyn callit Dessour and Thoissour set in tak.

Dalgarde   iii merkland. [2]

Our sovereign lady was Mary Queen of Scots. Dalgirdy was Crown land, in Breadalbane, in the district called Discher and Toyer. Dalgirdy was first in the list for its area!

So what does the name Dalgirdy mean?

There is Dalgirdy and Allt Ghaordaidh and Meall Ghaordie – the farm, the burn and the mountain. Say them aloud and you can see that they are all attempts to reproduce a similar sound. (The final ---*dh* is silent in Gaelic, as in *ceilidh*.) The original names were Gaelic, which is rich in landscape, farming and shieling words.[3] The problem is that Gaelic was a spoken rather than a written language, and there are no Gaelic records in this area. The names were first written down by English speakers and when they tried to Anglicize the Gaelic sounds, they all made up their own spelling. Over five centuries and with varying degrees of literacy, it got worse.

Ancient Celts often named rivers and water first because these were sites of pagan worship.[4] So *Allt Ghaordaidh* may come from *gaoir* or noise and means 'the noisy burn'. That makes sense, because the burn is noisy for its size, and can either keep you awake or lull you to sleep in the cottage. It is noisy not only in spate but even in summer when it tinkles down between the stones, perhaps because the ravine above the bridge acts as a funnel to amplify the sound.

The mountain and the farm were then named after the burn. Meall Ghaordie is 'the hill of the noisy burn'. The Gaelic *dail* means a piece of flat ground or meadow. Later it meant a field and the twelve-acre field below the road on the other side of the burn is still called the Dal. So Dalgirdy is 'the meadow or field at the foot of the noisy burn'.

We found sixteen spellings of Dalgirdy. Six were common.

Dalgardy or *Dalgardie* was the earliest spelling from 1476 to the mid-seventeenth century.

Dalgirdie first appeared in the late seventeenth century.

Dalgirdy has been the most common spelling since the mid-eighteenth century and is the standard form today.

In the mid- to late eighteenth century the Old Parish Records spelled it *Dalgardey* while in the Kirk Session Records it was *Dalegirdy*.

Some versions only occur once and some of these may be spelling errors. But some you would never guess: *Gildardie, Galgardie, Dallgairdu* and *Dalgourdea*.

Spelling is just one of the problems with old records. They were all hand-written and it is difficult to decipher pre-1650 'secretary hand' or just plain bad writing. And the key record may be missing, because many have been destroyed or lost or damaged in five hundred years. It all adds to the mystery!

Dalgirdy is in Glen Lochay, one of the most beautiful glens in the southern Highlands. The Minister of Kenmore picked it out in 1791 as *a beautiful and sequestered vale*.[5] The glen is about ten miles long and Dalgirdy lies in the upper glen, five miles from Killin.

Lochay is one of the few place names in the area from the old Pictish tongue, and means the river and the glen of the Black Goddess. She was a popular goddess and there are at least ten other rivers, lochs and glens of Lochy across the Highlands. Our River Lochay is a fitting site for a Black Goddess. Parts are dark and gloomy, with lurking corners to make you stop and ponder. There are small dark pools hidden in a ravine and huge dark pools in the lower glen. Yet elsewhere the river dances brightly over rocks in the sunshine.

Once again, the origins of the name are in the pagan worship of water in ancient Celtic society. Many precious archaeological finds have come from water, where they were perhaps gifts or sacrifices to the gods. Water is essential for life and there were old beliefs that people came from the seas. Before you laugh, think of how people came to Scotland and the theory of evolution. Mythical creatures also lived in water – water-horses, sprites and the beast that met St Columba in the River Ness. Again, it is not so long since people believed in mermaids and some still wonder about the Loch Ness Monster. The Christian Church adopted many of these pagan sites and turned them into holy wells.

Or perhaps it fits better with modern ideas of ecology if the Black Goddess was not a spirit who lived in the river but the living river itself.

The glen is in two halves, separated by a narrow pass where the river cuts its way through a ravine and drops over the Falls of Lochay into a different world. This is the *Coilig* - 'the wooded place' - where the road still winds carefully through the trees

18

between the river and the rock.

Lower Glen Lochay is flat and fertile, and the river *broad, stately and silent* as it winds its way down to Loch Tay. Dorothy Wordsworth and her brother, the poet William Wordsworth, spent a night in the Killin Hotel during their tour of Scotland in 1803. Next morning they went for a stroll up Glen Lochay. Even then, *that river - - - is bordered with tall trees and cornfields, bearing plentiful crops, the richest we had seen in Scotland. - - - The glen appeared to be short; indeed, we wondered how the river had grown so great all at once.*[6] They clearly did not get beyond the Coilig, like many tourists today. Everything in the lower glen lies within two miles of Killin and under its influence.

Upper Glen Lochay lies above the Coilig. It is eight miles long and the bottom of the glen is no more than quarter-of-a-mile wide. At one point on Dalgirdy it narrows to less than one hundred yards.

As late as the 1950s, locals felt that the upper glen still *lived in a world of its own* and the estate did not know all that went on there. It must have been really isolated before the first road in 1732. Maps still show it as a dead-end and only the more adventurous tourists and hillwalkers find it.

Breadalbane comes from the Gaelic *Bràghaid Albuinn* and means 'The Upland of Alba'. Alba was the old name for Scotland. The Gaels in Dal Riata on the west coast called the mountain range that separated them from the Picts in the east *Druim-alban* or 'the backbone of Alba'. Breadalbane is the mountainous country to the east of that divide and the name first appeared in the Irish chronicles about the end of the fourth century.

Breadalbane is a popular term but it was never an official province or district so it does not have fixed boundaries. The term is generally used for the district around Loch Tay and its headwaters. *Breadalbane may, therefore, be taken as that incomparably beautiful region in the very heart of Scotland, extending from the junction of the river Lyon with the Tay to the watershed west of Tyndrum. It includes the whole basin of the upper Tay with the noble loch, as well as the two great streams that feed it, the gentle Lochay and the wild, turbulent Dochart.*[7]

Breadalbane is famous in song and legend. It is landscape on a dramatic scale. Mountains, woods, lochs and rivers provide a majestic backdrop for history, folklore and leisure. Culturally, it is still Highland Perthshire. Sir Walter Scott described it as *a favoured region where Beauty lies in the lap of Terror. - - - The rivers find their way out of the mountainous region by the wildest leaps, and through the most romantic passes. Above, the vegetation of a happier clime and soil is mingled with the magnificent characteristics of mountain scenery. The woods, groves and thickets in profusion clothe the base of the hills, ascend up the ravines, and mingle with the precipices.*[8]

Fortunately for this story, Dalgirdy lies on the Breadalbane Estate. At one time this was one of the largest land-holdings in Britain, stretching a hundred miles from east to west. For more than five hundred years, from 1432 to 1948, it was in the hands of one family – the Campbell Lairds of Glen Orchy who later became the Earls of Breadalbane. They kept some of the best estate records in Scotland, which are now in the National Archives of Scotland.[9] There are tens of thousands of original documents, freely available for public access. This history of Dalgirdy would not have been possible without them.

The Lordship of Discher and Toyer dates from the time of King David II (1329-1371). It was part of the land around Loch Tay and in Glen Lochay. Discher was 'The South-facing Slope' and Toyer 'The North-facing Slope'. The south-facing slope got more sun and so was the better ground for farming. Dalgirdy, as you might expect, is on the south-facing slope.

So, what stories can Dalgirdy tell?

2. THE LAND

For these are my mountains
This is my glen

The people and the history of the Highlands have been shaped by geography, landscape and weather.

Titanic forces forged this land to withstand the puny efforts of man to tame it. In the abyss of time, four hundred million years ago, great masses of land came together to form Scotland. One of the joins is the Highland Boundary Fault, which runs from Helensburgh on the Clyde up to Stonehaven just south of Aberdeen. It marks a division between very different kinds of landscape, clearly visible on a satellite image from space. Southeast lie the Lowlands. Northwest are the Highlands. The forces of collision folded the Earth's crust to form the Caledonian mountains, higher than the Himalaya before erosion wore them down. Then the roots were thrust up again. They are still being worn down, ever so slowly, year-by-year. In our day, the summits are between three and four thousand feet above sea level.

Glen Lochay lies just west of the Highland Boundary Fault. Dalgirdy is only twenty miles as the crow flies from the Lowlands but this is truly a different land.

Most of the rock in Glen Lochay is mica-schist, formed by high temperature and pressure deep within the Earth's crust. It is a hard rock that does not split clean or work well, so it is not very good for building.

Scotland tilts down to the east so the watershed lies closer to the west coast. To the west, the rivers are short and steep as they rush down to the Atlantic. To the east, rivers are longer and larger as they flow to the North Sea with its fertile plains.

The River Tay stretches from Drum Alban to the North Sea and is the largest river in the UK, with an average flow throughout the year of 160 million litres/second. That is enough to fill 64 Olympic swimming pools every second. In flood it can be fifteen times greater. The Dochart and the Lochay are the headwaters of the Tay and flow together into the west end of Loch Tay at Killin. The River Tay flows out of the east end of the loch at Kenmore and down past Perth to the sea. The River Lochay is only 13 miles long but it has 250 miles of tributary burns. Coming from such an unspoilt glen, water quality in the Lochay is 80% excellent and 20% good.

Scotland was under ice for millions of years, with five or six major periods of glaciation over the past 750,000 years. Ice is the most powerful force of erosion in Nature and a single valley glacier can rip up and crush millions of tons of bedrock every year. The Highland landform of today is mainly the result of the last Ice Age from 116,000 – 15,000 years ago.

During each Ice Age, most of Scotland was covered in a sheet of ice. At times this was thick enough to bury the mountains and at other times it left the peaks exposed. Glaciers stripped the land bare, deepened the glens, and gouged out the hollows that now hold lochs. Glaciated valleys like Glen Lochay have a typical U-shape and eroded sides with polished bedrock and boulders. Frost shattered any rock exposed on the peaks above the ice to produce boulder fields. Shiehallion is the best local example but there is a small area on the summit of Meall Ghaordie.

The climate warmed up after 11,500 BC and by 11,000 BC Scotland was ice-free.

However, it then got colder again, with another brief period of glaciation about 8800 – 8300 BC. The temperature fell to 7-10°C in July and minus 20-25°C in January. Precipitation, mainly as snow, was one hundred inches per annum at the west coast but less than ten in the northeast. This produced an ice dome to the north of Loch Lomond, with its centre over Rannoch More. Glaciers from the ice dome flowed down the glens that fan south from Rannoch Moor. The ice in Glen Lochay was half a mile thick with the peaks sticking out like Greenland today. Yet at the same time there was arid tundra over the Cairngorms to the northeast.

When the ice retreated, the sea level was at first much lower than today. Most of the North Sea area was dry and formed a land bridge to Europe. Then, as the world heated up, more ice melted, sea levels rose, and the North Sea reached inland as far as Aberfoyle. Scotland was nearly cut in two. Later, the sea fell again but the area from Aberfoyle to Stirling was left as low lying marshland. This was Flanders Moss, from two Scots words for a 'quaking bog'. It was dotted with stagnant pools, and any slightly higher ground studded with birch and willow. Rivers meandered about and were difficult to navigate. Flanders Moss was not completely impassable, for excavations show prehistoric tracks made of cut logs and it was a rich source of fish and wildfowl for the people living on the edges of the Moss. But it was a major natural barrier to any invader. The best route into Scotland was up the eastern plains and the crossing of the River Forth at Stirling became a critical choke point.

Geology and weather determine the nature and condition of the soil. Glaciers leave behind a coarse soil of stones and boulders mixed with silt, sand and clay. The Scots word for this is *till*.[10] When the ice melted, it deposited *till* in the glens and often heaped it into ridges or mounds called moraines. Where rivers slowed in the lower glens, they deposited finer material like the large fan of fertile sediment where the Lochay and the Dochart enter Loch Tay.

Over time, weathering, plants and farming modified the *till* to produce the soil we have today. But 80% of the soil in Glen Lochay is still made up of broken down schist with less than 10% organic material or humus. Even at its best, it is poor and infertile soil.

Higher up the hillsides, on less steep areas, lower temperatures and higher rainfall produce cold, waterlogged ground. In some areas this is 'gley' which you can spot by the mottled grey or blue-green colour caused by its iron and chemical content. Early agricultural improvers knew all about gley. *Wherever the stones and rocks are granite, if the soil be wet, which happens in most cases on the face of hills that are not very abrupt, there is a pale coloured till which is more barren and more difficult to drain - -. Of all soils this is the most unfriendly, the most reluctant to reward the labours of the husbandman, and its natural fertility the worst to overcome - -.* [11]

Other gentler slopes up to two thousand feet carry a layer of peat. Peat is partly broken down plant material that forms in waterlogged conditions with a lack of oxygen. Most of it comes from sphagnum moss. It is a dark brown, acid soil. It is 90% water, which when wet is like firm mud but when it dries out it sets like a brick. Peat can form up to three feet thick in a thousand years.

Peat was the main fuel in the Highlands for most of the past four thousand years, from the clearing of the forests until coal became available in the nineteenth century. The dry carbon content of peat is 50-60% and its calorific value is quite high. However, it is not the best of fuels. Peat does not burn well on its own in an open fire but smoulders and gives off clouds of smoke. Mixed with wood in a modern stove, it burns quickly and leaves a lot of ash.

Plant growth is poor in gley and peat, unless you drain the soil and neutralize the acid with lime.

After the ice retreated, the ground was bare and rocky. The subsoil was frozen all year round and the growing season short. The only plants able to survive in these conditions were mosses, lichens and low-growing shrubs like crowberry. This was tundra and the closest we have in Scotland today is the Cairngorm plateau.

Arctic animals like reindeer, wolf, lemming and arctic foxes came first because only they could survive on the tundra.

Slowly, very slowly, humus built up to improve the soil and the first peat began to appear by 7600 BC. About the same time, as the climate got warmer and the soil improved, trees began to appear. The first were hardy shrubs like dwarf willow and juniper, then birch and hazel. Alder, oak and Scots pine came later.

As the climate here improved, the arctic animals moved north. By the time birch and hazel appeared, we had red deer and giant deer. But it was only with mixed woodland that we got the full range of woodland creatures. There were wild horses, aurochs, wild boar, beaver, roe and fallow deer, and brown bear. And hunters followed close behind: wolf, lynx, wildcat – and man.

The Caledonian Forest reached its peak around 4-5000 BC and there is a small remnant down in Glen Falloch. But it was not all Scots pine, like we sometimes imagine. Rather, it was a mosaic of some dense and some more open woodland, with areas of moorland and bog. There were pinewoods, birch woods, alder and willow swamps, and oak woods. But most of it was mixed. In 2500 BC trees grew at an altitude of more than two thousand feet on Creag na Caillich above Killin, and pollen studies show this was mainly hazel woodland with some rowan and birch.

The forest began to decrease from about 2500 BC. This was mainly due to colder, wetter weather, and you can still see tree stumps preserved under the peat. The tree line fell, bog and peat increased, and in wetter areas pine gave way to broad-leaved trees. But humans also accelerated the process. The first farmers burned forest to clear space for grassland where their animals could graze. These animals then killed any seedlings and stopped the forest re-generating. We felled more trees for timber and for fuel. By the time the Romans arrived, perhaps half the Caledonian Forest had gone.

By the early nineteenth century, woodland was at an all-time low. Large-scale sheep farming, increasing deer numbers on sporting estates, and muirburn on grouse moors stripped many areas of trees. Today the closest we have to native forest is in special protected areas or on crags and gorges where sheep and deer cannot reach. At last we realize what we have lost and we are trying to restore native woodland. The National Trust for Scotland enclosure on Ben Lawers is a good example, though it will be many years before it matures.

Today Glen Lochay has no arable land, 19% grassland and

only 1% improved pasture. The rest is 5% forestry and woodland, 55% heather moor and montane vegetation, and 17% bog land.[12] There are no crops apart from hay. Yet it does have more native broad-leaved woodland than most Highland glens, along the banks of the burns and scattered across the bottom of the glen. Half is birch and rowan, with one-third alder, and a scattering of oak and hazel. What little commercial forest there was in the upper glen has now been felled.

The trees end two miles up the glen from Dalgirdy, limited by altitude and rainfall. Fortunately, Dalgirdy is in the more attractive wooded part of the glen. However, the new landowner at the top of the glen has just got a grant to plant 600,000 saplings and re-establish native woodland. Time will tell how well these grow.

Weather is a constant topic of conversation in Scotland. Even the Romans spoke of the Scottish weather. *The sky in this country is deformed by clouds and frequent rains; but the cold is never extremely rigorous. - - - The soil, though improper for the olive, the vine, and other productions of warmer climates, is fertile and suitable for corn. Growth is quick, but maturation slow; both from the same cause, the great humidity of the ground and the atmosphere.*[13] That was the Lowlands, on a summer campaign!

Because we are close to the Atlantic, the Highlands have a maritime climate. The prevailing winds come from the west and funnel down Glen Lochay. Warmer air comes off the Atlantic laden with moisture. Swirling areas of low-pressure form depressions, hundreds of miles across, that all too often track across Scotland. Within a depression, the boundaries between warm and cold masses of air create 'fronts' that mark a change in the weather. These fronts are where we get bands of clouds and precipitation. In plain English, that means water falling from the sky. It comes as mist or fog, rain or drizzle, sleet, snow or hail, and in Scotland we get them all, sometimes in a single day!

If you live in the country you learn to keep one eye on the

sky and to recognize the cloud formations that tell what is coming your way. There are many sayings about the weather, often with a good meteorological basis. *Red sky at night is the shepherd's delight. Red sky at morning the shepherd's warning.* If the setting sun in the west lights up the trailing edge of the clouds that means the depression is passing. If the rising sun in the east lights the leading edge then the worst is yet to come. All too often, however, the clouds and drizzle just keep on coming. The Scots word is *dreich* – dismal, damp and dreary. There is no English equivalent!

The Gulf Stream brings warm water up the Atlantic and helps keep Scotland warm. Scotland is at the same level as Hudson Bay in northern Canada and without the Atlantic and the Gulf Stream its climate would be sub-arctic.

But mountains alter the weather passing over them and sometimes have a weather system of their own. Warm, moist air from the Atlantic hits high ground, rises, cools and releases its moisture as rain or snow. That is why clouds can sit on the hills even when the sun is shining in the glen. The top of Ben Nevis is in cloud 80% of the time between November and January, and 55% of May and June.

The result is that rainfall in the mountains at the head of Glen Lochay is 120 inches per annum while in Killin ten miles to the east it is only 53 inches. It then decreases one inch per annum for each mile you travel east along Loch Tay. For comparison, Perth and Glasgow in the Lowlands get 33-35 inches.

Altitude also has a major effect on climate. The average temperature falls 0.5-1°C for each three hundred feet you climb. Wind speed on the mountain tops can be double what it is at sea level. Even more important, there is much greater **variability** in the weather and the length of growing season as you move up the hill. Altitude and temperature set the upper limit for cultivation, but what matters most is the risk of complete crop failure in a bad year.

Weather in the Scottish mountains can also change very quickly. It can go from brilliant sunshine to heavy rain, hail or snow within an hour or two. And back again. There is a legend that an old shepherd died in a blizzard just a few hundred yards above Dalgirdy and locals still point out McPhail's stone. I have not been able to find any record of anyone of that name in Dalgirdy so I do not know if it is true. But climbers and walkers and even the occasional shepherd do still die on the Scottish mountains every year when they are caught out by the weather.

It is a harsh and forbidding land that, surprisingly, many Scots manage to love. For five months of the year the glen is bleak and the hills are desolate. The grass stops growing and hunkers down close to the ground. The trees are bare, dark skeletons dancing in the wind. Every living thing with any sense has left for warmer climes and those who stay spend most of their time sheltering from the elements. By midwinter it is dark, pitch dark, for 17 of the 24 hours.

Yet on a good day at any time of year you can - occasionally – bask in the sun on a mountaintop amidst the grandest views on Earth. Indeed, the views are often better in winter when the air is crystal clear.

Upper Glen Lochay has always been marginal farmland, vulnerable to the weather, and any change in the climate has most impact on marginal areas. We flatter ourselves that global warming is something new, but the climate of Scotland has varied a lot since the last Ice Age.[14]

The 'post-glacial climatic optimum' was between 6500 and 3000 BC, when temperatures were 1.5°C warmer than today. That does not sound much but it is enough to make a big difference to plant growth. It then became wetter, particularly in western Scotland, with milder winters but cool, damp summers.

Between 450 BC and 1000 AD, winters were often more severe but summers were warmer.

In 536 AD there was a massive volcanic eruption in Indonesia, which produced a worldwide blanket of cloud and ash. At the latitude of Scotland the sun was not visible for months on end. This was literally the Dark Ages. It caused the most sudden and severe cooling in the past two thousand years.

The Annals of Ulster tell of *a failure of bread* that lasted from 536 to 539. Irish and Anglo-Saxon chronicles tell of more harsh winters between 6-800 AD. In 763-4 the snow was heavy and lay well into the spring. Cattle died, crops could not be planted, and there was famine. There was another particularly bad year in 777, when there was *full winter in the summer*. To make matters worse, there were outbreaks of disease and *bloody flux*. Small wonder that people lost faith in the order of the ancient world.

From 1150 to 1300 AD there was a further warm spell when winters were mild and moist, and summers warmer and drier than today. This was the 'medieval climatic optimum'. It was the high water mark of upland cultivation, and farming would not match this again for five hundred years. Crops grew up to eleven hundred feet, with low risk of crop failure. There was prosperity. Population estimates for that time are little more than guesswork, but by 1300 AD there may have been between 500,000 and 1,000,000 people in Scotland. We do not really know, but it seems likely that the medieval farm and *baile* of Dalgirdy were established by this time. Scotland exported wool, sheepskins, hides and fish like cod and salmon. Wool was the medieval equivalent of North Sea oil even if lack of transport meant that Highland farms played no part in that trade.

From the middle of the fifteenth through the eighteenth centuries, there was a long spell of poor and erratic weather that became known as the 'Little Ice Age'.[15] It got much colder from 1645 and by 1675 - 1715 temperatures were 4-5⁰C lower than today. Severe storms were more frequent with heavy rain, deep snow, strong winds and floods. Winters were cold and stormy, springs late, summers cold and wet, and autumns early. The altitude limit for crops fell to 650 feet, and Dalgirdy at 610 feet was just about the limit. The chance of crop failure was as high as one-in-three years. In fact, bad years often came in clusters like the 'Seven Ill Years' from 1696-1702 when many people died of famine.

Into the eighteenth century, summers and winters got warmer. There was more rain in winter but less in summer. Cultivation was again possible up to a higher altitude. However, changes in farming practice and economic forces meant that most of this hill land was only used for grazing. Yet a government scheme for home food production during WWII showed that cultivation is still possible up to 800 feet in upper Glen Lochay.

Geological forces act over millions of years, and we often think of them as pre-historic. But they are still active today.

In 1883 the Indonesian island of Krakatoa saw the most violent volcanic eruption since modern records began. Half the island was vaporized and ash rose to a height of fifty miles. The explosion was so loud that it was heard two thousand miles away in Australia. There were several tsunamis, some more than one hundred feet high, larger than the Asian tsunami of 2004 or Japan's in 2011. Ash in the upper atmosphere affected global weather for several years. The sky was dark, the moon turned blue and there were spectacular sunsets. Edvard Munch's picture *The Scream* was inspired by the sky over Norway. *The sun was setting. Suddenly the sky turned blood red. - - - I stood there shaking with fear and I sensed an endless scream passing through nature.*[16] Over the next year world temperatures fell 1.2°C and took five years to recover. Farms in upper Glen Lochay suffered with the rest.

The nuclear disaster at Chernobyl in the Ukraine in 1986 affected Dalgirdy. Radioactive particles reached the upper atmosphere and blew across to Britain where they fell on upland pastures. Particles in the soil passed into the grass and so into sheep. For the next ten years, lambs from Dalgirdy land had to be fattened up in the Lowlands before they could be sold.

There was an earthquake in Glen Lochay at 10.13pm on 20 January 2005. The epicentre was only two miles down the glen and it had a magnitude of 2.7 on the Richter scale. Our neighbour felt a bang *as if a lorry hit the house.* Fortunately, we had no damage.

The River Tay transports more than a million tons of sediment to the sea every year.

We still get flash floods and landslides, like those that cut the Glen Ogle road in August 2004. Cars were trapped and people had to be rescued by helicopter. And there are still large-scale floods. The bridge over the Tay at Perth was washed away in 1621 and not rebuilt until 1771. 1814 saw the highest ever flood and there is a line carved on the bridge to prove it. In January 1993 heavy rain and melting snow flooded thirty square miles of farm-land as well as houses and businesses in Perth. In a few days the water caused £40 million of damage.

For all our imagined civilization, we still live on an unstable world at the mercy of Nature.

Land and weather made Dalgirdy what it is and will be major players in our story.

> *This is my country,*
> *The land that begat me.*
> *These windy places*
> *Are surely my own.*
> *And those who toil here*
> *In the sweat of their faces*
> *Are flesh of my flesh*
> *And bone of my bone.*[17]

3. EARLY PEOPLES
Before Scotland

Early humans came to Britain 500,000 years ago but each Ice Age drove them back. In Scotland the ice literally wiped the schist clean so there are no human traces before 8,500 BC.

Seven and a half thousand years ago a small group of people camped on the flanks of Ben Lawers. The camp lies high up in Corrie Odhar, looking out over Loch Tay. All you can see now are some turf mounds on a moraine bank above the Edramucky Burn, but excavations found three pieces of worked quartz and carbon dating puts the site around 5500 BC.[18] This is the first sign of humans in the area.

These were nomadic hunter-gatherers. This was a temporary campsite though it may have been re-used, perhaps even on a regular basis.

Because life has changed so much, it is easy to assume that Stone Age people were very different from us, but seven and a half thousand years is nothing in human evolution. Swap two new born babies and each would fit into the other's place without a whimper. These people had the same physical and mental abilities and emotions as we do. They might seem primitive and ignorant to us, yet they had the specialized knowledge and skills to cope in conditions where we would not survive.

From modern examples the group may have been 20 - 25 people, made up of a few families. It would function just like any small human group today. The leader would be the alpha male, based on his dominant personality and ability. His job was to make sure the group had food and security, and people would judge his leadership by the group's success. He would lead by consent of the group, even if nothing so crude as an election.

The group followed the animals that gave them food – deer, hares, wild boar, wildfowl, trout, salmon and fresh water mussels. They ate birds' eggs, edible roots, wild grain, nuts, berries and mushrooms as they came into season.

A single red deer could provide:

- Meat for the group for several days.
- Bones for soup.
- Skin to make a jacket and a pair of shoes.
- A mattock for digging.
- Barbed points for a spear or harpoon.
- Needles for stitching clothing, skin boats and netting.
- Skin-working tools, awls, punches and toggles.
- A pressure flaker for working flint.
- Two feet of strong sinew cords.
- Thirty feet of twisted gut cords.
- Containers for liquid, made from the stomach and intestine.
- Fat and hoof oil for lamps.
- Boiled hoof for glue.
- Brain for tanning hide.
- A tooth necklace.
- A ceremonial headdress. [19]

These people made tools and weapons of flint, antler, bone and wood, which were highly efficient for their purpose. They hunted with spears and harpoons, and effective bows and arrows were also invented about this time. Their flint working was highly sophisticated. A single flint core can give hundreds of fine flakes, each with a razor sharp edge. A flint edge blunts or chips quite quickly but a skilled flint worker can soon make more. The main limitation was a source of good flint and they must have brought a supply with them. Flint served for spear and arrow points, knives and scrapers. They also had fishhooks, and needles with an eye, and used traps for animals, birds and fish.

On the move, they had shelters or tents made of animal hides. In winter they probably went back down to mud and wattle huts on the coast.

Hunter-gatherers trod lightly on the land and left nothing but a few, faint traces.

The Neolithic – the New Stone Age – lasted from about 4000 to 2000 BC. This was a key stage in human history when we changed from hunting and gathering to farming and you can still see relics of this time in Glen Lochay.

There is a Neolithic long cairn at Kenknock, about two miles up the glen from Dalgirdy, on the north side of the glen at the bottom of the hill slope. Over the years it has been robbed of stones and is now difficult to see. However, there is still enough to show that it was a Clyde type cairn with burial chambers and 'horns' around a ceremonial entrance area. There are seven known cairns of this type in Perthshire. These are the earliest Neolithic remains in Breadalbane and date to about 4000 BC.

There is a Neolithic stone axe factory on the south face of Creag na Caillich – the crag of the old wife or old crone - which lies at a height of 2,500 feet on the hill above Killin. This was a source of hornfels – a hard grey-green rock with very fine grain that was ideal for axe heads. Although it is often called a 'factory', it was really cottage industry in scale. The site was in use between 2900 and 2300 BC.[20]

The vein of hornfels is only about twelve feet thick and runs across a steep hillside. Most of the stone was taken from a small outcrop a few yards wide, and close by there is a small man-made 'quarry' about ten yards across. Below these, stone debris still trickles down the hillside in a small burn. Quarrying was quite crude, by hammering to remove broken blocks and flakes of stone. These were taken down to a flat working area a hundred feet below, where the workers would choose the best stone by its appearance and test flaking, and then hammer and flake it into a rough shape. The 'axes' that left this site were still quite crude and had to be ground and polished to their final shape elsewhere. You can see the stages of the process at the

National Museum of Scotland.[21]

The stone from Craig na Caillich is easy to identify and axes from this site have been found over a wide area of northeast Scotland. There are even a few as far away as the southeast of England.

These axes were special and do not show any signs of wear. They were an enormous investment of time and labour - much too fine and precious to waste chopping wood. Also, the rock breaks naturally to give a sharp edge and you can pick up raw pieces of stone that would serve equally well as a working axe. These were objects of desire, symbols of wealth and status. It is also striking that they came from a site high in the hills, difficult to access, when there must have been easier sources. Perhaps this was a home of the gods and maybe that gave the axes magic powers.

Cup and ring marks are the most common Neolithic remains. They are sometimes called Neolithic rock art though that is probably a misnomer. Cup-marks are small circular hollows 1½ - 4 inches in diameter and ½ - 2 inches deep, carved on large flat boulders or exposed bedrock. They usually occur in groups and some have rings carved around them.

There are many cup and ring marks all along the south-facing slopes of Ben Lawers on the north side of Loch Tay. There is a very good set in upper Glen Lochay just below Duncroisk, close to some of the best farmland in the upper glen. A hundred yard stretch of exposed bedrock has 152 cup-marks, 17 of which have a single ring and two have double rings. No one has found any cup and ring marks further up the glen or on Dalgirdy land.

Cup and ring marks date from about 2-2500 BC. Pollen studies around these rocks show an open treeless landscape, which suggests that it may have been grazed. The meaning of cup and ring marks is lost but theories abound:

- Fairy footprints. (This was their old name.)
- Something about the land and farming.
- Boundary marks.

- Meeting places.
- Ceremonial sites.
- Religious symbols.
- Sites for exposing the dead.
- Decoration.
- An unknown language.
- Maps.

The real answer is that we do not know and never will.

There is a stone circle in a field near Kinnell House at Killin, with six stones of local schist standing about six feet high. The circle is thirty feet across, though the stones do not all fit exactly on the circle and they are not evenly spaced. All six stones were standing when Pennant saw them in 1769. Gillies said there were only five in their original position in the 1930s, but the sixth stone has now been replaced. The central space is smooth and level and does not appear to have been disturbed in ancient times. The central group of stones is a modern desecration.

There are at least ten known stone circles around Loch Tay.

These stone circles were not burial sites and no artefacts have been found in them, so they are difficult to date. The best guess is that they were built about 1500-2500 BC. They may have been some kind of meeting places, or ceremonial or religious sites. Unlike Stonehenge or in Orkney, the arrangement of the stones does not seem to have any astronomical meaning.

All of these Neolithic monuments took an enormous investment of time and effort, which would only be possible if people were settled. Cup and ring marks are near better ground for early farming. Burial cairns and stone circles took many people working together, with time to spare, commitment and leadership. Stone axes were the first, isolated examples of wealth. These are all evidence that society was beginning to change.

People were no longer 'living off the land' but were now shaping and changing the land for themselves. Slowly and with a lot of hard work, they cleared the forest. Farming began in the Middle East and came to Britain about 3500 BC though it would be much slower to reach the Highlands. The first cereals were oats and primitive barley. The first livestock were sheep, goats, cattle and horses. Neolithic cattle bones from Orkney show raised Nitrogen levels, so in at least some places they used manure to increase the fertility of the soil.

But farming also domesticated us. It changed our sense of the natural world and our ideas about time, life and death. Farming meant investment in the future. Increased productivity was a good survival strategy, but the price was 'working life' and 'the daily grind'. The phrase comes from grinding grain, which took about an hour a day for a family! It was also new to have a fixed abode or 'home' with 'neighbours'. The investment of blood, sweat and tears led to concepts of 'our' land that was passed on, to us from our ancestors, and from us to our descendants. The living and the dead were now bound together by the land.

The family was still the fundamental social unit but the tribe was also becoming important. 'Tribes' were groups defined by where they lived and by 'kith and kin' – one's 'country' and relatives by blood and marriage.

The living now **needed** the dead to prove who they were and their right to this land. But meeting the ancestors was a difficult and dangerous business, so they needed a new religion to reflect changed ideas about the land, the dead, time and the seasons. Cairns and stone circles may have been symbols of the group's power and ability to manipulate its landscape. Larger social groups now needed organization and strong leadership.

Within a few centuries the population of Scotland grew from hundreds of hunter-gatherers to thousands of farmers. Sheer numbers meant there was no going back. We could not have returned to hunting and gathering even if we wanted to.

People certainly lived in upper Glen Lochay by 2-2500 BC and perhaps earlier. We do not have any evidence if they lived on Dalgirdy. No evidence means just what it says. It does not necessarily mean there were no people here, just that we do not have the evidence to tell one way or the other. Farming was clearly possible at that time, just about the end of the post-glacial climatic optimum. The question is whether there were enough people to need Dalgirdy or if the better land around Duncroisk was sufficient?

The Bronze Age was the crucial shift from stone to metal tools and weapons, but it was much more than that. Bronze first came to Britain about 2500 BC but again would be slow to spread into the Highlands.

In 1868 a crofter near Killin found a buried hoard of bronze items.[22] There was a small fragment of a leaf-shaped sword or knife, a spear point, two axe-heads and a gouge, all with sockets for some kind of handle. There were eleven rings of various kinds. These had all been tied together with some kind of fastening. Sadly, the hoard is now broken up and it is no longer possible to date it precisely.

Bronze was much too rare and precious for everyday tools. Bronze was always the preserve of the social elite and never for practical use. These articles were symbols of wealth and status.

Farming might still be primitive and mainly pastoral, limited by stone and wooden tools, and supplemented by hunting and gathering. Yet it gave a much more reliable supply of food and could support many more people. Larger groups, settled living and spare time meant that some people could devote that time to other activities. Pottery and textile production began. People now wore woollen skirts and tunics and cloaks as well as animal skins. At least some people began to develop specialist skills and a few began to accumulate wealth and the power that went with it.

The Stone Age had been a time of vast communal monuments. In the Bronze Age this changed to individual burials, valuable possessions and status. Again, society was changing.

Around 7-800 BC iron began to appear and bronze may

have lost its symbolic value. Bronze objects were dumped in buried hoards. This was the date of most bronze items found in Scotland and now in the National Museum of Scotland, so it is likely this was the time of the Killin hoard.

This was also a time of social turmoil. From 600 BC we get hill forts in southern Britain and brochs in northern Scotland. About the same time, the first crannogs appeared on Loch Tay. A crannog is an artificial island, built on rocks or wooden piles and stilts driven into the loch bed. Many ancient people built houses on water or in marshes. Crannogs are common in Scotland and Ireland, some from as early as 3000 BC and some remained in use up to 1600 AD.

There are eighteen known crannog sites on Loch Tay. Even better, there is a modern example at the Scottish Crannog Centre at Kenmore, based on underwater archaeology.[23] The cold peaty water preserved ancient timbers, a log boat, plant remains, food, utensils and clothing. There was a butter dish with butter still inside it, a handful of sloes, pollen, seeds, herbs and even a midge! Through their long history, crannogs served mainly as homesteads working the nearby land and water and as refuges in times of trouble. The reconstruction at Kenmore shows how comfortable they could be.

A crannog has obvious advantages for defence but it was also a very visible symbol of power and prestige. This was probably some kind of local chief's house.

The Iron Age reached the Highlands some time about 250 BC. Even with early technology, iron was soon much more plentiful and cheaper than bronze. It was harder and stronger and lasted better. If you had an iron sword and your foe only had bronze, you had a definite advantage. But iron also led to a social revolution. Iron was not the preserve of the elite but was now widely available for everyday use. That meant ordinary people could begin to have iron weapons and tools.

There are more than fifty Iron Age homesteads in northwest Perthshire, with carbon dating between 250 BC and

250 AD. One has been excavated at Black Spout near Pitlochry.[24] It is circular, about sixty feet in diameter, with a dry-stone wall five to nine foot thick. The wall is well-built, with shelves and internal partitions. Stone paving survives in places. Within, archaeologists found fragments of a quern, a loom and thatch weights, and a glass toggle or pendant made from a Roman bottle. Another homestead near Loch Tummel yielded a small piece of iron, a bone bodkin, a stone spinning wheel, stone discs and the broken half of a well-worn quern. So the people who lived there had at least a few iron tools, grew and ground grain, and spun wool.

There are four roundhouses in upper Glen Lochay on what is now Kenknock.[25] All you can see today are faint circles in the grass about 40 feet in diameter, with no stone visible above ground. They are all on flat ground in areas of naturally drained land that shows faint signs of farming. This fits with Iron Age households being self-sufficient, living on their own lands, livestock and local resources for generations.

There is a much better Iron Age homestead on Dalgirdy, sitting on a hillock just above the road to the west of our cottage.[26] It is 45 feet in diameter, with dry-stone walls about three feet thick and in places still two feet high. The ground within is flat and in some areas there are faint traces of what may be stone structures. The entrance is to the northeast, facing a small burn that runs down the hillside about twelve feet away. There is a 12 X 16 foot, three-sided, 'entrance chamber' built into the circle, though that could be a later addition.

The Dalgirdy homestead is not built on flat ground like those up at Kenknock, though there is ground that could be cultivated on the hillside behind it. On the other hand, the hillock is quite gentle and this is clearly not a defensive structure. Perhaps it was placed to suit the terrain and take advantage of better drainage? Perhaps the better-preserved stone walls suggest a later date? Perhaps it was simply a better-built house like Black Spout?

Whatever, this is the first clear evidence of people living on Dalgirdy some time about 250 BC to 250 AD.

In the hills above Peebles in southern Scotland there is a settlement of four roundhouses, protected by curved enclosing walls.[27] Each had a courtyard, with enclosures for animals, a midden, and firewood and peat stacks. The houses were built of local materials to a well-established style. They had shallow founds and a wall of stone and turf three or four feet high. They had conical roofs with long branches resting on the walls and bound together at the peak, and thick insulating thatch of bracken and heather. Modern trials show that a pitch of about 45^0 is strongest and most waterproof. The floor was beaten earth with flagstones at the entrance. It was strewn with bracken, perhaps mixed with sweet smelling herbs. There were no windows and the only light came from the door, which faced east away from the prevailing wind and to catch the first rays of the morning sun. There would be a heavy leather flap to cover the door.

The fire was on a central stone hearth and in winter it would be kept burning 24 hours a day for warmth and cooking. Unlike Hollywood, there was no smoke hole at the peak, because that would create an updraft and set fire to the thatch! Rather, smoke hung in the air and seeped through the roof. This controlled vermin in the thatch and was good for drying herbsand preserving meat and fish. There was also enough carbon monoxide in the upper air to prevent sparks setting fire to the thatch. People sat or squatted in the clear air beneath the smoke.[28]

Here lived patriarch and matron, children, uncles and cousins, sharing each other's space, food and warmth. They also shared it with livestock, a small cow, dogs, chickens, rodents and a host of biting insects. Maybe even a slave or two.[29] It was a cramped but cosy world, where shared body heat kept you warm on a cold winter's night.

When you entered, the first thing to strike your modern nose would be the thick fug of smoke and the stench of close-packed human and animal bodies. No wonder that in summer people spent most of their time outdoors! Next would be the unbearable lack of privacy. There were wicker partitions but these were thin and low and did little more than mark out each space. Everyone lived, slept, made love, took sick, were born and died in sight and sound of the group. To maintain the peace, there must have been strict customs about eavesdropping, staring and invading each other's space. *Clan of the Cave Bear* tells it well.[30]

Sleeping spaces were filled with heather and bracken, covered with sheep and deer skins. The better class of roundhouse might have a thick bear skin, or wolf and beaver pelts, perhaps a few wooden seats and stools. Every nook and cranny was taken up with storage in woven baskets, clay pots and hanging from the roof. Cups and bowls were made of horn or carved hardwood. Apart from iron knives and perhaps a cauldron, most tools were still made of stone, wood or antler.

There are modern reconstructions of roundhouses in southern England.[31] Life in the roundhouse would be surprisingly comfortable. Housing in Dalgirdy would not do better than this until the eighteenth century.

When the Romans came, people in the Highlands still lived in tribes. Geography defined and separated each tribe from its neighbours. Many of the families in the tribe were related by blood or marriage, and this gave rise to myths about a common ancestor. They worked the land in common and thought of it as 'our land'. They shared a common language and religion and culture. They were able to undertake some communal tasks and had meeting places.

The Romans first used the term Caledonia at the end of the first century AD to describe northern Britain. One map suggests it was the fertile land down the east side of the country, beyond the Forth and Fife, and east of Drum Alban. As in later times, the heartland was probably the area of central Perthshire around Strathearn and the Tay. Dunkeld is the 'Fort of the Caledonians' and Schiehallion 'the Magic Mountain of the Caledonians'.

The Caledonii were ancient Celts.[32] The name might come from pre-Celtic *caled* or 'hard/tough' so the Caledonii were 'The

Hard Men' or 'Men from The Hard (Rocky) Place'.

Tacitus says the Caledonii had *ruddy hair and large limbs.* When they first met the Romans, they already had a warlike nature. Fighting was in their blood. *The various inhabitants of Caledonia immediately took up arms, with great preparations, magnified, however, by report, as usual where the truth is unknown; and by beginning hostilities, and attacking our fortresses, they inspired terror as daring to act offensively.*[33]

It really does seem that the early Caledonii fought naked. A distance slab on the Antonine Wall from 142 AD shows naked native warriors. In 210 AD, a Roman report said that Scottish warriors *do not wear clothes, so as not to cover the pictures on their bodies.* They were *protected only by a narrow shield and a spear, with a sword slung from their naked bodies.* In 297 AD they were still *accustomed to fight still half naked* but by 367-370 the practice seems to have stopped. They may have fought naked to display their war paint and tattoos, not only to terrify their enemies but perhaps for their magic powers.

The Romans called the people north of Hadrian's Wall *barbarians,* but remember that was a Roman perspective. Also, the Roman word simply meant 'outsiders' and did not carry modern connotations of savage, uncouth and dirty. When the Romans arrived the Celts were already skilled farmers and craftsmen and superb metal workers. The horse and the wheel gave improved communication and transport, even though travel by water was still easier. The simple rotary stone quern to grind grain must have been as welcome a household aid as the modern washing machine! Although they did not have writing, the Celts had a rich oral culture and religion, and distinctive Celtic art.

The Celts were also fierce fighters, who would fight a successful rearguard action against the Romans for eight hundred years, from northern Italy to what is still called the Celtic Fringe. And the Roman Empire would finally fall to us 'barbarians'.

We might be uncivilized compared to the Romans, but we were ready for our baptism of fire.

4. THE WOLF AND THE EAGLE
Fellow hunters

The history of the wolf in Scotland, more than any other animal, reflects the story of man.

Hunter-gatherers respected the wolf as a fellow hunter and gave him magical and spiritual properties. One of the Gaelic names for the wolf was *Mac Tire* or 'Earth's son'.

When men became farmers they took a much less tolerant view of the wolf. Despite old wives' tales, wolves do not attack people. But as man encroached on the wolves' habitat and their natural prey became scarce, they turned to livestock and this was a threat to our food supply that we could not tolerate. Boece said that *oure elders persewit this beist with gret hatreut, for the gret murdir of beistis done be the samin*. The problem continued in Breadalbane until the seventeenth century. In 1594 a cow was *slane be the wolf* at the foot of Ben Dorain. In 1622 there was another claim for compensation for the loss of three cows in Killin.

Much worse for their reputation, wolves ate human dead after battle. *There I saw the grey wolf gaping, o'er the wounded corpse of many a man.* They even dug up corpses, which to Christians was a terrible desecration.

The lean and hungry wolf,
With his fangs so sharp and white,
His starveling body pinched
By the frost of a northern night,
And his pitiless eyes that scare the dark
With their green and threatening light.
He climeth the guarding dyke,
He leapeth the hurdle bars,
He steals the sheep from the pen,
And the fish from the boat-house spars,
And he digs the dead from out of the sod,
And gnaws them under the stars.[34]

Folktales about wolves – and there are many - came to reflect a mixture of fear, admiration, awe and loathing.

As medieval man got a better grip on the land, he persecuted the wolf to extinction. In 1427, James I decreed that there should be three wolf hunts each year between St Mark's day (25 April) and Lammas (1 August). This was the breeding season, for maximum impact. No false emotion about animals in these days! Mary Queen of Scots herself took part in a wolf hunt in the forest of Atholl in 1563. In Breadalbane, in 1621, *it is statute and ordanit that evirie tennent within the saidis boundis respectiue mak four croscattis* (a kind of trap?) *of irone for slaying of the wolff yeirly in tyme.*[35]

Tradition says that the last wolf in Scotland was shot just south of Inverness in 1743. The last wolves in Breadalbane were probably gone before 1700.

Yet few animals have been so misjudged as the wolf. Despite its reputation, it is actually a shy, intelligent and elusive animal. Wolves are social animals that live and hunt in a pack with a well-developed social structure. Their survival depends on the strength of the pack, just like early humans.

Today, some people want to re-introduce wolves in Scotland. Experience in Yellowstone National Park shows that this top predator can help to restore the balance of Nature. Wolves would provide a natural control on the numbers of red deer and save us culling thousands every year. And they would do a better job of natural selection and so improve the fitness of the herd. They would compete with foxes and reduce their numbers. Of course there would be practical issues around sheep and perhaps it is only a dream. But Yellowstone shows it is possible without risk to humans.

What would it say about Scotland to have wolves roaming free once more in the Highlands?

But the wily old wolf had another trick up his sleeve. If you can't beat 'em, join them.

Man's best friend is none other than a domesticated wolf - the wolf in the living room. Remember, when next he licks your hand. We domesticated dogs more than ten thousand years ago and bred them for their hunting, herding, guarding and fighting traits. Wolves and dogs, like humans, retain child-like qualities so they learn well and are easy to train. Because they are such social animals they fit in well to a human pack.

The first hunter-gatherers and Neolithic farmers in Scotland already had dogs for hunting, as guards and as loyal companions. The Romans exported large hunting dogs from Britain, which may have been some kind of mastiff. Similar dogs were used until early medieval times as fighting dogs and many a battle started by *unleashing the dogs of war*.

Today, there are more than a million dogs in Scotland. And the wolf grins as he sleeps by our hearth.

The golden eagle is an icon of the Scottish mountains. It is wild and majestic, the king of birds. Its eagle eye and piercing gaze lets it spot prey far below as it soars over mountain ridges or glides down corries. With a six-foot wingspan and powerful talons, it can carry off hares, grouse and ptarmigan and even foxes and young deer. Eagles also eat carrion. But despite what farmers say, studies of their nests show that they only occasionally take healthy lambs.

There are now 450 pairs of eagles in Scotland and they stay together for years or even life. Each pair has a territory of up to sixty square miles. Golden eagles are shy and retiring and keep to the high and lonely places, well away from humans. The most eagles I ever saw in one day were in remote mountains south of Inverness, in the very glen where the last wolf was slain.

Eagle numbers fell greatly from persecution on shooting estates in the eighteenth and nineteenth centuries. In the 1960s they were also poisoned by DDT, which weakened the eggshells and led to breeding failure. The golden eagle is now a protected species and numbers are slowly recovering. But there are still areas of the Highlands where there are not as many eagles as we would expect and these areas just happen to coincide with grouse moors and their gamekeepers.

Meantime, the eagle passed into myth and legend.

In many cultures the eagle is a symbol of power and

royalty. The eagle is the national bird of many countries and appears in coats of arms. Roman legions fought under an eagle standard. Clan chiefs, like American Indians, still wear three eagle feathers in their bonnets as a badge of rank.

In Celtic mythology, the eagle was the oldest of all creatures and only the salmon was greater in wisdom. The eagle stands for swiftness, strength, keen eyesight and knowledge of magic. It helps you see hidden spiritual truths.

So, who got it right in the struggle for survival - the eagle or the wolf?

5. THE ROMANS
We arra peepul! We hate the Romans!

When the people in Glen Lochay were still living in Iron Age roundhouses, Rome built the greatest Empire the world had ever seen. At its peak it stretched from the Atlantic to the Middle East, from North Africa to the Rhine. It ruled 55 million people and lasted more than five hundred years. That was civilization.

But we only knew Rome by its army.

Rome was a military Empire based upon a professional army. Its strength lay in organization. A sophisticated command structure, good equipment and supply system, endless training and brutal discipline made it the most efficient fighting machine in the ancient world. Roman soldiers fought as a unit against enemies who fought as hordes of individuals. The Empire imposed order on a world of chaos. But most of all, Rome had a clear strength of purpose that it pursued with iron determination. It refused to admit defeat.

The Caledonii had no idea what was about to hit them.

Each Roman legion was a self-contained fighting force of about five thousand men. The basic unit was the century of eighty men - not the hundred we might imagine from the word. Each group of eight men ate and slept together, sharing a 160 square-foot room in barracks and a goatskin tent on campaign. They served and suffered, got drunk, laughed and wept together, in victory and defeat. These men grew closer than a family and literally trusted each other with their lives.

Six centuries made up a cohort and often operated together. Ten cohorts made a legion. Each legion also had four squadrons of thirty mounted men, who acted as scouts and messengers.

The legate or general in command usually held the post for

five years. He was from a senatorial family, in his thirties, with previous military experience. He hoped to make his name to further a political career and several went on to be Emperors. Second in command was the camp prefect. He was a grizzled veteran in his forties who had been a centurion for years and was at the peak of the professional soldier's career. Six tribunes served as staff officers. These were young men of aristocratic rank who served in the army as the first step to administrative posts in the Empire.

Each century was led by a centurion. Centurions were skilled and battle-hardened soldiers, with the scars to prove it. They were promoted from the ranks for their leadership qualities, but above all for their sheer fighting ability. The sixty centurions were the backbone of the legion and provided its training, discipline and esprit de corps. Each carried a vine cane as symbol of his authority and to provide more physical encouragement to those recruits who might need it. Centurions led from the front and had the highest casualty rate in the Roman army.

Each legionary signed on for 25 years. If he survived that long, he retired with a pension. At first only Roman citizens could join the legions. But as time passed the army drew more recruits from the provinces and gave them Roman citizenship.

There were also auxiliary cohorts who were recruited from the provinces and had lower status and pay than the legionaries. They were not as highly trained and were more lightly armoured. They often filled specialist roles. Cavalrymen from the northern European plains lived in the saddle. Bowmen from Syria could put an arrow through your eye at fifty paces. Light infantry from Batavia could swim like otters and called themselves the River Rats. Auxiliaries only got Roman citizenship at the end of their service or for outstanding bravery in battle.

Legates often looked on the auxiliaries as more expendable, so put them at the front on the march or in battle.

The Roman army did not have what we would call a uniform but the men did have standard dress and equipment.

They wore a loincloth and a tunic of red or un-dyed wool. A neck cloth could also serve as a towel, sweat rag or bandage when required. They had belts to carry weapons, a leather harness for decorations, and hob-nailed sandals. In the cold north, they wore long-sleeved tunics, breeches and a woollen cape smeared with fat in a vain attempt to keep out the rain.

Legionaries were heavily armoured by the standards of the day. They had a rounded steel helmet with a neck guard, hinged cheek guards and a forehead ridge, worn over a felt liner that was fiendishly sweaty in hot weather. The centurion's helmet had a cross plume of crimson horsehair, a beacon for men to follow in the dust and confusion of battle. In their early days in Britain, legionaries wore a chain mail vest. By the end they had segmented armour with broad, overlapping strips of iron. They had metal greaves to protect their shins. But their best defence was the shield. Each legionary had a large rectangular shield, four feet high, two-and-a-half feet wide, and curved from side to side. It was made of laminated wood with its outer surface covered in hide, a central iron boss and iron rims top and bottom. In battle, each man carried sixty pounds or more of armour and gear.

The legionary's main weapon was a wicked short stabbing sword or *gladius*. It was designed for close-quarter battle, where a few inches of razor sharp point is more deadly than any length of edge. Each man also had a large dagger and various spears.

In close combat the legionaries formed a shield wall, each shield in the front row overlapping the one on its right. Each man worked with his comrades on either side. He thrust his sword between the shields to stab into the body or groin of the enemy to his right, relying on the man on his left to protect that side. The heavy, iron-rimmed shield also made a formidable weapon to bludgeon an opponent or slam down on any exposed part.

On the march, each man carried a pack hung from a wooden carrying-pole or yoke, holding his water-skin, bedding, rations, cooking equipment, spare clothes and few personal things. Each carried part of the tent, a pickaxe, and two stakes for the overnight camp. Even in these days the Roman army knew all about loading up the poor bloody footslogger! They called themselves Marius' Mules - with pride and affection - after the general who founded the professional army. On campaign, each century had a mule-drawn cart for tools, stakes, spare weapons and, of course, the centurion's personal baggage.

The legions fought as heavy infantry. They practiced *shock and awe* long before the US used the term. They had the deadly efficiency of a well-oiled machine - the relentless killing machine that was Rome.

Can you imagine the arrival of a Roman legion in Scotland? It would be unlike anything the native people had ever seen. The sheer mass of men would be terrifying, as the deep red of their tunics spread across the land like a river of blood.

Cavalry scouts rode ahead and wide out to the sides, sweeping the way ahead for hostile forces or ambush. Auxiliary cohorts led the column, to bear the brunt of any surprise attack. Next came the command group, with its bodyguard, messengers and trumpeters. Then the main body of legionaries, marching six abreast in their centuries, armour polished, eagle standards glinting in the sun. Behind came the baggage train with its carts, animals, camp followers and slaves. Last of all was the rearguard.

The column would be more than two miles long. To the native watcher it must have seemed like a scaled serpent winding endlessly across the land. The legions did not sing as most armies do but marched in silence to save their breath for fighting. But the thunder of ten thousand iron-shod feet made the very earth quake. It was awe-inspiring and terrifying, which was of course the purpose, to instil fear and discourage any resistance.

On campaign, the legion marched about fifteen miles a day. Each night it dug a marching camp. Surveyors went ahead to select a site and measure out the classic playing card shape - rectangular with rounded corners. When the legionaries arrived, all was ready for them to dig a ditch and use the spoil to form a rampart. They hammered their stakes into the rampart so that thousands of jagged points tilted out like porcupine quills. They scattered caltrops in the ditch – four vicious iron spikes arranged so that whichever way it lay, one pointed up to impale the foot or hoof of an attacker. Within a couple of hours the legion could create a fortified camp for the night. The layout of the camp was standardized, so wherever he might be in the world each man knew where everything was and his place within it, which could be vital in a sudden alarm.

To natives who had never seen a town before, it must have seemed magic when a Roman city appeared on their doorstep. It would be another 1600 years before Perth reached that size.

Next morning, groups of men took down the stakes and collected the caltrops. Others shovelled the soil of the rampart back in to level the ditch. Nothing was left for an enemy. But the scars on the land still show on aerial photographs two thousand years later.

The Romans held southern Britain from 55 BC until 410 AD and there they had a profound and lasting impact. But most of that time they stayed south of Hadrian's Wall. They had a much more difficult time with the people of the north. The Romans were only able to 'conquer' the north for short periods and at times impose rather shaky peace treaties but they never had any real control. Turf and wooden forts soon rotted away and there are few Romans remains left in Scotland.

To the Romans, this was the end of the known world. They described the north as a dark foreboding forest, full of screaming savages, six months darkness and a frozen sea. So what did they want with such a useless place? They might dream of slaves and trade and minerals, but these were poor return for the effort of conquest. The real reason was Glory – expansion of the Empire and the Fame that went with it.

The Romans made three major campaigns in northern Britain.

From the early 70s AD they fought a difficult, running war

beyond their northern frontier and perhaps got as far as the Forth – Clyde isthmus. Then, in 82-83 AD, the Roman general Agricola led an army further north. His main line of advance ran northeast from Stirling on the Forth, up the line of the Gask ridge, to cross the Tay near Perth. The Gask Ridge may have been an old frontier between the tribes in the plains and the Caledonii in the hills. Agricola now built a line of Roman forts along that ridge. He also set up outposts at the mouths of the Highland glens, just west of Callander, at Comrie, and at the Sma' Glen, all within about twenty miles of Glen Lochay.

This new Roman frontier was very different from anything the native people had ever seen before. It spoke of a power that could tame the very landscape. The Lowland tribes made treaties with the Romans and lived within their protected area. The Caledonii were outside the frontier, beyond the pale.

Tacitus, Agricola's son-in-law, wrote an account of the campaign.

The various inhabitants of Caledonia immediately took up arms, - - - (They) had assembled the strength of all their tribes by embassies and confederacies. Upwards of thirty thousand men in arms were now descried; and the youth, together with those of a hale and vigorous age, renowned in war, and bearing their several honorary decorations, were still flocking in - - -. Their military strength consists in infantry; - - - (They) also make use of chariots in war - - -.[36]

The numbers are almost certainly exaggerated, as in most ancient wars. Even so, it is clear that the Caledonii managed to gather a large force from throughout their land. But compared to the Roman legions, this was an ill-equipped rabble. Once battle commenced, the Caledonian leaders would have little control over their forces.

The Romans brought the Caledonii to battle in 83 AD at Mons Graupius, though Tacitus does not tell us exactly where this was. It used to be thought it was further north, perhaps at Bennachie in Aberdeenshire, but modern scholars think it more likely it was in Strathearn, at Dunning or the Gask ridge.[37] That would bring it much closer to home, and means that the men of

Glen Lochay probably took part.

Calgacus, 'The Swordsman', led the Caledonii into battle. Tacitus gave him a rousing pre-battle speech. It is pure literary invention but it does show that at least one Roman had some empathy for the Caledonii.

For we are all un-debased by slavery; and there is no land behind us, nor does even the sea afford a refuge, whilst the Roman fleet hovers around. Thus the use of arms, which is at all times honourable to the brave, now offers the only safety even to cowards. - - - For we, the noblest sons of Britain, stationed in its last recesses, far from the view of servile shores, have preserved even our eyes unpolluted by the contact of subjection. We, at the furthest limits both of land and liberty, have been defended to this day by the remoteness of our situation and by our fame. - - - But there is no nation beyond us; nothing but waves and rocks, and the still more hostile Romans, whose arrogance we cannot escape by obsequiousness and submission. These plunderers of the world - - - To ravage, to slaughter, to usurp under false titles, they call empire; and where they make a desert, they call it peace.

Our children and relations are by the appointment of nature the dearest of all things to us. These are torn away by levies to serve in foreign lands. Our wives and sisters, though they should escape the violation of hostile force, are polluted under names of friendship and hospitality. Our estates and possessions are consumed in tributes; our grain in contributions. Even our bodies are worn down amidst stripes and insults in clearing woods and draining marshes. - - - Since then all hopes of mercy are vain, at length assume courage, both you to whom safety and you to whom glory is dear.

Every incitement to victory is on our side. The Romans have no wives to animate them; no parents to upbraid their flight. Most of them have either no home, or a distant one. Few in number, ignorant of the country, looking around in silent horror at woods, seas, and a heaven itself unknown to them, they are delivered by the gods, as it were imprisoned and bound, into our hands. - - - March then to battle, and think of your ancestors and your posterity. [38]

Tacitus' account of the battle is more straightforward reporting, and it is brutal.

(The Caledonii) - - - *received this harangue with alacrity, and testified their applause after the barbarian manner, with songs, and yells, and dissonant shouts. And now the several divisions were in motion, the glittering of arms was beheld, while the most daring and impetuous were hurrying to the front, and the line of battle was forming. - - - The troops, for the greater display of their numbers, and more formidable appearance, were ranged upon the rising grounds, so that the first line stood upon the plain, the rest, as if linked together, rose above one another upon the ascent. The charioteers and horsemen filled the middle of the field with their tumult and careering.*

At first the action was carried on at a distance. The Britons, armed with long swords and short targets, with steadiness and dexterity avoided or struck down our missile weapons, and at the same time poured in a torrent of their own. Agricola then encouraged five auxiliary cohorts to fall in and come to close quarters; a method of fighting familiar to these veteran soldiers, but embarrassing to the enemy from the nature of their armour; for the enormous British swords, blunt at the point, are unfit for close grappling, and engaging in a confined space. When the Batavians, therefore, began to redouble their blows, to strike with the bosses of their shields, and mangle the faces of the enemy; and, bearing down all those who resisted them on the plain, were advancing their lines up the ascent; the other cohorts, fired with ardour and emulation, joined in the charge, and overthrew all who came in their way: and so great was their impetuosity in the pursuit of victory, that they left many of their foes half dead or unhurt behind them.

- - - The squadrons were ordered to wheel from the front of the battle and fall upon the enemy's rear. A striking and hideous spectacle now appeared on the plain: some pursuing; some striking: some making prisoners, whom they slaughtered as others came in their way. Now, as their several dispositions prompted, crowds of armed Britons fled before inferior numbers, or a few, even unarmed, rushed upon their foes, and offered themselves to

a voluntary death. Arms, and carcasses, and mangled limbs, were promiscuously strewed, and the field was dyed in blood. Even among the vanquished were seen instances of rage and valour. When the fugitives approached the woods, they collected, and surrounded the foremost of the pursuers, advancing incautiously, and unacquainted with the country. And had not Agricola, who was everywhere present, caused some strong and lightly-equipped cohorts to encompass the ground, while part of the cavalry dismounted made way through the thickets, and part on horseback scoured the open woods, some disaster would have proceeded from the excess of confidence. But when the enemy saw their pursuers again formed in compact order, they renewed their flight, not in bodies as before, or waiting for their companions, but scattered and mutually avoiding each other; and thus took their way to the most distant and devious retreats. Night and satiety of slaughter put an end to the pursuit.

Of the enemy ten thousand were slain: on our part three hundred and sixty fell.[39]

In most ancient battles, hand-to-hand fighting only lasted between 15 and 30 minutes. There would be some casualties during that stage of the battle, as shown by the Roman losses, but most of the Caledonian casualties would occur during the rout. Even if we do not accept the figure of ten thousand, the Caledonii may well have lost a third of their warriors, which would be a devastating loss for their society.

The outcome was probably inevitable, but it taught us a painful lesson. After Mons Graupius, we never fought another set battle against the Romans. Instead, we stuck to guerrilla war, hit and run tactics, and raiding.

Agricola continued north, perhaps as far as the River Spey, but his campaign was really over. He claimed that he had subjugated the Caledonii but they were not pacified and the Romans never managed to secure control of the Highlands. Within three years, demands in other parts of the Empire forced the Romans to withdraw because they could not spare the forces to control northern Britain. The Romans may have won the battle of Mons Graupius but we won the war!

That was the closest the Romans ever came to Glen Lochay. The myth that Pontius Pilate was born at Fortingal in Glen Lyon is just that – a myth. The Romans were nowhere near the Highlands before 70 AD. During Agricola's campaign, none of the Roman outposts were that far into the glens. The claimed 'Roman camps' at Fortingal are actually a later Pictish fort and a medieval homestead.

Over the next forty years the north continued to consume men and resources. This was the time of the original 'Lost Legion' – the famous IX Hispana of five thousand battle-hardened veterans. Legend has it that they disappeared into the Scottish mist. Did they really fall victim to the Caledonii and their allies? Or is that just another myth?

By 122 AD the Emperor Hadrian accepted that *the* (northern) *Britons are incapable of being held under Roman authority.* So he built Hadrian's Wall across north England from the Solway Firth to the Tyne to keep us out. There is a nice postscript. A few years ago an Italian construction firm got the contract to upgrade the M74 motorway just north of Hadrian's Wall. With all their modern machinery, they took longer to build a few miles of road than the legions took to build the Wall from coast to coast. There is no better testament to the power and determination of the legions.

The second Roman invasion of the north came in 139-142 AD.

Despite setbacks, the Romans *drove back the barbarians, and built a new wall.* This was the Antonine Wall, which ran forty miles from the Forth to the Clyde. Despite its appearance, this was not a static defence. The Roman legions really did not do 'defence' but relied on armed might to crush their enemies in open battle. Rather, the Wall marked the frontier in a way that no one – inside or out - could ignore. It was a potent symbol of the might of Rome. It controlled movement and trade in and out of Roman territory and collected tariffs and customs duty. It was a psychological as much as a physical barrier.

The Romans only held the Antonine Wall for about twenty

years. But the cost was high, the gain was little, and men were needed on the Rhine. So they abandoned it and withdrew once more to Hadrian's Wall.

In 197 AD war bands from the north raided Roman Britain - - - *laying waste the countryside, carrying off plunder and wrecking almost everything.* Once more, in 207 AD, *the barbarians there were rebelling, over-running the land, taking booty and creating destruction.*[40]

So, in 208-09, the Emperor Severus personally led a third invasion. They came up the eastern plains, through the Caledonian heartlands, and as far north as Moray. It is doubtful if Severus really expected to 'defeat' the northern tribes and this was more likely a punitive raid to teach us a lesson. This time we refused a set-piece battle and used guerrilla tactics to cause heavy Roman losses. *It was easy for the Britons to slip away; putting their knowledge of the surrounding area to good use, they disappeared in the woods and marshes.*[41] Severus did manage to get another peace treaty, but he died in 211 and the Romans withdrew.

By 360 AD the end was nigh. *The wild tribes of the Scots and the Picts broke their undertaking to keep peace, were causing destruction in those areas near the frontiers, and the provincials, exhausted by the repeated disasters they had already suffered, were caught in the grip of fear.*[42]

The Barbarian Conspiracy in 367-370 was an alliance of Picts from Scotland, Gaels from Ireland, and Franks and Saxons from across the North Sea. The barbarians over-ran the Roman province of Britain and devastated farms and settlements. Free men, women and children were killed or enslaved. This ruined the economy, did great harm to Rome's prestige, and strained the Empire's military resources to breaking point.

The Picts continued to cause trouble and by 410 the Romans had had enough and withdrew from Britain. Later accounts were clear that the end of Roman government in Britain could be blamed on *two exceedingly savage peoples: Gaels from the northwest and Picts from the north.*

The world shifted on its axis.

After the Romans left, Britain suffered an economic recession that lasted for three hundred years. Coin fell out of use and people went back to barter. Manufacture stopped and urban life shrank. It took nearly six hundred years to restore the level of production and prosperity that southern Britain had under the Romans.

Caledonia kept its independence and was never brought into the Roman Empire. The price was that we missed out on the benefits of Roman civilization. But that does not mean we escaped the influence of Rome.

Agricola came close and must have caused a few years' panic in Glen Lochay. Men of Glen Lochay may well have taken part in the battle of Mons Graupius and, if they did, many were killed or wounded.

For the next three hundred years the Caledonii must have been very conscious of the Roman presence to the south. At times they got trade goods or bribes to keep the peace, though probably little of that reached Glen Lochay.

Yet the very presence of the Romans forced Caledonian society to respond. Three invasions and the ever-present threat from the south created social turmoil in the north. Cultural, political and military interaction with Rome helped to shape northern society. It transformed our material culture, our awareness of the wider world and our religion. Rome was a catalyst for change, whether we liked it or not.

From now on we would be part of the wider world.

6. BIRTH OF A NATION
Scotland was born fighting

Scotland was never inevitable. It could so easily not have been.

When the Romans came, the Caledonii were a loose collection of large and small groups. They were some kind of large population grouping but they were certainly not what we would call a nation. They were clearly able to get together and muster a large fighting force, but the battle of Mons Graupius was a harsh lesson on their limitations. The Caledonii fought as hordes of individuals and did not have the organization, training or discipline to fight as an army.

If the Caledonii wanted to remain free, they must learn to fight more effectively. In organizing their society for war, they began to develop the structures of a state.

The Barbarian Conspiracy shows how much had changed by 367-370. The barbarians were now able to build an alliance – even if short-lived – with other peoples from Ireland and across the North Sea. They could muster an army that campaigned for months on end into southern Britain, with all that implies in men and supplies. And they had the leadership to organize such an invasion.

The Romans gave us our first common sense of purpose, even if it was just the shared will to resist an invader. By the end of the struggle against Rome we had bonds of shared campaigns and battles. Is it just romantic to think that perhaps we even took pride in the Roman view of us as barbarians? In the words of Billy Connolly: *We arra peepul! We hate the Romans!*

Between the sixth and ninth centuries, the tribes began to coalesce into petty kingdoms. The first record of a king in Scotland was in 576 AD, when Aedan became king of southern Argyll. There were kings in southern Pictland from at least 586 and a king of Strathclyde in 657. Dalriada was one kingdom before the end of the seventh century. However, most of these petty 'kings' were really just rulers of provinces. The first *Rex Pictorum* or 'King of the Picts' did not appear until the end of the seventh century.

The Picts played a key role in the birth of this nation, yet they remain a shadowy and mysterious people. They did not leave any written records and we do not have a single sentence of their language. All that remains are a few words like the place name *Pit* as in Pitlochry, or *Dun* which meant fort in early Celtic languages. The Picts left impressive carved stones but they are hard to interpret. We can identify Pictish sites but few have been excavated. Much of what we know about the Picts comes from the Irish and Anglo-Saxon chronicles.

Picts means 'The Painted Ones'. The people of Roman Britain first used the name in the third century to describe the peoples beyond the Roman frontier. When the Romans first came to Britain in 54 BC, Julius Caesar wrote that the people there *dye their bodies with woad.* Later accounts said that the Caledonii *tattoo their bodies with various patterns and pictures of all sorts of animals.* Isidore of Seville summed it up in the early seventh century. (The Picts) - - - *whose name is taken from their painted bodies, because an artisan, with the tiny point of a pin and the juice squeezed from a native plant, marks them with tattoos of various figures to serve as identifying marks, and their nobility are distinguished by their tattooed limbs.*[43]

Who were the Picts? The clue lies in a Roman report of 305 AD about *the Calidones and the other Picts.* There are other similar accounts. These were not newcomers from overseas but the very same natives of this land. Picts was not the name of a new people, but rather the name for a new and larger population group that included the Caledonii.

It took until 685 AD before Pictland emerged as a distinct and stable territory. It was then most of the land north of the Forth and east of Drum Alban. By the eighth century, Pictland was **the** military and political super-power of northern Britain.

The Mounth – that part of the Grampian mountains

sloping east just north of Aberdeen – forms a natural divide between north and south Pictland. From early times these were two rival centres of power, with distinct identities and at times separate kings. But after 685 there was no doubt that they were one country and it was more a question of who should be king.

Pictland was a loose group of seven provinces. Fortriu was the most powerful and always led or dominated the others to varying degree. Despite what you see on the Internet, Fortriu was in the south, based on the rich and fertile lands of Strathearn and the Tay basin. The centre of royal power was around Perth, at Moncrief Hill, Forteviot and Scone.

The only other province that we know from contemporary records is Fodla, which would become *ath Fhotla* in Gaelic and then Atholl in English. Fodla was the mountainous area to the west of Fortriu leading up to Drum Alban. Glen Lochay was in the western edge of Fodla.

Pictland was only one part of what is now Scotland. The two other parts important for our story were the kingdoms of *Dal Riata* and Strathclyde. All three were Celtic peoples.

Old history books said that the Gaels came from Ireland about 500 AD and settled on the west coast of Scotland to found Dalriada. That is unlikely. In early times the sea was by far the best method of travel. Dalriada was much closer to Ireland by sea than going by land over Drum Alban to the Picts in the east. So people of the west coast simply had stronger links and more in common with the people of Ireland than with the Picts.

Dalriada was the fertile coastal plains of Argyll, with their gentle maritime climate. Kilmartin is the richest prehistoric landscape in Scotland, with Neolithic and Bronze Age burial chambers, cup and ring marks, and standing stone circles.[44] As soon as ancient people had sea-going boats, there would be links between the people on the west coast and the Gaels in Ireland. For as long as we have records, the Gaelic language, culture and political influence were strong in Dalriada. They became dominant after about 500 AD.

Dunadd was the main fort of Dalriada. It stands on a rocky

outcrop 175 feet high with wide views over Kilmartin and it is still impressive. You enter through a natural rocky defile, with terraces and four sets of walls at different levels. Between about 500 and 736 AD this was one of the most important power centres in Scotland and it has given us some of the best archaeology from that time. Excavations revealed tools, weapons, quern stones, imported pottery, and moulds for fine metalwork and jewellery. On the summit of Dunadd there is a carved footprint in the rock. Was this part of some early kingship rites – in which a new king planted his foot and made his mark in the land?

Strathclyde was the area around the Clyde and the shores of Loch Lomond. It was home to the Britons, with its royal centre at *Al Clut* or 'Clyde Rock', what is now Dumbarton.

Pictland, Dalriada and Strathclyde met at the southern end of Drum Alban, around Tyndrum, Crianlarich and Strathfillan. That is just over the hills from the head of Glen Lochay. From the seventh to the ninth centuries, Glen Lochay was Pictish frontier land facing the Gaels to the west and the Britons to the south. It was right in the middle of the action and must have been a very uncomfortable place to live. There would be constant threat of minor raids – minor in the grand scheme of things but not for the people who were killed, had their cattle stolen, or their families enslaved. At times they were on the receiving end of a larger war band. Even when one's own army passed through on the way to war, there might be indiscipline and looting.

Glen Lochay was also one of the first parts of Pictland to be Gaelicized[45] and that would bring an ethnic dimension to the struggle. Bosnia in the 1990s gives some idea of what it might be like.

There are more than fifteen hundred hill forts in Scotland, dating from the Iron Age and Pictish times. Forts from the different periods are very alike and were often re-used, so they are difficult to date. But the annals tell us that the larger Pictish hill forts were military and political centres, where kings and great lords lived and ruled.

Dundurn was a major Pictish hill fort at the east end of Loch Earn, just over Glen Ogle. The place names Dun Locha at Killin and Duncroisk in upper Glen Lochay show that these were also forts. Nothing remains on the ground, but they may have been part of a chain of Pictish forts guarding the western frontier. Duncroisk means 'Fort of the Crossing' which could guard the hill pass or *lairig* over from Glen Lyon and the lowest ford on the River Lochay.

There are remains of two smaller hill forts in upper Glen Lochay. One lies a mile west of Dalgirdy, on the south side of the river. The other is another mile further west, on the north side of the river. They are both on moraine mounds, about thirty feet high, with a good outlook up the glen. The sides are too steep to be natural and the tops have been flattened. Each has obvious remains of a rampart and ditch, and a defended approach from the hillside. The nearer fort is the larger, with an oval top that measures fifteen-by-thirty paces. The other is rectangular and only measures eight-by-fifteen paces. These hill forts are clearly defensive and quite unlike the Iron Age homestead. Were they some kind of outpost?

They have not been excavated so we cannot tell if they are Iron Age or Pictish. But even if they were from the Iron Age, the Picts would re-use them as part of their frontier system.

Let me jump ahead for a moment. On top of the nearer hill fort are the rectangular stone footings of one or more buildings. Local legend says that James V used it when hunting in the royal forest of Mamlorn at the head of Glen Lochay, and it would make practical and romantic sense to re-use an old hill fort in this way. Sadly, there is no record that James V ever hunted in Mamlorn. This seems to be one of the host of myths that 'James V was here', which arose after Sir Walter Scott wrote *The Lady of the Lake*. But we need not give up. There are records that both James I and James II did hunt in Mamlorn and we know they had hunting lodges, which were usually built of wood, with a hall and one or two chambers or separate buildings. James II did have a hunting lodge in Glen Finglas, where there is still a mound with a flat top and a ditch and rampart on two sides. So perhaps an earlier King James did indeed lodge in Glen Lochay![46]

Frontier land! In 642 the Gaels tried to invade Stirlingshire but the Picts defeated them at Strathyre. In 682 the Britons laid siege to Dundurn in Pictland and Dunadd in Dalriada. In 693 the Gaels took their turn laying siege to Dundurn. *Clach nam Breatann* or 'Stone of the Britons' is a tall boulder that still stands in Glen Falloch, just south of Crianlarich. This was a boundary stone between Strathclyde and Dalriada, where Britons and Gaels fought a battle in 717. Local legend has it that part of Tyndrum is built on the 'Field of Kings' where Picts fought Gaels in 729. In 736 the Picts invaded Dalriada, going down the western glens to Dunadd and laying waste to the whole region.

The Hollywood image of battle at that time is a horde of barbarians going crazy in a frenzied charge. That is wrong.

By this time Pictish and Dalriada societies were organized for war. The core of the army was made up of the war bands of the king and his great lords - professional warriors who rode to war.

A warlord's gear was heavy and hot and sweaty, so you only put it on when the time for battle was close. Over a thin tunic and trews, you pull a leather tunic that falls to your knees. The hide is thick and hard, and should blunt a sword slash though not a spear. A rich warlord might have some old Roman chain mail, polished until the links shine, which might even block a spear thrust. Knee-length leather boots are sewn with iron strips to cheat the blade that comes beneath the shield wall. Elbow-length leather gloves sewn with metal plates protect your forearms and serve as a maul of last resort. Your helmet is richly adorned in silver or gold, with a mail flap to protect the back of your neck, and gilded cheek pieces. So all your enemy sees is a dazzling, iron-clad killer with dark, soul-less pits for eyes.

Strap on your sword belt and scabbard, heft your shield and largest war spear, and you are ready. This is the rich armour of a great warlord dressed for battle, striking fear into the heart of an enemy.

But the bulk of the army was made up of common foot soldiers. These were men who spent most of their time working the land but owed military service to their lord. The *Senchus fer nAlban* from Dalriada in the seventh century is the oldest civil list in Britain and pre-dates the Domesday Book by nearly five centuries. It shows that *military service always goes with the soil* and that the unit of assessment was the 'household', which might be a tenancy and an extended family. Each household had to supply one or two men for military duty, though we do not know how often or for how long.[47]

Summer was the season for war. The weather was better, the ground dried out and the grass grew lush. It was easier to travel, to sleep out, and to graze horses on the way. A war band could move further and faster to catch the enemy unaware. In the time between sowing and harvest, farmers were free to take up their spears and follow their lords. Chronicles tell how the green, green grass of June and July was often spattered with gore. But when autumn came, then men must head home to gather the harvest that would see their families through the winter.

Most battles were fought to control resources - land or people or power. In territorial battles, opposing sides fought to acquire or defend land. Battles for power were often civil wars between rivals to the throne or between great lords. But many battles had mixed motives. And there were always the spoils of war - booty and glory.

By that time battle was well organized - at least to start. The sculpted stones show that the Picts fought in a classic shield wall up to three ranks deep.

A young man of fifteen or sixteen was not a warrior until he had fought in the shield wall.

'Shield wall!' bellows the warlord. You shuffle into place, lined up shoulder to shoulder with the men on either side, shields overlapping. Warlords and hardened warriors are in the front rank. Others press close behind to add weight and help push forward like a rugby scrum, ready to take the place of those who fall. For any gap in the shield wall can be fatal if the enemy manage to break through and come amongst you.

The enemy shield wall forms up to face you, fifty paces away. The icy grip of fear tightens on your chest, your heart thumps faster, your legs are like jelly and your bowels turn to water. Your palms are sweating and you grip your spear tight. You try to scream your hatred at the enemy but your mouth is dry and all that comes out is a croak. Any man who does not feel fear is a liar or a fool, and you would flee if you could but honour and comradeship bind you fast. Ale before battle gives many men courage, but great warriors fight cold sober because they know that even a small amount of alcohol can slow your reactions.

For a while, both sides shout and hurl insults at each other as they work up courage. Sometimes that is as far as it goes, if neither side is sure enough of victory to start the attack, and the shouts and jeers continue until both sides drift away.

But if the order comes to advance then you all shuffle forward, holding the shield wall intact as you go, spears levelled. Men shout and beat spears against their shields, and the din rises until no orders can be heard but only the blare of war trumpets. The shield walls crash together with a mighty noise like thunder overhead that rents the sky asunder. Then the beast of war howls and the battle rage takes over and you see and hear nothing but the enemy face in front of you – the man whom you must kill or be killed by. Great warriors fight with a savage joy. It is not just adrenaline, more a feeling of power and strength and euphoria as if only in that moment close to death you are truly alive.

As the walls clash, your spear takes one man in the throat. Your shield crashes against the opposing shield and you put your weight into your shield and shove to keep momentum while the men behind add their weight to your back and your feet scrabble for purchase. You all heave as hard as you can, with a terrible rhythmic grunting. There is no space to use your spear so you abandon it and draw your sword. An axe crashes on to your shield but you see it coming and manage to deflect it, and while the axe jams in your shield you thrust forward with your sword but cannot feel if it strikes home. You heave, you sweat, you curse, and you strike when you can - above, below, between the shields. You thrust and you kill. Your shield and sword become parts of your body, and you ward off blows with one then strike with the other. You stamp on the face of a fallen enemy as you step over him and rely on the man behind to finish him off before he can make a last thrust up at you.

Then an enemy spear strikes your helmet and you are dazed for a moment, but the man behind you chops the spear down and the crush holds you up until your head clears. It is just as well, because to fall to the ground is to be trampled or stabbed to death.

A pause while you draw breath, gazing stupefied at the blood-spattered faces of friend and foe around you. Then throw yourself back into the fray, hissing and spitting like a wild animal.

You ram your shield forward and manage to knock a man off balance, and as he turns away you thrust your sword into his belly, twist and wrench it free in the classic gutting stroke. Suddenly the opposing shield wall gives way and you are through and into the midst of the enemy. And then it is all a glory of slam and smash and slash, until the world is full of blood and gore and offal.

Until suddenly there are no more enemies and only a savage exultation that you are still alive. Only then does the battle madness fade and the world slow down to normal. You suddenly become aware of your exhaustion and can barely lift the shield and sword that a moment ago you were wielding with such enthusiasm. You are parched with thirst. You are drenched in sweat, gasping for breath, throat raw and hoarse from shouting and screaming, arms and legs aching from exertion, cuts and bruises that you never noticed at the time. If you are lucky you have no more serious injury.

Only then do you see the tidemark of dead and dying men

where the shield walls met. Only then do you smell the blood and piss and shit - the dreadful aftermath of battle. Later, you only have disjointed, frozen images from the heat of battle. And the haunting thought: why me? Why do I survive when so many perish? But those brief moments are the source of all reputation and honour and glory in Celtic society.[48]

Most men did not die in battle but in the rout that followed, like at Mons Graupius. That was when cavalry came into its own, to turn the flank and pursue the fleeing enemy. In defeat the only outcomes were death, flight or enslavement. The chronicles make little mention of wounded. If you did manage to escape, clean wounds could be dressed and simple fractures splinted and you might recover if you did not die of blood loss, shock or infection. Many men drowned as they tried to escape. If you were too badly injured to run, the victors would finish you off. Open fractures and penetrating wounds of the chest or belly were almost always fatal, so putting you out of your misery might be a mercy.

The chronicles speak of *devastatio* during an invasion or after victory in battle. *Devastatio* was savage and brutal 'laying waste' or 'ravaging' of an area. The army plundered everything valuable that they could take away and destroyed all they could not carry - forts, churches, houses and crops.

In the 730s, in a single decade, the Picts invaded Dalriada three times, won five battles, toppled three kings and destroyed Dunadd. The damage to the people and the economy was immense. The kingdom of Dalriada crumbled and after 741 had to accept the king of Picts as overlord. It was to all intents and purposes a province of Pictland. The king of Dalriada was appointed by or paid homage to the king of the Picts. The royal families inter-married and inter-twined.

Then the Vikings came.

AD 793. This year came dreadful fore-warnings over the land of the Northumbrians, terrifying the people most woefully: these were immense sheets of light rushing through the air, and whirlwinds, and fiery dragons flying across the firmament. These tremendous tokens were soon followed by a great famine: and not long after, on the sixth day before the ides of January in the same year, the harrowing inroads of heathen men made lamentable havoc in the church of God in Holy-island, by rapine and slaughter.[49]

In the same year, of a truth, the pagans from the Northern region came with a naval armament to Britain, like stinging hornets, and overran the country in all directions, like fierce wolves, plundering, tearing, and killing not only sheep and oxen, but priests and Levites, and choirs of monks and nuns. They came, as we before said, to the church of Lindisfarne, and laid all waste with dreadful havoc, trod with unhallowed feet the holy places, dug up the altars, and carried off all the treasures of the holy church. Some of the brethren they killed; some they carried off in chains; many they cast out, naked and loaded with insults; some they drowned in the sea.[50]

We think of the Vikings as raiders from the sea who attacked places on the coast, so we might imagine that Glen Lochay in the centre of the country was safe. But that was only the start of it. The Norsemen devastated Dalriada early in the ninth century. In 839 a Viking fleet came up the Rivers Tay and Earn where *the heathens won a battle over the men of Fortriu* in which *almost innumerable fell*. In the 860s the heathens *wasted all Pictavia*. They defeated the Picts at Dollar, spent a whole year in Pictland, and defeated the Picts again in Ath Fothla. In 870 they destroyed Dumbarton after a four-month siege and plundered the whole of Strathclyde. In 903 *the Norsemen plundered Dunkeld and all Alba* before they were finally defeated the next year at a battle in *Strath Erenn*.

There had had always been slaves, captives of raids or war, but the Vikings practiced slavery on an industrial scale. After the sack of Dumbarton in 870, it took two hundred galleys to carry the captives to the slave markets at Dublin. We do not know if the Vikings reached Glen Lochay but they were close for long periods, so perhaps they did. It really depends if there were enough people in the glens to make it worth the bother, or did they get enough easier plunder in the lowlands? Whichever, the people of Glen Lochay certainly lived in fear of the Vikings.

A slave is someone who is the legal property of another person and must obey them. He owns you, just like his dog or his horse, and he may treat them better than he treats you. Can we even begin to imagine what it was like to be a slave?

Men burst into your hovel in the middle of the night and drag you out. You see your man struck down as he tries to defend you and you do not know what happened to your children. Now you are in chains, stumbling along in a row of helpless others. You do not know where they are taking you, but you will never see your home and family again. You do not know what they will do to you, but you know it will be bad. They can work you till you drop. They can beat you, brand you, rape you, kill you, and there is nothing you can do about it. No one cares. You have no rights and there is no Court of Human Rights for any appeal. This is the rest of your life.

The Vikings destabilized the country. When they attacked Fortriu in 839, they surprised a royal council and killed the king of the Picts, the king of Dalriada and many leading nobles. The Pictish kingdom fell apart. Into this power vacuum stepped *Cinaed mac Alpin* – Kenneth MacAlpin. He was probably a lesser member of the Dalriada royal family who had links and claim to the Pictish throne. He was also a skilled military leader and politician. He united Dalriada and Pictland into a single kingdom and created a dynasty that lasted until 1034. Under Viking pressure, he moved his royal centre to Forteviot in Strathearn and took St Columba's relics from Iona to Dunkeld.

The question is how the Gaelic language and culture took over so completely in this new kingdom, while Pictish disappeared. Remember that the Picts were the dominant military and economic power and out-numbered the Gaels ten-to-one. So it cannot be just because a Gaelic king took over. Usually, in that situation, the native language and culture prevail and foreign rulers go native – like the Norman conquerors. Much stronger forces must have been at work. Between 793 and 904, Pictish society and its leadership were largely destroyed and the Gaelic elite moved into a vacuum. The Gaelic church had already been spreading across Pictland since the sixth century, bringing Christianity, the Gaelic language and culture, and support for the king's authority. After the Vikings devastated Dalriada in the ninth century, there would be a flood of Gaelic refugees. All of these forces probably came together to create a perfect storm for the Picts.

Perhaps it was also because the Gaelic language, church and culture were richer and more dynamic, just like English would replace Gaelic a thousand years later.

The Gaelic takeover was complete by the end of the ninth century and in 900 AD they first used the term 'Alba' for the new kingdom. But Alba was still not a 'nation' as we think of it today – an organized political community under one government. Rather, it was a loose confederation of the peoples and lands of Pictland and Dalriada, across most of what is now mainland Scotland north of the Forth and Clyde. And even the idea of one nation of Alba was still very much in the minds of the political and church elite, who of course had a vested interest. The common people probably gave it little thought.

We can skim quickly over the next four hundred years. Strathclyde and the lands in the south were brought into the fold and the present border with England was agreed in 1237. The Norsemen were finally driven out of the western isles in 1266. Scotland was more or less the shape it is today.

During the thirteenth century, Scotland began to develop a sense of national identity. It was now one land with stable borders. It had one king and one church, who between them held all political and spiritual authority. Alexander II and III now addressed their charters to 'the Scots' where earlier kings of Alba had listed the French (Norman), English, Gaelic and other peoples who made up their kingdom. In 1249-60 there was a 'Community of the Realm of Scotland' made up of the earls, bishops and nobles, who spoke for the nation and *governed in the name of the king on behalf of the community of Scotland* until the king came of age. In the 1290s the king held the first 'parliaments' with the *three estates* of clergy, nobility and burgesses. At the national and political level, Scotland was becoming a nation.

We should pause here to say that this was still very far from what we would call democracy. The three estates were all members of the privileged classes and there were no elections. The common people had no place in parliament and would not even dream of it. Even so, it was a step in the right direction.

We still call them the Wars of Independence. When the Scottish royal line died out in 1290, there were fourteen claimants for the throne and Edward I of England was brought in to adjudicate. If he had shown more restraint, the Scots might have accepted Edward as overlord and in due course Scotland would have come under English rule, much like Wales. But Edward could not resist the temptation to take advantage of the situation. This sparked uprisings that he crushed without mercy.

King Edward I, 'Longshanks', 'The Hammer of The Scots' led the mightiest medieval army in Europe. The heavy horse was the medieval tank. The steel-clad knight was almost invulnerable, reaching down to slash and crush his foe. His warhorse stood fourteen or fifteen hands high like a modern Clydesdale, was itself armoured, and trained to kick and bite. It was so weighed down that it could not really charge but at best could only manage a kind of half trot. Yet even plodding slowly across the battlefield it swept all before it. But if the knight could be unhorsed he was like a lobster on its back. All you need do is crack the shell to get at the soft creature within. A simple bodkin through the visor could pierce his eye and into his brain.

William Wallace was only one of many leaders of the uprisings and the politics that followed. He did not achieve any lasting success and could easily have been forgotten, like most other leaders of that time. Mel Gibson would never have heard of him and there would be no *Braveheart* - even if the film is full of historical nonsense!

Two things changed that. On 11 September 1297 at the

battle of Stirling Bridge, Wallace out-manoeuvred the invincible English army and proved they could indeed be beaten. 9/11 was a famous date in Scottish history, long before the Twin Towers. It gave Scots hope in the bitter years to come, but Edward never forgave Wallace for this insult. The peace treaty, when it came, excluded him by name and demanded that he be hunted down and handed over for execution.

They dragged him off to London and held a mockery of a trial. Wallace denied the charge. *I could not be a traitor to Edward, for I was never his subject.* But the verdict was a foregone conclusion.

It was a barbaric death. They stripped him naked, tied him on a wooden hurdle and dragged him through the streets to Smithfield where the butchers awaited. The citizens of London made great sport, throwing dirt and stones and filth. The executioners hanged him by a rope around his neck but cut him down while he was still (just) alive. They emasculated him and disembowelled him and burnt his entrails before his eyes, and at some point during this he died. They cut off his head and stuck it on a pike on London Bridge. They quartered his body and sent his limbs to hang in public warning at Newcastle, Berwick, Stirling and Aberdeen. They not only killed him in this life but in the next life too. To the medieval mind, dismembering his body meant that he lost all hope of resurrection.

In real life Wallace became a martyr and his name lived on forever more. Blind Harry's poem *Wallace* would become the best-loved book in Scotland after the Bible.[51]

If Edward had such a mighty army, why was he unable to subdue the Scots? The trouble was that most of the time he was fighting on at least two fronts, and the war in France was always his main priority. Scotland was a sideshow. The English also failed to grasp the full geography of Scotland and never established garrisons beyond Stirling and Perth. The Scots always had the Highlands and the north as a secure base and could import war materials through Aberdeen. England was never going to conquer Scotland by military force alone.

The battle of Bannockburn took place before Stirling on 23-

24 June 1314. The main force of the Scottish army was 4,500-5,000 spearmen, in four divisions. Robert the Bruce, King of Scots, led the largest division with the Highlanders and the men of the clans. Edward II was no military leader like his father Longshanks and Bruce took full advantage of the land. Soft ground bogged down the English heavy horse. The Scots dug pits and spread caltrops. The Scottish schiltrons were like hedgehogs bristling with twelve-foot spears braced into the ground and horses, unlike tanks, could refuse the obstacle. So a block of well-trained infantry who stood their ground could hold off a frontal charge by cavalry.

Scots Wha Hae
Scots, wha hæ wi' Wallace bled,
Scots, wham Bruce has aften led,
Welcome tæ yer gory bed,
Or tæ victorie.

Now's the day, and now's the hour:
See the front o' battle lour,
See approach proud Edward's power -
Chains and Slavery.

Wha will be a traitor knave?
Wha will fill a coward's grave?
Wha sæ base as be a slave?
Let him turn and flee.

Wha, for Scotland's king and law,
Freedom's sword will strongly draw,
Freeman stand, or Freeman fa',
Let him on wi' me.

By Oppression's woes and pains,
By your sons in servile chains!
We will drain our dearest veins,
But they shall be free.

Lay the proud usurpers low,
Tyrants fall in every foe,
Liberty's in every blow! -
Let us do or dee.[52]

Bannockburn was a decisive military victory but of course that wasn't really the end of it, despite what myth would have us believe. It was not until Edward II was deposed in 1328 that England recognized Scotland as an independent country and Bruce as King of Scots. Then the Pope granted Scottish kings the right to be anointed, which gave them divine blessing. Please note too that it is *King of Scots*, not 'King of Scotland'. It is the people who matter rather than the place.

Even then, the struggle with *the auld inemie* would continue off and on for the next 150 years. It was the longest Cold War in history, even if the flare-ups were only occasional. But one thing was clear. We defined ourselves to a large extent as *not English*. And, whatever the English might think, we now had a very clear sense of our Scottish identity and *the liberties of Scotland*.

For so long as one hundred of us are left alive, we will never submit to English dominion. We fight not for glory nor riches nor honours, but for freedom alone, which no good man surrenders but with his life.[53]

7. THE EARLY CHURCH
The three orders of society:
Those who fight, those who pray and those who labour

Early people saw themselves as part of Nature and the land was alive to them in a very real sense that is hard for us to imagine. They shared this world with all other living beings. And behind the physical world was another spirit world. Every moving thing had a force or spirit of its own, be it animal, water, wind, sun or moon. Every event had its magic, every landmark its tales of local people and history. The boundaries were blurred and permeable between the natural and the supernatural, this world and the next, the living and the dead.

At the same time, life was hard and natural disasters were common. No one knew what fate might bring. Any strange events were signs from the gods or foretold calamities to come.

Even the earliest people had some kind of religion, to help them make sense of a bewildering world. It gave comfort in times of need. It charted the passage of time in the natural world. It provided a bridge between this world and the next.

Pagan Celts believed in a whole pantheon of gods and spirits, good and evil, who lived in every nook and cranny of this world and the other. Like most primitive societies, they had festivals to mark the natural cycle and bring fertility.

High up at the head of Glen Lyon is the only surviving pagan shrine in Scotland to the Celtic earth mother.[54] This is the *House of the Cailleach*. It is a small stone house about six feet by four and two feet high. The door faces east to the rising sun. In it live a family of little stone figures – mother, father, daughter and two smaller children. At the start of summer on the festival of Beltane (1 May) a local gamekeeper brings them out to the door and at Halloween he puts them back into the house for the winter. Some years ago an academic took one of the children to Edinburgh to study it, but she suffered so much misfortune that she had to bring him home. Then a new landowner threatened to flood the house under a small-scale hydroelectric scheme. He died, suddenly, unexpectedly, in his forties, before work could begin. Do not mess with the *Cailleach*!

Christianity came to Scotland with the Romans and their camp followers. We would first become aware of the new religion through contact with ordinary Christians. But it was a low status religion for women and slaves and had little impact in northern Britain.

St Ninian was said to be the first bishop in Scotland, around 400 AD, with a base at Whithorn in Galloway. He has also been called *The Apostle to the Southern Picts*. However, there is doubt about Ninian's very existence and no historical evidence that he ever came to Pictland. The churches dedicated to St Ninian were founded many centuries later.[55]

Nevertheless, Christianity did have a firm hold in Ireland by the fifth century and a score of Irish missionaries came to Scotland. Several sites around Loch Tay are linked to the names of early saints. Corrycharmaig in Glen Lochay means the 'Corrie of Cormac', which suggests that he had a church there, though no trace remains.[56] Moreover, there were several saints of that name and we do not know which one this was.

There used to be an early Christian gravestone on the hillside above Tullich farm. It was an upright slab of schist with a disc shaped head. You could not make out any carving or inscription but it looked very like a fifth century gravestone in Luss graveyard.[57] Sadly, someone stole it at the end of the twentieth century.

There is also a 'preacher's stone' with carved crosses above Duncroisk but no one knows when that was from.

We cannot tell what impact these early Christian missionaries had.

All changed with the arrival of St Columba or *Colum Cille,* which was Old Irish for 'Dove of the Church'.

Columba was a member of the Irish royal family and came

to Scotland as a missionary in the year of our Lord AD 563. He founded a monastery in Iona, which seems remote today but in these days of sea travel was a major communication hub. It would become the most important religious centre in Scotland. Iona was the religious cloister, Dalriada its pastoral role, and Pictland its main area of missionary work. But its influence spread as far as Lindisfarne in Northumbria. And Iona played a key role in the preservation of Christianity in northern Europe after the fall of the Roman Empire.

St Columba was *the teacher who would teach the peoples of the Tay*. He *subdued with a blessing, the arrogant ones who surrounded the great king of the Tay.*[58] This was probably Fortriu and he would pass through Glen Dochart and Atholl on his missionary journeys.

The classic tales are about royal conversions but it was not just a matter of winning the king. You had to convince the king's household. Bede described how it worked. *When the king heard his words, he answered that he was willing to accept the faith that Paulinus taught. He said, however, that he would confer about this with his loyal chief men and his counsellors - - -. A meeting of his council was held, and each one was asked in turn what he thought. - - - (Only once they all had their say) - - - The king publicly accepted the gospel.*[59]

But even then, converting the king was only the first step. Taking Christian teaching to the common people was much more difficult and challenging. Bishops and priests would struggle with that for the next thousand years.

Columba was also active in politics. Columba's royal status, Iona's success and hard political graft changed the social status of the Celtic church. Christianity was now a religion fit for kings, not just women and slaves.

The church became an important force for change in Pictish society. By the middle of the ninth century it had displaced pagan beliefs throughout Alba. It brought not only a new religion but also Gaelic language and culture. Its impact was not only spiritual but cultural and economic too.

Leading churchmen became rich and powerful landowners,

who were deeply involved in running the country. Kings and church leaders worked together to their mutual advantage. Churchmen – clerics – clerks – had a monopoly on reading and writing up to the fifteenth century and this gave them a powerful tool for controlling and changing society. They wrote the early chronicles and histories. They helped to run the court and the country, which placed them in positions of trust and influence.

The church also contributed to a profound change in the nature of kingship. Early kings were little more than successful warlords. For many centuries to come, kings would still need to be military leaders but that alone was no longer enough. The greater goal now was to create a more peaceful society. Kings were anointed by God so they ruled by divine grace, which made them sacrosanct. In return, kings promised before God to rule according to law and custom. Kings were answerable to God and some churchmen had the courage to tell them when God disapproved of their actions. Succession should be lawful and orderly rather than by feud and bloodshed. As early as 697 AD, St Adomnan laid out his 'Law of Innocents' to protect non-combatants in war.

The church was the first national organization and that made it a powerful force to support the king's authority. The network of parishes and churchmen let the church spread the message throughout the land.

The church even got into international politics. Senior churchmen were educated abroad, were part of an international network, and had contacts across Europe. They served as diplomats and ambassadors, negotiating with the kings of England and France and the Pope in Rome.

For many centuries the Scottish church struggled to be independent of the Archbishopric of York. On the surface, the dispute was about who should appoint Scottish bishops. The real issues were the links between the Scottish king and church, and relations with England. That struggle only ended in 1192 when the Pope made the Scottish church a *special daughter of Rome*. No other country ever got this honour.

St Columba was the national figure but it was St Fillan who brought Christianity to Breadalbane. St Fillan settled in Glen Dochart in the late seventh or early eighth century, in the part now known as Strathfillan, which lies just over the lairig from the head of Glen Lochay. St Adomnan, who was the ninth abbot of Iona and biographer of St. Columba, founded the monastery and seat of learning in Dull.

Legend says that Fillan and Adomnan crossed Drum Alban together and when they came to Tyndrum they cast lots to see who should go where. The west part fell to Fillan, the east to Adomnan. Perhaps the real story is that Adomnan was the boss and took the plum job, while Fillan was junior and got the outpost! In any case, St Fillan's Priory became a centre for Christian teaching and missionary work throughout the Killin district. It was only after the Reformation that it gradually lost its lands and income and died away. The medieval ruins were still there in 1898.[60]

St Fillan left a lasting and gracious memory across the district. His left arm had a luminous glow, which let him study and write Scriptures in the dark. When Fillan was ploughing in the fields near Killin a wolf killed his ox, but the saint got the wolf to take the ox's place and finish the job. Is that a parable about the Picts and the Gaels? Or is it about farmers and raiders? He also had powers to heal the sick. As late as the nineteenth century, mentally ill people were dunked in St Fillan's Pool on the River Dochart, bound and left overnight in the old priory. If the bonds were loose by morning, they were cured!

St Fillan left some powerful relics.

The *Mayne* was the saint's arm bone, enclosed in a silver casket. Presumably it was from his luminous left arm, though history does not say. Legend has it that Bruce wanted the *Mayne* brought to Bannockburn. The Abbot and the Dewar - the keeper of the relic - brought the casket but left the bone at home in case it fell into the hands of the English. On the eve of battle, the abbot, the Dewar and the Bruce knelt in prayer. A noise came from the casket, the lid fell open and to the churchmen's amazement there was the saint's relic. It was a miracle and showed the Scots had the favour of the Lord. After they won the battle, Bruce was duly grateful and granted lands to support the Priory. Sadly, the *Mayne* is now lost.

St Fillan's staff or crozier is the *coigreach*. The keepers were another family of Dewars, recognized by King James III in 1487. The head of the crozier is silver-gilt and within it is a smaller, older crozier of bronze. It is now in the Museum of Scotland.

The *Bernane* is a cast bronze bell and legend says it would come when St. Fillan called. One day a stranger who was not used to seeing bells flying though the air shot it down with an arrow and the bell is cracked to this day. The *Bernane* was used in the coronation of James IV. About two hundred years ago an English tourist stole the bell, but seventy years later it was found in Canada and brought home. It also is now in the Museum of Scotland.

The eight healing stones of St Fillan are still in Killin. They are water-worn and two are 'socket stones' with smooth holes. Each stone looks like the part of the body it is supposed to heal. So the stone for headaches is shaped like a skull. You rub the stone round the painful head, three times one-way, three times the other, then three times right around the head. All the while, you have to chant the correct Gaelic incantation, except the words are now lost. The socket stones are applied to the nipples of inflamed breasts. The local schoolchildren still give the stones a fresh bed of reeds and grass from the river bank each Christmas Eve.

Over the years St Fillan's Priory was granted revenue from lands in the area. The prior became a lay abbot, which was common at that time. By the twelfth century King William the Lion appointed the Abbot of Glen Dochart with the Earl of Atholl to recover stolen cattle. The abbot was now a local lord.

The Macnabs were the 'sons of the abbot' who descended from the lay abbots of Glen Dochart. The MacGregors were the 'sons of Gregor' who claimed descent from a son of one of the early MacAlpin kings. All such origin myths should, of course, be taken with a large pinch of salt! All we can really say is that both the Macnabs and the MacGregors were clans from this area.

The churches at Killin and Lochearnhead are dedicated to St Fillan and may have been founded by him in the eighth century.[61]

The name Killin comes from the Gaelic *cill* and may mean *the chapel, churchyard, or burying place of the pool.* In earlier times, Killin was a tiny village in a poor area and must have struggled to support a church. In 1317, Robert the Bruce made the Abbot of Inchadney (modern Kenmore) responsible for the vicarage at Killin and a canon in Strathfillan. But as late as 1557, just before the Reformation, the Bishop of Dunkeld had to order the curate of Killin to summon the people of the parish to pay their dues.

The pre-Reformation church at Killin was in the old churchyard beside the River Lochay. It was in use until the present church was built in 1744 and its ruins were still standing in 1842, though nothing now remains. People often went on using a site that was made sacred by worship from ancient times, so that could be a much older site and would fit with the name Killin.

But even Killin was a long way from upper Glen Lochay, especially in winter. So what kind of religion did ordinary people get in a remote place like upper Glen Lochay?

The work of the medieval church was to save souls and the way to salvation was through the sacraments of baptism, confession, communion and the last rites. These were in Latin, which ordinary people did not understand, but they would be impressive and awe-inspiring ceremonies.

Religion also added much-needed spice to life. English accounts tell of rich pageants, with saints' days and holy days adding colour and fun to peasant life. Religion offered comfort, as well as opium, for the very real trials of life. As a final consolation there was faith in a better life hereafter and people spent much time praying for the dead. Yet there can have been little grandeur or pageantry in a small church in Killin, never mind Glen Lochay.

Then there were the cults of the Scottish saints.

Kenneth MacAlpin brought the relics of St Columba to Dunkeld in 849 AD for safe keeping from the Vikings. Dunkeld cathedral became the centre of the diocese in which Killin lay. Columba's relics were carried into battle, used to bless the troops and given credit for victory. The men of Alba prayed to God and St Columba before battle and his Crozier was their battle standard against the Vikings. The Abbot of Arbroath carried his relics at Bannockburn.

Saint Andrew is the patron saint of Scotland. St Andrew was the first disciple and was supposedly crucified on a diagonal or Saltire cross. His bones were taken to Constantinople in the fourth century. That much is history. Then the legend begins. An angel appeared to a monk called Regulus and told him to take the saint's relics *to the ends of the earth*. He got as far as Fife, where he was shipwrecked, and that (centuries later) became the monastery of St Andrews. In the eighth century a Pictish king dreamt of St Andrew the night before a battle with Northumbria. Next morning, before the battle, a huge cross of white cloud appeared against a brilliant blue sky. The Scots won the battle and the Saltire became the flag of Scotland.

Yet it was not until the thirteenth century that the Scottish legend of St Andrew was written to support growing nationalism. St Andrew wasn't even at Bannockburn. It was only after the battle that the new cathedral of St Andrews was consecrated *for the notable victory granted to the Scottish people by the blessed Andrew*.

In the same kind of way, out of the mists of time, the thistle became the emblem of Scotland. Some say it is because it is such a common flower in Scotland. Others because it is prickly, just like the Scots. The real story is that once upon a time a band of Vikings tried to creep up on a Scottish camp under cover of darkness. They took off their boots to make less noise but as they crossed the field they ran into a patch of thistles. Their cries of pain awakened the Scots who were able to fight off the bare-footed Vikings. And so the thistle became the emblem of Scotland. Of course, you must remember the pinch of salt!

To come back to more mundane matters, what was the church actually like in upper Glen Lochay before the fifteenth century? St Fillan's Priory lay just over the lairig from the head of Glen Lochay, so we must have been within its sphere of influence from the very beginning.

Any church buildings in Glen Lochay, if there were any, would be pretty basic. Rod diviners claim there was an ancient church at a junction of ley lines just above Kenknock, though the local archaeologist does not believe this. Indeed, given the number of people, it seems more likely that services were held outdoors and that would fit with the preacher's stone.

Parish priests were very different from leading churchmen. They came from a much poorer background, more like better-off peasant families. They had little education. They made a modest living, if a little bit more comfortable than their flock.

The parish priest's main job was to administer the sacraments. The Mass was *the salvation of the living and the redemption of the dead.* Hearing it regularly and devoutly *built up credit against the dangers of dying un-confessed, reduced the devil's power, temporarily suspended the aging process, protected against sudden death or blindness, improved digestion, and facilitated childbirth.*[62] But there was no organized system of preaching or religious instruction. As late as 1460, the church had to bring a hundred and fifty Franciscan friars to Scotland to meet the need for preachers.

There is a great deal of doubt about how often ordinary people went to church. Baptism was almost universal. But many people would only attend confession and communion once a year at Easter.

Yet even if people did not go to church very often or get any preaching when they did, they had clear ideas of sin, penance, heaven, hell and purgatory. God and the Devil were much more real to them than they seem to us today.

In Glenlochay, about three miles from Killin in a clearing in the wood, you can see the ruins of a cottage, where dwelt a well-known weaver. One Hogmanay he was returning home when whom should he meet but the Devil. Of course he took to his heels and ran for his life in the direction of home, and the Devil after him. He had almost reached the door when the Gentleman with the Horns made a snatch at him, but the weaver ducked, the Devil missed and his hand struck a tree and left its print on the trunk, where it was to be seen for many a day and especially many a night, for it shone in the dark![63] Shades of Tam o' Shanter!

Christianity adopted many pagan ideas and festivals into its rituals. Others survived as superstitions and continued happily alongside the church until the nineteenth century.

Superstition played a part in every aspect of peasant life and was strongest and most persistent in remote areas. There were superstitions about every daily event – birth, death, the illness of a cow, milk turning sour, going on a journey. Mysterious signs foretold good or ill, and rites or charms could promote or prevent it. People placed their trust in charms, omens, incantations and magic.

Old Highland peasants were as sure of the existence of fairies, kelpies, urisks and witches as they were of their own. The wee folk lived below ground in green knolls or 'fairy hills', in water and in wild recesses all over the Highlands.

Fairies were originally minor gods in pagan religions. These were the most active sprites. If you did not perform the right ceremony the fairies might steal a new-born baby and replace it with a changeling.

There were many tales of people visiting fairyland. The Rev Robert Kirk, minister in Aberfoyle, was the seventh son of a seventh son and had the second sight. In 1691 he wrote *The Secret Commonwealth* about the lives and customs of the fairies.

Every day he used to walk up Doon Hill, about a mile from the village. There he collapsed and died on 14 May 1692 and you can still visit his grave in the local graveyard. Legend says that he appeared to his cousin after the funeral to say that he was not really dead but had only swooned and been carried off to fairyland. His wife was pregnant when he died and he said he would come to the child's baptism. If his cousin threw a knife over the ghost, the fairies would release him. At the baptism the Rev duly appeared but his cousin was too shocked to throw the knife so the fairies took Rev Kirk back to fairyland and there he has lived ever since.

There is still an old pine tree – the fairy tree - on top of Doon Hill where tourists tie ribbons and leave silver coins for the fairies.

The kelpie or water-horse was the most dangerous creature. He would lure women and children to his underwater haunts and devour them. He could cause a spate and drown the careless traveller.

Urisks were more benign, a curious mixture of mortal man and spirit. They also lived in water and haunted deep ravines, waterfalls and lonely lochs. Urisks were solitary beings, but became more sociable about the time of the harvest, when they hung around mills and farmyards. They loved dairy products, and people often left out a bowl of milk for the urisk. They were lazy and mischievous, but would sometimes help with hard work in the kitchen, barn or stable. Many a family got the benefit of their help, but only if they treated the urisk with respect and left his place open at the side of the fire.

Whatever you might think of these spirits, witches were real people. But witches were thought to be familiars of the devil. They caused stillbirths, made a cow's or a woman's milk dry up, and stole a neighbour's milk. Between the Reformation in 1560 and the Union of the Crowns in 1707, nearly three thousand people were killed in Scotland because other people thought they were witches. Most of the victims were women, often old, living alone, and usually from the lower social classes.

Belief in witchcraft and the evil eye was as deep-rooted in Breadalbane as in other parts of the country, but they did not burn any witches here. Kenmore Kirk Session records tell of several old women accused of witchcraft. Yet though they might scold them for improper behaviour, they did not convict any of witchcraft. More often they rebuked the accuser!

In 1662 Donald M'Gillechrist accused his neighbour N'Vane of bewitching him. *She brought a pock of earth - - - to his house; since which, his gear has not luckit with him, and his corns grow not. The judge, with sense beyond the age, acquitted the woman at this time, but forbade all persons from the use of the pock of earth "seeing it inclines to no good, but to an evil custom".*[64]

Highlanders perhaps held to older beliefs that some witches did good and only some were bad. You should tolerate them all for fear of stirring up the supernatural, and the best approach was to bribe her with milk and oatmeal. Indeed, many an old widow with a good line in curses, charms and herbal remedies might make a good living as a witch!

The crime of witchcraft was abolished from the statute book in 1736, but long after that there was a widespread belief in the evil eye.

Yet not all spirits were bad and there were many lucky charms too. With superstition and Christianity all mixed up!

Cross your fingers. Wear a cross around your neck to protect you from the evil eye. A rabbit's foot is lucky. Wear a sprig of white heather at a wedding. Young women can spot a seductive kelpie by the sand or weed in his hair. If you kill the first adder you see in the spring you will be able to overcome your enemies for the rest of the year. Do not stamp on a beetle because that will bring rain and if you do it in the house there may be a death in the family. Dogs can see ghosts, know when someone is about to die, and can tell you who is a good person and who is bad. Two rowan trees at the front door will protect the house from evil. A white cockerel keeps ghosts and evil spirits away.

There were even magic cures for illness. We have already seen the holy pool of Strathfillan, which could cure madness. Until recent times, there was a pagan healing well on Sròn a Chlachain above Killin and a whooping cough stone in Achmore woods.[65]

Do not dismiss it all too readily. Have you never done anything to bring good luck or guard against misfortune?

Human beings throughout history have felt a need to believe in something greater than themselves. Religion in all its forms has met the same basic needs: to help make sense of the world and to provide comfort in times of need. In turbulent times, these needs were even more pressing.

Christianity was a powerful force that helped to shape the society we call Scotland. And superstition was important in people's lives until at least the nineteenth century. The question is how that legacy would shape the years ahead.

8. THE LAIRDS OF GLENORCHY
The Campbells are coming!

In the fourteenth century, Glen Lochay was still part of Atholl.

In 1306, Robert the Bruce murdered his rival John Comyn and grabbed the Scottish throne. This led to a bitter blood feud with the Comyn supporters, who included the MacDougalls of Lorne, the Macnabs and the MacGregors. It plunged Scotland into civil war and re-ignited the war with England.

Bruce was soon defeated by the English in a battle at Methven near Perth. As he fled west, a force of MacDougalls and Macnabs caught him in a skirmish at Dalrigh in Strathfillan and Bruce barely escaped with his life. He suffered six defeats in a row. By now, most of his supporters had been killed or captured. At this point no one would have given much for his chances of survival, never mind holding on to the crown.

But Bruce was not a man to give up easily. Legend says that while on the run hiding in a cave he watched a spider trying to climb its thread. Six times it failed but it tried and tried and tried again until the seventh time it succeeded. If a tiny spider could do it, so could he. Bruce took heart and persevered. Oh, by the way, Sir Walter Scott only made up that story in the nineteenth century!

In real life, Bruce fell back to the west, re-grouped his forces and fought back. He had the support of the Scottish church. He won a series of battles against the English and the Comyn supporters, and built a reputation as a skilled general. He was lucky, favoured by God, and popular among ordinary Scots. Within two years, by 1308, he was undisputed king.

These fortunes of war changed land holding across Breadalbane. In 1306 the Earl of Atholl supported Bruce, but he was captured and hanged in London. His son switched to the English side but lost to Bruce forces and forfeited his title and his land. In 1308, Bruce got his revenge on the MacDougalls at the Pass of Brander up at Loch Awe so the MacDougalls and Macnabs also forfeited their land. The Macnabs and the MacGregors had a bad habit of choosing the losing side.

This brings us to the Campbells who are key players in the Breadalbane story. They claimed descent from a Norman knight who came to Scotland some time in the twelfth century. Legend says they came to Loch Awe in the thirteenth century when a knight called Cambuel married an heiress of the old castle at Innischonel. The first definite historic figure was Sir Colin Campbell or *Caelian Mor* – 'Big Colin' – who held the Barony of Loch Awe. He died about 1296 and may have been a cousin of Robert the Bruce.

Caelian Mor's son Niall was a faithful supporter of Bruce and fought in his war band from 1306 until Bannockburn. In 1315, Bruce re-granted the Barony of Loch Awe to one of Sir Niall's sons. Niall himself married Bruce's sister and Bruce made their son John – his nephew - Earl of Atholl. However, John died without an heir so Atholl reverted to the Crown. By 1342, Atholl went to Robert the Steward, who was Robert the Bruce's grandson and later became King Robert II. Atholl would stay in the hands of the Stewart family until 1625, even if there was a lot of power play within the family at different times.

By 1336 the lairds of Macnabs got back in favour with Bruce's son King David II. Over the next five hundred years they held various small parcels of land around Killin but they were never major players again.

If you are confused by now, then you have a pretty good idea what it was like. Confusing! And that was only a small part of the picture. It was all a game of feudal musical chairs in which the players jockeyed for position and land. There were all the layers of feudal superiority. Many land holdings were split up and inter-mingled. So there was plenty of scope for dispute.

The key facts for our story are that by the middle of the fourteenth century Glen Lochay was still part of Atholl, but the Crown had a finger in the feudal pie and the Campbells were poised to the west.

What kind of men were these? First and foremost, they were warlords who led from the front.

Recent work at Stirling Castle unearthed nine graves from the thirteenth and fourteenth centuries.[66] There were men and women and most had died of blunt injury. The most interesting skeleton was a man in his mid-twenties who died about 1300 AD. His upper body was very well-muscled and he was bow-legged from horse riding. He had an injury to the front of his skull caused by a sword or axe, but that was healed so he had survived to fight again. Lodged within his ribcage was the barbed arrowhead that killed him. This man had a short, strenuous and violent life.

Forensic scientists re-built his face upon the skull to see what he might have looked like, just as they do with crime victims today. He was thickset, with a bullet head and a deep scar on his forehead. He was built like a front-row forward from a rugby scrum. To our eyes, he looks a real thug. What, in Glasgow, we call a hard man. If you saw him coming down the street you would cross to the other side. Yet these scars were the badges of his profession and he would wear them with pride.

We do not know who he was but his burial place suggests he was a leading knight. This is the closest we will ever get to seeing what Lords of that time were like.

Meantime, what about the ordinary men of Glen Lochay? We know that Atholl split and fought for both sides at different times. So did they go with the rising tide of popular opinion and join Bruce? Or did they go with the forfeited Earl of Atholl and the Macnabs and MacGregors and fight on the wrong side? Did the men of Dalgirdy fight with Bruce at Bannockburn, or on the English side, or did they manage to keep out of it and stay at home? We simply do not know.

But not to worry, there would be plenty other battles to come.

The Campbell Lairds of Glenorchy dominate the rest of our story.[67]

The first Laird of Glenorchy (1432-1475) was Sir Colin Campbell, third son of Lord Campbell of Lochaw. By feudal right, Lord Campbell passed most of his lands to his eldest son Archibald, whose descendants would become the Dukes of Argyll. For some reason that is not very clear, he gave Sir Colin the lands of Glenorchy by a charter dated 20 October 1432[68]. Glenorchy was a small, poor land in the hills to the east of Loch Awe. It could have been worse, because as a younger son he had no right to any land of his own. But the lairds of Glenorchy would always be the junior or cadet branch of the Campbell family. However much they might resent it and however hard they strived, Glenorchy would always live in the shadow of the House of Argyll. It gave our lairds a powerful motive to better their lot.

For the next five hundred years the Campbells spread across Breadalbane like an irresistible tide. Sir Colin's descendants would become the Earls of Breadalbane and at their peak owned one of the largest land holdings in Britain.

There are many tales of adventure and romance about the first Laird. He visited Rome three times and was a Knight Templar of Rhodes.

His first wife, like his mother, was a Stewart of Atholl. Altogether, he had five wives and two of them brought him dowries of more land.

During one of Sir Colin's times abroad, his wife spent seven years' income from the lands to build a new castle at Kilchurn. This is a famous picture postcard castle that still stands on a rocky knoll at the east end of Loch Awe, with views over the loch and Ben Cruachan. It is a magical place. On a good day you can stand on the battlements and imagine you are lord of all you survey.

The legend goes that while in Rome Sir Colin had a dream. A monk interpreted it to mean that he should go home as fast as he could to prevent a domestic tragedy. He duly came home dressed as a beggar and sought food and shelter from his old nurse. She only knew him by a scar on his arm, showing how much he had changed in his years away. She told him that MacCorquodale, a local chief, had intercepted all his messages and spread rumours that he had died in the Holy Land. Lady Glenorchy, thinking she was a widow, was to marry MacCorquodale the very next day.

Still dressed as a beggar, Sir Colin rushed to Kilchurn Castle, which was wide open for the wedding feast. With the other guests he got food and drink, but said he would only drink from milady's fair hand. She took pity on the beggar and handed him a cup of wine. He drank her health and handed back the empty cup with his ring in the bottom. Of course she recognized the ring (even if not her husband!) and threw herself into his arms. Sir Colin was the hero of the hour and got a prodigal's welcome from his wife, his family and his people. Some accounts say that he slew the wicked suitor and others that he simply threw him out, but that does not really matter. All agree on the more important point that Sir Colin grabbed MacCorquodale's land!

A similar tale is told of other knights so it may well be apocryphal. But it does tell of a very real problem. When crusaders were away for years with no word of their fates, their lonely wives must have faced many fears and temptations.

Sir Colin first came to Breadalbane by getting blocks of land in *tack*. Tacks were a Highland system of holding land under lease. A *tackman* was a chief tenant, often kin to the lord, who held land directly from him for a period of years or for life. He then sublet the land to lesser tenants who farmed it. The tackman took responsibility for running this land. He paid rent to his lord in cash, produce or military service, and got a larger rent from the tenants, taking his profit between the two. Sometimes, he also farmed on his own account.

The Exchequer Roll of 1454 mentions *Sir Colin Campbell - - - said to be of Deschyr & Towyr*[69] though we do not know how long he had already held it. The key word here is *of* which means that he held the land, but did not necessarily live there.

When the old records said that someone was *in* a place that meant he did actually live there.

Sir Colin died in 1475 and the first listing of Dalgirdy in the Exchequer Rolls was in 1476[70]. However, a partial list of farms in 1451 did include neighbouring Tullich and Tirai, so the farms were established before then. And the amount of the 1451 rental for the *Farm of the lands of Tullich* suggests it may have included Dalgirdy, as it sometimes did over the years ahead.[71] So there is a fair chance that Sir Colin held Dalgirdy from the early 1450s.

By Sir Colin's death in 1475, the Campbells had a firm toehold in Breadalbane. He started the family motto of *Conquess and keepit things conquessit.*[72]

Sir Colin's eldest son Sir Duncan Campbell was second Laird of Glenorchy from 1475-1513.

Soon after his father's death, Sir Duncan became the king's Chamberlain for the crown lands of Discher and Toyer, responsible for collecting rents, running the estates, and submitting an annual return to the Exchequer Roll. Then, in 1488, the king made him Baron Buillie of Discher and Toyer.[73] Later he got the same position for Glen Lyon and Glen Dochart. He bought Finlarig, which became the baronial seat of Discher and Toyer.

In 1479-80, Sir Duncan was the first person of whom we have a record holding the rentals of *Corycarmac, Tullich et Gildardy, Terartor.*[74] *Gildardy* is Dalgirdy.

The second laird died at the battle of Flodden in 1513, along with King James IV and his cousin the Earl of Argyll. Flodden was a black day for Scotland. It was the final, disastrous mistake of James IV's flamboyant reign. It was a pointless battle against the English, in support of a far-off French king, fought for no good purpose. James had a large army but it was badly led and the battle went wrong from the start. James personally led a gallant but foolish charge into the centre of the English ranks. It was death or glory on a throw of the dice and you can guess the outcome.

The lairds of Clan Campbell and the men of the west ranged behind Earl Archibald, chief of Clan Campbell and head of the Gael, at their head. Argyll and Lennox seem to have been outflanked and driven across the hill through the shambles of James IV's already defeated battle. Somewhere in the grim and bloody mess Earl Archibald and his cousins Duncan of Glenorchy and John of Lawers fell.[75]

The Scots were badly mauled. - - - Particularly badly cut up was the division commanded by the Earls of Lennox and Argyll. - - - Stanley and his men inflicted fearful casualties on the Highlanders, driving them pell-mell across the battlefield over the ground on which already the Scottish King lay stiff and stark. - - - Scottish losses were horrendous. Clan Campbell was hard hit, even in comparison with the slaughter all around. - - - The men from Argyll had been with their Chief in the division that had been broken and comprehensively destroyed.[76]

Scotland lost most of her leading nobles – *the Flowers of the Forest.* Overall Scottish casualties were 20-30%. There were a thousand men of Clan Campbell at the battle and perhaps as many as half died. Records from that time only gave the names of kings and lords, so we do not know about the ordinary men of Glen Lochay or Dalgirdy who died on Flodden field.

Sir John Campbell was fifth Laird from 1536-1550 and this is when we begin to find out more about Dalgirdy.

Renunciation and resignation by John Earl of Atholl of the lands of Dalgardie, Tullich, Teray, Corecharmick - - - and all other lands, steadings and possessions pertaining to the King in property within the Lordship of Deschoir and Toyer, and of all investments, charter and writs thereof made to the said Earl or his deceased father or grandfather by the King or his predecessors or by any other person whatever, and that in favour of John Campbell of Glenwrquhay his heirs or assignees whomsoever. Dated 7th Dec 1536.[77]

These four farms seem to have been some kind of group, which sometimes also included Murlagganmore. Each time they changed hands, Atholl 'renounced' its rights and this continued as late as 1784. Although the lairds of Glenorchy held Dalgirdy, Atholl clearly still had some kind of feudal rights in this part of Glen Lochay.

Just a year after Sir John became laird he faced a legal challenge about who had power to hold Courts in the area. The Privy Council held a hearing in the case of *Patrick Makgrogain, Patrick Makstalkar and Sir Crystal Rouch and other tenants of lands of Discher and Toyer, v. John, earl of Athole, and John Campbell of Glenurquhay.*

Whereby the lords ordain the tenants to obey said John Campbell in holding of courts upon said lands in time to come, because he produced a charter under the great seal, where deceased Sir Duncan Campbell, his predecessor (the second laird), *was infeft in said office of bailiery, at Perth, 3 December 1488, which was long before date of feuferme made of said lands to said John, earl of Atholl.*[78]

Duncan McCarbre was *wadsetter* in Dalgirdy and Tullich in 1536-1541.[79] Wadsets were a kind of mortgage in which the laird mortgaged some of his land to raise capital. The lender became the wadsetter who got the rent or free use of the land until the capital was repaid. Wadsetters were often fellow lairds or cadet members of the laird's family, and wadsets helped to maintain their social ties. For as long as the wadset lasted, the wadsetter had more freedom and standing than a tackman. However, McCarbre seems to have left after 1541, so presumably the wadset was paid off.

That is when we learn that Dalgirdy was a three merkland.[80] That was about average. Most farms in upper Glen Lochay were between two and four merklands.

A merk was two-thirds of a Scots pound. Under the feudal system, starting in the twelfth century, land was granted for a Knight's Service. The land to support one knight was worth thirty merks, so a three merkland was about one-tenth of a knight's value. On Loch Tay side, a three merkland would have about 20-30 acres of infield land. That was about the same as the Lowland *ploughgate*, which was the amount of land that a plough team could work.

There is a romantic tale from that time. King James V went to Paris in 1537 to marry his first French bride Madeleine of Valois, daughter of Francis I of France. Sir John Campbell and his brother Colin were in the bridal party. But the story goes that Duncan McCarbre in Dalgirdy and Finlay in Tirai were also in the king's escort.[81] The archives show that the king did indeed issue 'letters of protection' under the Privy Seal to look after the property and interests of various men. And the list includes *Finlay McCarbre, Donald McCarbre, Johne McCarbre, Duncane McCarbre, younger* and nine other men from Glen Lochay.[82]

Sadly, Dr Norman MacDougall, today's expert on King James V, thinks such letters of protection were actually to protect those at home while their laird was away.[83] So our man from Dalgirdy wasn't invited to the royal wedding after all!

Sir John left no male heir, so his younger brother Colin succeeded him.

Sir Colin Campbell, the 'Grey Laird', was the sixth Laird of Glenorchy from 1550-1583. He was aged fifty when he became laird, but then held the lands for thirty-three years. Sir Colin was an ambitious and ruthless man who took full advantage of turbulent times to add to his lands. He *conquessit the superiority of M'Nabb his heil landis.*

At the age of eleven, his grandfather sent him as a foster child to a lowly family of MacGregors.[84] This was an old Gaelic custom that helped to broaden the education of future chiefs and to bind the social classes to each other. But the Grey Laird would prove no friend to the MacGregors.

As soon as Grey Colin became laird he set about building a castle at Taymouth. This was only quarter of a mile from the eastern edge of Glenorchy land but when Sir Colin was asked why, he replied: *Och, we might just push beyond.* An insatiable lust for land!

The *Great Seal Feu Charter in favour of Colin Campbell of Glenurchuay and Katherine Ruthven his spouse in lands of Dalgardie and many others in lordship of Disher and Toyer, in Sherriffdom of Perth* was dated 1564.[85]

Four years later, Grey Colin and his wife granted various lands including Dalgirdy to their younger son Archibald Campbell and his wife Margaret Toscheoch, who lived in Murlagan Moir.[86] Archibald held these lands until 1623, probably as tackman under the laird. The lands then returned to the laird, perhaps on Archibald' death.

Grey Colin took a leading role in persecuting the MacGregors, much to his own advantage. The Black Book of Taymouth summed it up. He was *ane great justiciar all his tyme, thoch the quhilk he sustenit the deidlie feid of the clan-gregour ane lang space.*[87]

Branches of Clan MacGregor had occupied much of this area from early times. Indeed, their heartlands of Glenorchy, Glenlyon and Glenstrae were at one time known as 'MacGregor's Glens'. And the very first tenant of Dalgirdy whose name we know was one Patrick MacGregor in 1527.[88] However, clans only held a loose area. Critically, too, the old clan chiefs did not 'own' the land, which was held in common by the whole clan 'by right of the sword'.

But the MacGregors were naïve. They relied on their right to the land by possession from ancient days and failed to understand or adapt to changing times. This placed them at the mercy of 'Charter Lords' like the Campbells who used lowland law charters, tacks and tenancy agreements – to expand their empire. The power of the broadsword was replaced by the thousand pricks of sharp little pens. The MacGregors put up a futile and doomed resistance that would be fatal for them and play into the hands of Glenorchy.

The Campbells and the MacGregors had earlier shared the lands of Loch Awe on friendly terms. But when the Campbells began to expand to the east, they encroached more and more on MacGregor lands. The Campbells wanted to put the MacGregors in their place. The MacGregors saw the Campbells as outsiders invading their space. They became bitter enemies.

Some men were persuaded or forced into submitting to their new lord. Some were tolerated for a time as 'kindly tenants' based on bonds of kinship. Some changed their names, like *Calum McKerlich alias Campbell* in Dalgirdy.[89]

Some tried to hold on to their land by the old 'right of the sword' but they had no chance. Many lost their lands, and were driven to lawlessness. For example, there was a *Decreet of removal* against *Patrick MacGregour in Dalgardy and others - - - tenants of the said ward lands charging them to cease occupying the same.*[90]

Dispossessed or 'broken men' of Clan MacGregor became outlaws and moved into empty land on Rannoch as *Clan a Cheatheaich* – Children of the Mist. They lived on plunder and took most delight in raiding the lands they had lost.

In response, the government appointed the Campbells of Argyll and Glenorchy to restore peace. 'Letters of Fire and Sword' gave them legal powers to evict, brand and exterminate MacGregors. They should *be esteemed publick enemies to God, the King and all his trewe and faithful subjectes, and to be persewed with fire and sword, quhair ever they be apprehended, without crime, paine or danger, to be incurred be the doers there-throw.*[91]

The Grey Laird and his son Black Duncan were relentless in the persecution of the MacGregors. They abused their powers so badly that the Privy Council had to rein them in on more than one occasion. The MacGregors retaliated with larger raids on Glenorchy land but that brought the law down on them even harder. To bring it to an end, in the early 1600s, Acts of Parliament placed a bounty on MacGregor heads and outlawed the very name MacGregor.

The name Macgregoure suld be altogidder abolisched, and the haill persounes of that Clan sulde renounce thair name, and tak them some other name, and that thai nor nane of their posterities sulde call thame selffis Gregoure or McGregoure thair efter under paine of deade.[92]

Glenorchy completed the 'cleansing' of the MacGregors about 1613.

Sir Duncan Campbell succeeded his father and was seventh Laird from 1583 to 1631. He was another greedy and grasping man who was known as 'Black Duncan'. His first wife was yet another Stuart of Atholl. (Just to confuse things, Mary Queen of Scots changed the spelling of the family name from Stewart to Stuart.)

Sir Duncan was a royal favourite. In 1590, King James VI chose him as one of the barons to assist in his marriage to Anne of Denmark. He was involved in court plots all his life, particularly against his kinsmen the Earls of Argyll and Atholl. He even had a hand in murder but was protected by his friend the king. He was said to be so devious that he tricked the fairies into the impossible task of making a rope out of sand!

Black Duncan added so much land to the estate that he is sometimes mistaken for its founder. In 1596, James VI made him Keeper of the Royal Forest of Mamlorn. Later, Charles I made him Sheriff of Perthshire.

By this time the feudal system was changing. Kings now needed money as much as military service and when Sir Duncan renewed the Lordship of Discher and Toyer he had to pay two thousand Scots merks. At the same time, many of the old noble families had died out and the link between land and titles was broken. And kings no longer had enough land to reward supporters, so began to give titles separately from land. These changes would in due course lead to land 'ownership' and the modern peerage system.

As a great lord, Black Duncan lived in style. He built or extended seven great houses on the estate, including Finlarig Castle whose ruins stand outside Killin. He employed artists and had rich fabric hangings. The fare was sumptuous. There was fresh and salt beef, salmon and trout from Loch Tay, herring from Loch Fyne, dried fish, mutton, capons, geese, venison, partridge, blackcock and rabbits. The laird, his family and guests drank claret and white wine. The household drank enormous quantities of ale, of three grades for different ranks.

This lifestyle was costly and he raised the money by oppressing the poor and conspiring against the rich.

Yet in some ways Black Duncan was ahead of his times. He was an early pioneer of 'improving' his estate. He planted forests and great avenues of trees that stood into the twentieth century. He built the first Bridge of Lochay. The first school in Killin was in his time.

By 1640 the Campbells of Glenorchy were a wealthy family. Among the *Jewells, silver plaitt and vther silver work* at Balloch were *ane stone of the quantitye of half a hen's egg set in silver* said to have been worn by the first laird on the Crusades. There was *ane targatt of gold sett with thrie diamondis, four topaces, ane rubbie and ane saphyre, enameled,* from James V. Queen Anne, wife of James VI, was even more generous with *ane round Jewell of gold sett with precious stones conteining tuentie nyne diamonds and four great rubbies* and also *ane gold ring sett with ane great diamond schapine lyke a heart and vther four small diamonds.*[93]

They were also a prolific bunch.

The ninth Laird had a large family of eight sons and nine daughters. He got the estates free of debt but soon ran into financial difficulty. He had to support his large family and the widows of his father and brother. Then came the Civil War. He personally fought for the Covenanters and had to pay for arms and supplies for the army raised from his men. He might just have managed all that, but the devastation of his estates by the Raid of Montrose in 1644-45 brought him to the verge of ruin. More of that anon.

The House of Glenorchy had fallen upon evil days.

The tenth Laird took over a bankrupt estate. His wealth was spent, his land mortgaged, and his debtors were pressing for payment. To make things worse, he married three times and had twelve sons and fifteen daughters! He also fell out with his eldest son who bit-by-bit wrested control of the estate away from him. Yet his major achievement was to preserve the estate intact for his son to inherit and rebuild the family fortunes.

By the mid-seventeenth century, the Lairds of Glenorchy had a secure hold on Breadalbane. They drew income from its lands. They were the feudal superiors who exercised the king's authority and held courts of justice across the land. They had the power to raise military forces. Everything was in place to become legal owners of the estate in due course.

It had been an untidy process rather than a pre-planned strategy. They often gained control step-wise: first a tack, then a wadset and later feudal superiority. But the steps were often opportunistic and messy. They and their lawyers used every dirty legal trick they could dream up. They spun a complex web of tacks, wadsets, loans and debts, options and defaults, and obscure land deals that no one else could understand. And they had their own courts to enforce them.

They also made a lot of advantageous marriages. They planted kinsmen – younger sons, brothers, cousins – across the land to keep it all within the family. They were very fertile of sons, which helped to maintain the family lineage over many generations. And their many daughters created more ties of marriage and kinship.

It was like a living, growing organism that kept changing shape. And it was a greedy beast that consumed all it could grab and sucked it dry.

But it had worked. The cadet branch of the family was well on the way from poor wee Glenorchy to mighty Breadalbane. And the best was yet to come.

9. PEASANT LIFE
Nasty, brutish and short

Meantime, what was rural life like for the common folk? Nine out of ten Scots lived on the land. Most were peasants. The Latin *paganus* simply meant 'a country person' though today it also suggests poverty and subsistence living in an undeveloped country. 'Pagan' comes from the same root.

Rural life did not change much between the eleventh and mid-eighteenth centuries. People lived like their forebears, in the same area. Most people had never been more than a few miles from home. Customs and beliefs were passed on from one generation to the next and slow to change. Tradition!

At its peak in the eleventh century, Gaelic was the language of Scotland from the far north down to Fife in the east and Galloway in the west. Only the people of Lothian spoke English. That changed with the Anglo-Normans. Norman lords spoke French and English while their clerks wrote in Latin. The new burghs spoke English. By the fourteenth century, English became the language of government while Gaelic retreated to the Highlands and became a second-rate language. Yet 50% of Scots still spoke Gaelic and it would remain the language of the Highlands until the nineteenth century.

Up to the fourteenth century there was little social divide between Highlands and Lowlands. It was only as lowland Scotland developed and the Highlands were slow to follow that the rift got wider. The first mention of 'Highlanders' as a distinct identity was by John of Fordun in the late fourteenth century.

The manners and customs of the Scots vary with the diversity of their speech. For two languages are spoken amongst them, the Scottish (Gaelic) and the Teutonic (English); the latter of which is the language of those who occupy the seaboard and plains, while the race of Scottish speech inhabits the highlands and outlying islands. The people of the coast are of domestic and civilized habits, trusty, patient, and urbane, decent in their attire, affable, and peaceful, devout in Divine worship, yet always prone to resist a wrong at the hand of their enemies. The highlanders and people of the islands, on the other hand, are a savage and untamed nation, rude and independent, given to rapine, ease-loving, of a docile and warm disposition, comely in person, but unsightly in dress, hostile to the English people and language, and, owing to diversity of speech, even to their own nation, and exceedingly cruel. They are, however, faithful and obedient to their king and country, and easily made to submit to law, if properly governed.[94]

Geography, language and way of life divided the Highlands and the Lowlands. The geographic divide was not just between mountains and plains, but soil and climate and farming too. The mountains were a physical barrier to travel and economic development. Language was a major barrier to communication. The whole way of life, traditions and culture were different. Gaelic society was still based on kinship and the clan while the Lowlands was now a feudal society based on the rule of law.

Against that background, Fordun thought the Highlanders were *savage and untamed* and *hostile to the English.* That was new. Before the fourteenth century, Highlanders were not considered to be any different or any worse than other Scots. From now on, there was growing concern about law and order in general and in the Highlands in particular. Royal and church authority struggled to reach into the Highlands. When the Norsemen were driven out of the west in 1266, the Lords of the Isles filled the power vacuum and there was a resurgence of Gaelic power and confidence. But when James IV toppled the Lords of the Isles in 1493, he failed to replace them with any effective authority of his own and that led to a further period of lawlessness.

The divide of economy and language and culture between Lowland Scots and Highland Gaels made tension inevitable. Lack of law and order gave real cause for conflict, and the Gaelic custom of raiding only made things worse. But this was really a clash between two kinds and stages of society. It is easy to see how the conflict became ethnic as well as cultural.

Many accounts up to the seventeenth century continued to talk of *wyld wykkyd Helandemen.*

Gaelic society was based on kinship, real or imagined. All members of the clan felt they were related, however distantly. All felt pride in their good name, whatever their social position. Early travellers joked that any ragged Scotsman could call himself a lord but what he really claimed was that his ancestry was as good as anyone else. He could pay respect to social status without losing pride in his own worth.

Gaelic culture is rich in song and legend. In earlier times it was all about Highland blood and feuds and military prowess. More recently it told of the history, customs and lives of ordinary people in a close-knit community.[95] Today it often seems to be looking back to the past. And the real Gaelic culture is now almost lost in Victorian myth.

Before the eighteenth century, Highland peasants lived in what can only be called hovels. Some did not improve until the late nineteenth century.

There were no traces of inhabitants, except perhaps a rude pile of clods - - -.[96]

It was a wretched little hovel of earth only, I think, and for a window had only a small hole, which was stopped with a piece of turf, that was taken out occasionally to let in light. In the middle of the space which we entered was a fire of peat, the smoke going out at a hole in the roof.[97]

The walls were built of turf and stone and were no more than five feet high. They were not strong enough to carry weight, so the roof rested on wooden arches called 'crucks' and in a land short of timber these were the most valuable part of the house. The thatch was turf, heather, reeds, bracken and broom. Straw was food for livestock and much too valuable to waste on buildings. You had to replace the thatch every few years, but it could be re-cycled because old thatch full of soot from the fire made good fertiliser for the fields.

By the seventeenth and eighteenth centuries, the walls were mainly rough stone gathered from the fields. Yet in 1730 this was still an issue in our area. *The Baily decreed that the present way of constructing houses by building gable walls only is very destructive and expensive of timber. Therefore enacts that - - - all houses, barns, byres, etc. in need of rebuilding or repairing shall be made of sufficient stone Gavills to the very top and with a single gauge of feall (turf). - - - under pain of twelve pounds Scots of which the informer is to have four pounds.*[98]

When Samuel Johnson journeyed through the Highlands in 1773 he *found a village, consisting of many huts, perhaps twenty, built all of dry-stone, that is, stones piled up without mortar. - - - The wall of a common hut is always built without mortar, by a skilful adaptation of loose stones.*[99]

Few houses had chimneys and smoke escaped though the thatch or a hole in the roof. Most had floors of beaten earth or clay and few had wood or stone floors or any form of ceiling. Windows, if there were any, were small openings in the wall with wooden shutters rather than glass. A flap of hide served for a door.

Of course there were no modern conveniences. Water had to be carried from the burn, ice cold in winter, a little warmer in summer. There was no soap, though mutton fat mixed with wood ash might be a primitive alternative. There were no proper razors or scissors so most men did not shave and even trimming hair was an ordeal. The chewed end of a hazel twig served as a toothbrush.

No wonder their skin was ingrained with dirt and sweat and smoke!

What about toilet arrangements? Surely 20-30 people did not go behind the nearest bush or use the burn, though in some primitive societies today that is exactly what they do. Did they simply shit in the fields? Or did they add their human waste to the dunghill, because on poor soil every little helps? Early travellers do not say, though even cities paid little heed to sanitation in these days. Whatever, moss serves surprisingly well for toilet paper and nappies.

By the eighteenth century the better houses were 'longhouses' where people and livestock shared a roof and each other's heat. People lived at one end, animals at the other, with a partition between. Cottars at the bottom of the social scale had a single-roomed house or bothy. They had few possessions and the family slept on the floor around the fire in the centre of the room.

All of these houses had serious faults: damp floors, leaking roofs, smoky, dirty and dark. The thatch was thick with smoke and soot, so in heavy rain filthy black drips landed on your head. Gaelic even had a special word – *snighe* – for rain coming through the roof! You had to keep a fire going all the time to dry out the roof or it became waterlogged and collapsed.

Yet for all their faults these houses also had some merits. They were cheap, simple and quick to build with materials close to hand. *If the English do burn our houses, what consequence is it to us? We can rebuild them cheap enough, for we only require three days to do so, provided we have five or six poles and boughs to cover them.*[100] The turf and thatch roof kept them cool in summer and warm in winter. Dry-stone walls gave ventilation without draughts.

What about household goods? Mallcolme Gait was a Perthshire tenant in 1576. He had 40 sheep, 20 goats, 15 cattle and 4 horses, so he was a modestly successful tenant farmer. Yet when he died, his total possessions were one iron pot, a kettle, a brass pan, one chair, two cups, two dishes, four wooden plates and a chest. There was no mention of any other furniture, though he must have had some kind of seating and bedding.[101]

People made their own clothing from wool and later flax that they grew themselves. Contrary to myth, they did not wear kilts at that time. Their main garment was the plaid – a rough-woven woollen cloth about seven or eight yards long, used as a cloak during the day and a blanket at night. This was wrapped round the body from neck to knees and held in place with a belt, leaving the right arm bare. Beneath it, they wore a loincloth and a long shirt. They might have some kind of bonnet. Only the better off wore trews and shoes. Even the poorest liked to dress up but their only finery would be a good bonnet or a fancy brooch or pin.

Peasant life was full of fear. Life was insecure and death was ever present. The Bible spoke of the *Four Horsemen of the Apocalypse*: War, Famine, Pestilence and Death.

War, feud and raiding were endemic. One example will suffice.

In the 1640s, Breadalbane got caught up in the Civil War. In Scotland the main flashpoint was religion. Charles I tried to impose Anglican forms of worship on the Scottish Kirk, which was a red flag to the Presbyterian bull. Scots of all ranks including the laird and people of Breadalbane signed a 'National Covenant' to defend their faith.[102]

In 1638 the Scots drew up the Muster Roll of the Covenanters. This was the 'common army of Scotland' ready to be called out and led by their lords. All freemen were duty-bound to leave their land, pick up their weapons and serve without pay for forty days.

The Laird of Glenorchy for himself and his domestic servantis ar sufficientlie provydit with muskets, thair rests and bandeliers, with pouder and lead, some steill targets, some horsemen and footmen at armes, headpieces and steilbannetts, some hakbuts of found (early firearms), *and twa fielding pieces on thair carriages.*

The Laird of Glenurquhay - - - hes about ane hundrethe ablemen or therby to beare weapons, and ar alreadie provydit, some with hakbuts, some with swords and targetts, some with bowes and arrowes, and some with siclyk swordis, so that thair is non of them for the present but ar provydit with some of thir sortis of weapones.[103]

The names of all the able men within the parish of Inchaddin (Kenmore) *which are the Laird of Glenurquay's vassals:*
The list included:

In Dalgardie:
Callum M'Kerlich, 1 sword, 1 target, 1 steillbonnet.
Johne M'Onauchtan, 1 sword, 1 bow and arrowes.
Duncan McBaine,
Ewine McCloylan McIliyar.[104]

By the time the Civil War broke out, Covenanter armies joined the parliamentarians. We do not know the fate of these four men of Dalgirdy who went marching off to war but more than two hundred Breadalbane men died on the English campaigns.

Meantime, Montrose's Royalist army rampaged across Scotland. Many of his men were Macdonalds, MacGregors and Macnabs, whose main interest was raiding and seizing the chance to get their own back on the hated Campbells. Between December 1644 and February 1645 they indulged in a savage whirlwind of rape, pillage and murder which became known as *the Burning of Lochtayside* and *the Ravaging of Argyll.* From Blair Atholl they swept down both sides of Loch Tay, up Glen Lochay and Glen Dochart, and west to Argyll. They killed 895 people. They burned every house on Lochtayside but one and they only missed that because it was hidden among trees. They destroyed the corn stores and drove away the cattle. This *devastatio* left the survivors – mainly women and children – without food or fuel or shelter to face the worst of the winter. There is no record of how many more died in the months to follow.

The Laird had to borrow money to help his tenants rebuild their houses and buy seed corn for the next spring. Later, he put in a claim for damages to the government.

Compt of the loss of the waistlands in the laird of Glenurchy's tenants in Perthshire (pages of lists, including):
Dalgardie 3 merkland £5-0-2[105].

That was equivalent to 60% of the annual rent.

History records the broad sweep of events but history is the sum of many small parts. That brief entry shows that Dalgirdy *baile*, like its neighbours, was ravaged. Its houses and peat stacks would be burned, livestock killed or driven off, and grain destroyed. We have no names for any killed or injured. There was no compensation in these days for loss of life or limb, never mind stress or mental anguish.

Encouraged by this success, the MacDonalds of Lochaber raided Killin again on 4 June 1646. They killed four nephews of the Laird, including Colin Campbell of Murlaganmor with *32 of his ablest tenants and servants killed and 21 dangerously wounded.*[106] Patrick McVean in Tullich and Dalgirdy was one of those killed.

The second Horseman is Famine. Peasants were only ever a few meals away from hunger and one harvest away from starvation. They could just about survive one poor harvest, but several bad harvests in a row were lethal.

The last national famine in Scotland was in the 1690s.[107] The Little Ice Age caused seven failed harvests in a row from 1696-1702, which became known as the 'Seven Ill Years'. To the Jacobites, they were 'King William's Years'. The rich farmlands of the lower Tay may have got off relatively lightly but the glens were hit as badly as anywhere in Scotland.

Low grain yields led to food shortages. Lack of fodder meant that cattle and sheep were in poor condition and could not be kept over the winter. But if you slaughter them now, you lose your source of meat and dairy products. And less livestock means fewer young born next year. When all else fails, you have no choice but to eat next year's seed corn even if that means you starve next year. It was a vicious circle.

Peasants fell back on what they could. Some tried to live on cheese instead of grain but that caused bowel upsets. Some bled their cattle and mixed it with meal to produce the famous Scottish 'black pudding'. But the cattle were already weak and that weakened them further, so some tried to steal from their neighbours instead. In an earlier famine, the baron court fined Patrik M'Woyllen and Widow Kaithren M'Comey for *blooding of the Lairdis ky.*[108]

Many people starved. The old and the young died first. Starving people have lower resistance, so there were outbreaks of disease. And when people did get ill, recovery was slow and they were more likely to die. It was always worst by the end of the winter when food ran out and before the spring brought fresh supplies. And even when they did survive, they were weak and less able to work the farm.

The population of Scotland fell by 10%, half by deaths and half by a fall in the birth rate. There are no good figures for Breadalbane but it may have been hit even worse. In one church the number of burials rose from an average of 21 a year, to 114 in 1697 and 81 in 1699. The birth rate may be a better measure of population health. Baptisms in the parish of Kenmore halved from 1694 to 1699.[109]

There was a breakdown of social order. Starving people become desperate and the normal rules of behaviour do not apply. In that earlier famine the baron court found Johnne McIntheir guilty of *letting Finlay M'Keissiks bairnis die for hunger and haifing thair geir to sustene tham thairwith.*[110] When the last food had gone, hordes of starving people left their homes and wandered the country begging for food.

The Breadalbane estate came close to ruin due to massive rent arrears and the expense of supporting its tenants. The 'Scroll of Rests' is a list of arrears in rent that were waived for 1696.[111]

Tomochrocher & Badour	*John McNab*	*£20.00.00*
Lariganlochan	*The Bowmen of Clochern*	*£20.00.00*
Botwarniebeg	*Finlay McDiarmid*	*£6.10.00*
Dalgirdie	*John McBoure(?) & others*	*£2.01.04*
Tullich	*D/ Mch ick(?)*	*£2.18.00*
Tirai	*James Campbell*	*£1.05.00*

Dalgirdy clearly had problems that year but was able to pay most of its rent. It did not need a Rest in the next few years, though Tullich and Tirai did. The farms at the head of the glen had it much worse than those just a few miles and a hundred feet lower down. So perhaps the people in Dalgirdy did survive.

Shortages drove up grain prices. The Breadalbane estate spent vast sums buying meal and supplying it to starving tenants below market price. Many tenants left, with a further fall in rent income. By the spring of 1699 the estate had to supply seed to those who remained, otherwise *the land had lyen waist.*

The famine was a terrible sign of the vulnerability of subsistence farming. It made people begin to think about agricultural improvements, even if these would take decades to come.

The third Horseman is Pestilence, which came in many forms. Fleas on the black rat carried bubonic plague. Lice carried typhus. Typhoid spread by contaminated drinking water. Smallpox just seemed to come and go and was a major cause of death in childhood. Summer diarrhoea spread by flies and spoilt food, and killed many babies.

History tells of epidemics ever since the first towns and wars. Plague struck Britain in 686 and 688 AD, though Scotland escaped.

Scotia and Britannia were twice utterly ravaged by a terrible pestilence, save two peoples only, the Picts and the Gaels - - - Although neither people is without great sins, by which the eternal judge is often provoked to wrath, none the less he has until now spared them both - - - To whom else can this favour, conferred by God, be attributed than St Columba?[112]

The Great Plague of 1349 was quite simply the most horrific event in human history. Today we take it for granted that most infectious diseases can be treated, and we can hardly imagine the destruction that plague wrought on medieval society.

People then did not know anything about germs or infection or hygiene. But they did believe without doubt in God's direct intervention on earth and bible stories of the destruction of cities and peoples. So everyone agreed that the plague must be a sign of God's wrath, to punish mankind for its sins. And you can't fight God's will. People had always lived on close terms with death but the plague heightened their concerns. There was a sense of doom, despair and fatalistic resignation. Imagination ran riot. Life as they knew it seemed about to end.

The Great Plague, only later called 'The Black Death', was a worldwide epidemic of bubonic plague. It came from the east, reached the south coast of England in 1348, and spread remorselessly north. It came to Scotland in late 1349. *God and St Mungo, St Ninian and St Andrew shield us this day and ilka day from God's grace and the foul death that English men die upon.* Prayer to St Cuthbert was even better, because he had actually caught the plague and been saved by God's grace.[113]

By spring 1350 the plague spread throughout Scotland. Over a few years it killed up to a third of the people of Scotland – men, women and children. To put this in perspective, WWI is the greatest loss of life in living memory. Twenty-five per cent of soldiers died, yet that was only 3.1% of the Scottish population. *Every* medieval peasant had a lower chance of surviving the Plague than a soldier in the trenches had of surviving the war.

In the year 1350, there was, in the kingdom of Scotland, so great a pestilence and plague among men (which also prevailed for a great many years before and after, in divers parts of the world — nay, all over the whole earth), as, from the beginning of the world even unto modern times, had never been heard of by man, nor is found in books, for the enlightenment of those who come after. For, to such a pitch did that plague wreck its cruel spite that nearly a third of mankind were thereby made to pay the debt of nature.

Moreover, by God's will, this evil led to a strange and unwonted kind of death, insomuch that the flesh of the sick was somehow puffed out and swollen, and they dragged out their earthly life for barely two days. Now this everywhere attacked especially the meaner sort and common people; — seldom the magnates. Men shrank from it so much that, through fear of contagion, sons, fleeing as from the face of leprosy or from an adder, durst not go and see their parents in the throes of death.[114]

If a third of the people died **on average** that means some small *bailes* were wiped out. A stone still stands in the field before the village of Fortingall in Glen Lyon. *Here lie the victims of the Great Plague of the 14th Century, taken here on a sledge drawn by a white horse led by an old lady.*

There are three forms of bubonic plague. The 'standard' form gave the plague its name from the buboes - painful, swollen, infected glands. *In men and women alike it first betrayed itself by the emergence of certain tumours in the groin or the armpits, some of which grew as large as a common apple, others as an egg.*[115] Within two to five days of infection, the victim developed high fever, chills, muscle cramp and seizures. They had bleeding from the bowel, in the urine, from the nose and even from the ears. Bleeding under the skin caused a rash and as the disease wore on the skin rotted while the person was still alive, causing severe pain. Only delirium and coma brought relief, to the victim if not the relatives. Most people died within five days and only 5% survived. The more severe pneumonic form of the disease infected the lungs and spread by coughing and breathing in germs. It was always fatal within two or three days. The rare septicaemic form was an overwhelming blood infection that killed within hours.

The cold statistics are bad enough but do not begin to express the horror. Can you imagine waking to find your husband or wife lying dead beside you? Or your children - whom you put to bed last night with a kiss - feverish, vomiting blood, and drowning in their own fluids?

You have no idea what caused this evil visitation. Why pick yours? And there is nothing you can do about it. Medieval medicine is useless, even if you could get any. At first you may try to kid yourself this isn't really the plague but that forlorn hope soon fades. Then all you can do is attend your loved ones as they die, watching helplessly with feelings of despair and dread. Nearly everyone who takes ill will die. Most survivors only lived because they did not catch it due to natural immunity or simply because they were lucky.

So when you get a fever with rose-pink spots, and painful swellings in your armpits and groins, all you can do is prepare to meet your Maker. The old nursery rhyme sums it up:

Ring a ring o' roses
A pocketful of posies
Atishoo! Atishoo!
We all fall down -
Modern PC leaves out the last word - *dead.*

What can you say to the old lady in Fortingall who buried her family, her friends and her neighbours in a mass grave, without even the comfort of a Christian service? Can you blame her if she prays that she will die too and join them in heaven? In the worst places, bodies lay unburied to be eaten by starving dogs and rats. Crops wasted in the fields and cattle wandered lost and untended. The stench of death and decay hung over all.

Even when the outbreak passes your troubles are not over. In some places there were not enough adults left to care for the children, the animals or the crops. So plague is followed by famine. And the plague kept coming back. By 1400 the population of Scotland was only about half what it had been in 1349 and it would not recover until 1700.

Over the next few years there was an economic recession. Output and demand fell. But the shortage of labour put peasants in a stronger position and rents also fell. Serfdom came to an end. In the long run – the very long run – ordinary people's situation got better than it was before. Yet there was little social unrest in Scotland and nothing like the 1381 Peasants' Revolt in England.

There were many epidemics over the next three hundred years. Most were worst in the towns or only hit parts of Scotland. But the three great outbreaks of 1349, 1606-9 and 1644-49 spread to all parts of the countryside.

The last of these was spread by armies and refugees in the Civil War. We still have Breadalbane's bill from *John Tayllor, chirurgian, and the burgesses of Perth.*

For cleaning of several rooms infested at the visitation of the plague of pestilence, during their service from 15 November to 15 December 1647. Finlarig.[116]

So the pestilence certainly came to Killin. There is no record about individual farms like Dalgirdy but it is unlikely that we escaped.

It all sounds horrendous. How could anyone live through all of that? But of course War, Famine and Plague did not happen every day. These are the worst events that we know

116

about in four hundred years. Smaller raids, poor harvests and minor outbreaks of disease were much more common but if you were lucky there might be nothing serious in your lifetime. The real trouble was that you never knew when fate might strike.

So, if there is no disaster, how long might you expect to live?

The birth rate was double what it is today, and the average family had five to seven children. But at least one child in every three died in the first year or two of life. Of those who survived, half died before the age of twenty. For those who reached adulthood, life expectancy was less than the age of forty and few people lived beyond sixty.

Smout wrote of *the fatalism and hopelessness of peasant existence*. Grinding poverty was never romantic. Peasants lived in squalor with their animals, dirty and lousy, riddled with superstition and disease, struggling to live and dying young. At times, life must have seemed an endless cycle of inevitable catastrophe. What is the point of working hard if you never know when all you have will be destroyed?

Even at the start of the eighteenth century - - - *the people of the parish were rather averse to industry. The spirit of clanship which prevailed was very unfavourable to it. The different clans spent a great deal of their time avenging themselves of each other; the man who could best handle his sword and his gun was deemed the prettiest fellow; and the attentive industrious man was a character held in a degree of contempt. The people, in general, were consequently poor, rents ill paid and sometimes not at all.*[117]

Yet human beings are amazingly resilient. When death stares you in the face every day, all you can do is grin back and get on with your life.

By the time of the Union in 1707, the population of Scotland had risen to about one million. Eight out of ten still lived in the country. Just over half lived north of a line from the Firth of Tay to the Firth of Clyde. There were four towns of more than ten thousand people – Glasgow, Edinburgh, Dundee and Aberdeen. Perth had about five thousand.

Two travellers from Europe in the fifteenth century gave quite positive pictures of the people.

The men are small in stature, bold and forward in temper: the women fair in complexion, comely and pleasing, but not distinguished for their chastity, giving their kisses more readily than Italian women their hands.[118] The writer went on to be Pope Pius II, so that may be a misogamist's view of the gentle sex!

The women are courteous in the extreme. I mention this because they are really honest, though bold. They are absolute mistresses of their houses, even of their husbands, in all things concerning the administration of their property - -.[119]

When Johnson and Boswell visited one old woman in her hovel, Johnson was curious and asked where the family slept. She was affronted. *She answered with a tone of emotion, saying she was afraid we wanted to go to bed with her. This coquetry, or whatever it may be called, of so wretched a being, was truly ludicrous. Dr Johnson and I afterwards were merry upon it.*[120]

Johnson found more to admire in another peasant house. *To enter a habitation without leave, seems to be not considered here as rudeness or intrusion. The old laws of hospitality still give this license to a stranger.*[121]

Even the poorest can have pride and honour. It is amazing how people not only survived in these conditions, but even thrived.

And things could only get better. With the Reformation, the Scottish Enlightenment and the Industrial Revolution, all was about to change. We were going to escape from the social and economic stagnation of peasant life.

10. SUBSISTENCE FARMING
The bare necessities of life

Farming, like rural life, had not changed for centuries. Young people learned the skills from their parents and got the benefit of generations of experience about how best to work their farm. But medieval farming was also hidebound by tradition and slow to adapt to new ideas.

Subsistence farming was self-sufficient, in contrast to modern commercial farming which produces for the market place. It always struggled to grow enough to feed the people who lived on the land.

It was a hand-to-mouth existence. They consumed most of what they produced. What little surplus they had went to pay the rent and for the few outside goods they could not produce themselves, like salt and a few iron tools.

Subsistence farming gave little chance to build up reserves and that made it vulnerable to bad years. Poor communications and lack of money meant there was little outside help when times were hard.

Dalgirdy is a rare example of a medieval Highland farm. Because it is such rough and difficult ground, much of it was never 'Improved'. Most of the land has never been drained nor ploughed. So you can still see traces of the pre-Improvement farm in terraces, earth banks, small enclosures and the faint footings of buildings. It is an archaeological treasure trove.[122]

One glance at Dalgirdy shows you how poor it must have been. Today the modern farm of Tullich supports one family and even that would be uneconomic without the hill farm subsidies. Dalgirdy was only about one-third, and the poorest third, of modern Tullich. Most of the land was only fit for grazing. The only arable ground lay in small terraces on the lower hillside, yet that had to support twenty to thirty people.

It was a basic existence and we have forgotten the effort it took each day just to keep body and soul together. Yet for all the difficulties, people lived here for centuries.

Dalgirdy was home to a small community who all lived and worked on the farm.

There were usually three tenants who rented the farm either direct from the laird or through a tackman like the laird's younger son Archibald Campbell in Murlaganmor. These were the farmers. They were the more prosperous peasants who had some capital and status in the community. Of course 'prosperous' is a relative term.

Farming was a communal affair. The joint tenants worked the farm 'in common', which meant that all farm tasks had to be done together and they had to cooperate with each other. So it is no surprise that a group of relatives often farmed together.

One or two crofters were sub-tenants on the farm. They each got an acre or so to graze a cow or a few sheep for themselves. They did not pay a money rent but had to labour on the farm without wages for so many days a week.

There was always a Crofter in Dalgirdy who occupied a separate and distinct pendicle of land - - -. All he had was - - - but a house and Kail yard- - -. He described his - - - present poor scanty Cottage, which is in every respect exceedingly inconveniently situated, at a distance from the arable land of the Farm and separated there from by a rapid large Burn, and is moreover so small that it is with the utmost difficulty he is able to hows his Furniture and Family therein.[123]

Then there were a few cottars. Most were farm labourers but there might also be a widow or an elderly or disabled person. These were the lowest level of society. They and their families worked on the farm, for which they got a house, some food and perhaps a pittance of a wage.

By the 1760s, Dalgirdy had three tenants, two crofters and three cottars.[124] Many of them had wives and families, to make up the total of twenty to thirty people.

They all lived together in the *baile* or fermtoun. The Roy Military map of 1747 showed a cluster of houses on the east side of the burn.[125] The *baile* would originally have six or eight turf houses and you can still see some faint outlines of a few rocks and turf banks that look man-made and could be the remains of some dwellings. It is hard to tell.

There is a small group of ruined dry-stone buildings just above the road. This has been built and rebuilt many times and spans at least four periods of use.[126] Two small buildings at right angles may be earliest as this L-shape was a common medieval pattern for a house and barn. That was replaced by a longhouse and then in turn by a simple house, though that takes us up to post-Improvement times and we will come back to that later. The deserted walls now form part of a sheepfold.

The ground around the *baile* shows signs of human working. There are many small piles and rows of stones that have been cleared from the land. There are small enclosures and short stretches of field boundaries, either to keep animals in or to keep them out of growing plants. There are outlines of smaller buildings that could be stores. Much of the ground is very wet so there may have been some crude paths, though no sign of these remains.

The landscape looked very different from today. There was no neat chequerboard of fields, no hedges or dykes, only the most primitive of small enclosures. There were few trees. The small groups of houses were well scattered and blended into the land. All you could see was bare, open hillside with little shelter and a lot of moorland and bog.

Thomas Kirke described the Scottish landscape in 1679. The mountains and glens - - - *are freed from the charge and the incumbrance of inclosures, the whole being but one large waste, surrounded with the sea. Indeed in many places you may see half a rood of land divided by an earthen bank, into many different apartments, according to the quality of the beasts that are to possess them. The whole country will make a park, forest, or chase, as you'll please to call it; but if you desire an account of particular parks, they are innumerable, every small house having a few sods thrown into a little bank about it, and this for the state of the business (forsooth) must be called a park, though not a pole of land in't.*[127]

The soil and the weather of the Highlands have always been more suitable for raising livestock than for the cultivation of crops. This was pastoral farming. Cattle were always most important, to pay the rent and to sell as the only source of income. Sheep and goats were for the family's own use. Cattle were the main measure of wealth, which meant the land was often over-stocked.

The original 'black cattle' were a small, rough-haired breed that dated back to the sixth century. They were less than half the weight of today's 'Highland cattle'. Most of them were black and it was only later that the breed turned red and gold. The best that can be said of them was that they were hardy and well suited to the harsh terrain and weather. *The cows in general are of a bad breed, not so well haired and shaped as the Argyle breed, nor giving so much milk as the southern breed.*[128]

Today we would call these beef cattle, reared for meat and fattened up for autumn. Cattle were traditionally sold or slaughtered by Martinmas, 11 November, which was the old Halloween. This was the time to complete preparations for winter and to celebrate the Earth's bounty, much like the American Thanksgiving.

Lairds might preserve meat by salting, pickling or smoking. Salted meat kept best but then had to be boiled for several hours to make it edible. Meat pickled in weak ale or vinegar tasted better but did not keep as well. However, peasants in a turf hovel had no facilities to preserve meat. Perhaps the one method they might use was smoking but there is no record of that. In reality, cattle would be too valuable to eat unless they died by accident or starvation. Then everyone would help to eat the meat before it spoiled.

The main limit on the number of cattle was the lack of winter-feed. The grazing was used up by early winter and then the land was *gnawed to the quick*. Even in normal years about one in five of the cattle kept outside died during the winter. The milk cow was kept indoors – in the house. Even then, by spring her condition was so poor that she often had to be lifted out to pasture.

Cattle kept in these conditions grew slowly and were not fit for market until they were four years of age. Cows only calved every second year, could only suckle for a short time, and only gave about a pint of milk a day. Compare that to a modern dairy cow that produces two gallons a day. Many calves must have died and building a herd was a slow and painful business.

The old Highland sheep were small, less than half the size of a modern Blackface. They were white, dun or mixed in colour, with four or six horns, long legs, short tails and prominent eyes. They were a primitive breed, rather like the Soay sheep from St Kilda or skeletons of Bronze Age sheep. They are now extinct.

They had a very fine but scanty fleece that was not much thicker than a goat's hair. So people often plucked the wool rather than sheared them, and got less than a quarter of the wool from a modern breed.

They were delicate little beasts that were housed at night in sheepfolds and often tethered by day. Farmers smeared them with a tarry substance to protect them from the weather but this was a magnet for dirt and twigs and made them filthy. It also made it difficult to gather and clean the wool.

People kept sheep mainly for their milk. They weaned them in May so that they could get the limited milk yield, but this was very hard on the lambs.

Goats are such hardy creatures and their milk is so nutritious that at one period they were very much reared over all the Highlands of Scotland.[129] However, they were less profitable than sheep. They also did a lot of damage to young trees, so as landowners began to value their woods they banned goats. In 1728 tenants in the neighbouring farms were fined for their goats eating trees. By 1762 Mgt McNab in Dalgirdy was fined just for keeping goats.[130] By the end of the century they *have almost disappeared entirely in this part of the kingdom.*

In 1769 Dalgirdy was recorded to have grass for seventy-two cattle and four horses. The column for sheep was left blank.[131]

Oxen were the main beasts of burden in the Lowlands but they were never used in Highland Perthshire. Here, horses were the main draught animals. Highland horses in medieval times were medium-sized, about twelve or thirteen hands high. They had a hollow back, flat sides, wide buttocks, deep wide chest and good legs. The most common colour was grey. They were hardy and all-purpose packhorses, but too small for heavy draught work. To a foreign traveller, they were *ill-groomed, small and clumsy brutes*. In 1640, Finlarig grazed the estate horses in Glenlochay and there were still forty wild mares in Glenlochay and Glenorchy.[132]

People also kept *an extraordinary number of chickens*. These often lived in the house and roosted in the rafters. There would not be any grain to spare for poultry so they would have to forage for themselves and gather what would otherwise go to waste.

All the livestock wandered freely, limited only by the head dyke and by children chasing them out of the crops. This was a most inefficient system and inevitably some crops were eaten or trampled. Grazing was on common land so the livestock inter-bred freely and no one could try to improve their stock.

What about the arable land?

The Dal is now the best twelve acres of arable land on Dalgirdy but in earlier times it would be pretty useless. There is a small area of ground like this further up the glen that has never been drained or ploughed. Even sheep and deer that are free to roam do not graze there but prefer the grass on the open hillside.

A considerable part of the soil of the parish too is wet and muddy. This kind abounds most in the plain which lies at the west end of Loch Tay, and in the bottoms of the valleys of Glenlochay and Glendochart, which are subject to the overflowings of the rivers of the Lochay and Dochart running through them.[133]

In many places these meadows are very much neglected.

They are overcharged with water a great part of the year. The grass is coarse, unpalatable and unfit for hay. Little or nothing grows except rushes, flags, willows and other aquatic plants. In many part of the country the meadows are abandoned as incurable - - -.[134]

Tho' they have many fine valleys, which might be improved into a competitorship with our English meadows, yet for want of sufficient industry and care they become almost useless, on the account of frequent bogs and waters in such places.[135]

If you climb the opposite side of the glen and look across to Dalgirdy, you can see the medieval farm.[136]

The faint remains of a ruined head dyke mark off the hillside on the west side of the Allt Ghaordaidh, from 250 yards up the side of the burn to 350 yards along the road. Within this area there are many small terraces that look man-made or at least modified. Most of them are 15-40 yards long by 3-5 yards wide, with two slightly larger areas of flat ground. These are all on areas where the hill slope provides natural drainage. If you take a spade to them, the soil is quite good; there are few large stones and the ground looks as if it has been worked.

There are many clearance cairns where the field stones have been piled aside. Dalgirdy has more of these cairns that anywhere else in the glen. Is that because the ground was stonier? At times it must have seemed to grow more stones than grain! Or is it because this land was abandoned at the time of the Improvements, while on better ground the stones were re-used for dykes and tracks?

There are several small enclosures and short stretches of what could be boundaries of small fields. There are the footings of many small agricultural huts or stores and a few larger buildings that could be dwellings.

Just above the road there is an area of lazybeds that measures 30 X 25 yards. In low morning light in winter when the grass is short you can just make out the ridges running down the slight slope. This was a traditional form of cultivation in the Highlands and Islands. The beds are five to six yards wide and would be one or two feet high when in use. Between them are drainage ditches where the rushes still grow stronger. This would be the most fertile and productive ground on the farm.

Most of these patches of arable land are so small that they must have been worked by hand. At first, people probably used the *cas chrom* or 'crooked foot' which was a curved piece of wood about five feet long with a pointed front to dig into the ground and a wooden peg at the side for the user's foot. It was a crude and back-breaking tool. A metal 'foot' for the *cas chrom* came later.

Some of the larger patches might just have taken a horse-drawn plough, though I doubt if the usual team of four horses could squeeze in. The old Scots plough was made of wood, with the parts fixed together with wooden pins and leather straps. The only metal part was the coulter or cutting tip, which was worth more than the rest put together. It did not turn the soil over like a modern plough but was *a very singular and feeble instrument, and made a rut in the ground rather than a furrow, leaving the ground on either side undisturbed.*[137]

This was all very small-scale and crop yields were low. Medieval farmers could only try to get as much as possible out of these small areas by labour-intensive cultivation.

The tenants worked the land on a 'runrig' system[138] in which each got different patches of ground, all mixed up together. Each year they changed round. The idea was that everyone got a share of the better and poorer ground. In one sense this was fair, in that no one got an unfair advantage, but it meant there was little incentive to improve. If you worked hard this year, your neighbour got the benefit next year. And if you tried to do something different, he might object or change it back next year. It was the same with common grazing. No one could change the old ways of doing things or bring in new ideas unless everyone else agreed and that was unlikely if it went against tradition.

Short leases had the same effect. If you did not know how long you would have the farm it was not worth trying to improve it. Robertson summed it up. In 1750 *the country was unenclosed, the fields uncultivated, and the farmers spiritless and poor. The husbandry - - - was in a most wretched condition.*[139]

Up to the eighteenth century the common crops were oats and bere. 'Grey' or 'small' oats had seeds more like wild oats than modern fat grains of corn. It had a shorter stem, which stood up better to wind but gave less straw. Bere was a primitive form of barley. Oats were hardier and did not suffer as badly in a poor year. Yields were little more than three times the grain sown - *ane to saw, ane to gnaw and ain to pay the laird withaw.* Compare that with 20:1 today. Breadalbane always struggled to produce enough grain to feed its people and often had to import meal.

Peasants harvested the grain with a sickle rather than a scythe, which was slower and harder labour but gave less waste. If the grain was wet, they dried it in small corn kilns. Once dry, they used a hand flail to separate the grain from the chaff. Then they ground the grain in a stone quern or circular hand mill to give 'wholemeal' but that left stone dust in the meal and wore down your teeth by old age.

There was only a limited amount of straw, which was used as animal feed in the winter. They did not grow hay as a crop but would gather coarse natural grass and weeds. They had no clover or turnips or potatoes.

The farm had an 'infield' and an 'outfield', divided by the head dyke.

The head dyke was the first field boundary in the Highlands and dates from at least the sixteenth century. Its main purpose was to keep livestock out of the crops. It was part turf and part stone, and perhaps three or four feet high. The earliest Baron Bailie Court statutes were written in 1574 but probably date from even earlier.[140] They laid down that all tenants had to build and maintain their head dykes. *All heiddykis and faulddykis within the foirsaidis boundis respectiue be yeirly beittit bigit and upholdin be the awnaris and possessouris thairof sufficiently with divot earth and stane, under the pane of ten pundis money.*[141] Several tenants in Dalgirdy were taken to Court for not keeping their head dykes.[142] The original Dalgirdy head dyke is now broken down and in places almost gone.

The infield was the more fertile land near the *baile*. This was kept in constant cultivation and got most of the manure, mainly for bere. The outfield was the higher, poorer ground – *wretched, ill-kept, untended ground*. The only crop in the outfield was occasional oats. It might get a single dose of manure, then be re-sown for a few years until the ground was exhausted, and then lay fallow. The upper limit of cultivation was the furthest extent of outfield oats with the 'natural grasses' on the hill above for grazing. In upper Glen Lochay that was most of the farm.

Some parts of Highland Perthshire used a double head dyke system and there do appear to be upper and lower head dykes on Dalgirdy. The lower head dyke enclosed the infield from the outfield. The upper dyke divided the outfield from the hill grazing. Or perhaps this reflects more land being taken into cultivation with population growth in the eighteenth century?

In summer everyone moved up to the shielings, which kept the cattle away from the growing crops and took advantage of the high pastures. The Dalgirdy shielings lie at a height of 1500 feet in a hollow in the hills beside the Allt Ghaordaidh. The estate set strict rules about going to the shielings between 1 May and 15 July.

Eviry tennent sail put out thair heall ky hors nolt and scheip outwith thair heid dykis fra the first of Maii and reinane quhill the aucht day of Junii yeirly, and fra the 8 day of Junii to pas to scheillingis and remane quhill the fyftene day of Julii yeirly, and nane to cum hame befoir ane uther, except a kow that is a lifting, or ane seik man or ane seik woman to hauld ane kow besyd thame to gif milk.[143]

The shielings were summer dwellings for the women and children, who tended the animals and made butter and cheese. Because the Dalgirdy shielings were so isolated they have never been disturbed and are well preserved. There are three larger buildings about twelve to fifteen feet long by six feet wide with stone walls that still stand three to five feet high. There are four smaller stone ruins and at least four grass-covered outlines.

On a good summer day it is an idyllic situation with views to the head of the glen and down to Loch Tay. Life at the shielings was happy for the people as well as the beasts. Leaving for the shielings was one of the big adventures of the year: *The people looked so glad and contented for they rejoice at going up.*[144]

The peasant diet was monotonously poor, mainly oatmeal and *knockit bere* - 'everlasting oatcake'. *Oat meal is the great support and strength of the Highlander, and is probably the most substantial of vegetable food.*[145] Samuel Johnson defined oats in his Dictionary as *a grain, which in England is generally given to horses, but in Scotland supports the people.*

Meal often made up a large part of the wages of cottars and servants. They could mix it with milk to make porridge or with water to make gruel. They could bake it into oatcakes or bannocks. Like the Swedes with herring, you must have looked for a wife who knew twenty ways of cooking meal!

Bere also made broth and there would always be a pot of soup to use up the scraps and leftovers of food. Nothing went to waste.

By the sixteenth century and perhaps earlier, each house had a kailyard, which was the only source of green vegetables. Kail was a primitive form of cabbage that could survive cold weather. People ate it as a vegetable or added it to broth. In late winter it saved many children from the 'spring disease' of scurvy.

Every family had a cow, sheep or goats to provide a little milk in summer, and butter and cheese for the winter. Poultry was a welcome source of extra protein, both meat and eggs. Only the better off tenants ate beef or mutton, and even that very occasionally. Poor cottars would never taste meat unless a cow or sheep died.

The main drink must have been fresh running water from the burn. Milk was scarce because of the low yield, and most of it was used for butter and cheese. Fermented whey would be a special treat. Each home could make home-brewed ale from bere, but no beer because they did not have hops. Brewing was usually women's work and a good 'ale-wife' must have been another great prize!

Scotch whisky is *uisge beatha* or the 'water of life'. The ancient Celts distilled fermented grain but what we now call whisky only dates from the fifteenth century. As whisky improved and became more popular, the Scottish parliament tried to tax it from 1644. Then, when the UK parliament imposed law and order after 1707 and the Risings, production was driven underground. For many years more than half the whisky drunk in Scotland tasted better because it was duty-free. In 1747 the Baron Baillie Court fined three men from Kenknock, Botourniemor and Duncroisk for selling illicit whisky.[146] Even worse, they had to destroy their remaining stock. Distilleries were licensed in 1823, and fourteen thousand illicit stills were confiscated in Scotland in a single year! There is a small man-made platform hidden deep in the Allt Duncroisk gorge that may have been an illicit still.[147]

But then some genius dreamt up an escape clause. We managed to convince the London lawmakers that while whisky is maturing in wooden casks, 2% evaporates each year. That sounds negligible. It is 'the angel's share'. But good malt whisky needs to mature for ten years. So that means one whole fifth of all the whisky made in Scotland somehow, magically, disappears into the Highland mist. And if some of it should find its way down good Highland gullets - - -.

The other major task of the farming year was to gather peat for fuel. Digging, drying and bringing in the peat is **very** labour intensive, as anyone who has tried knows only too well. Peat-cutters say that peat heats you three times over - first when you cut it, again when you carry it home, and finally when you burn it in the fire!

Each family needed 15,000 peats to last the year. It took a good man to cut 1,000 a day, while the women and children spread them out to dry. Everyone got filthy. The kids thought it was great fun and in some parts of the Highlands it was the only day in the year they got jam. If the weather was good the peat could dry in three weeks, during which it had to be turned and stacked up. Then it was carried home in baskets, either on the women's backs, in horse panniers, or on a horse-drawn sled. The peat stack was as big as the house, with the outer layer built like tiles to keep out the rain. The problem is this all takes a great deal of time and labour during the best summer weather, time that could be better spent improving the farm.[148]

They must be cut by the 20th or the latter end of June, otherwise there will be no drought to dry the peats. They must be brought home in July, for if the August rains come on they are commonly lost for that season.[149] Global warming seems to be bringing that forward! In a wet summer *the peats never dry properly and a great discomfort is entailed upon the people.*[150] So, ideally, you built up an extra year's supply in reserve.

The rent was due at Martinmas, after the harvest was in.

There was no coinage in Scotland until the twelfth century and even then it took several hundred years before money was common. Rents were originally paid in kind with produce from the land. In 1682, Catharin McGrigor, Jon Gilmartine and Murdo McLimartine paid £57-10s in cash and made up the balance of the rent by two sheep, a quart of butter, a large quantity of straw and hay, forty pounds of oats, and four hens. They also had to carry in 36 loads of peats for the laird.[151] By the way, Catharin is the only woman tenant we know of in Dalgirdy.

By 1776 all rents were paid in cash but the lease still included service to the laird. Each of the Dalgirdy tenants had to *furnish a man and a horse for carriage to his Lordship for ten days yearly when required thereto seed and harvest time excepted.* There was a footnote, that they - - - *are to carry sixty loads of peats to Finlarig over and above the Carriage within mentioned.*[152]

Today we take inflation for granted, but the rent of Dalgirdy never changed from 1555 to 1733. It then rose 50% between 1733 and 1770, but that was still only 1-2% a year.

131

It was a life close to Nature.

Winter was the hardest time, when the glen was cut off by floods and blizzards, the nights were long and dark, and the rain dripped through the thatch. Spring brought new life and fresh hope, so long as your food did not run out before the new growth came. Long summer days were the time to enjoy the best that life could bring. And autumn was the time of plenty, provided you had a good harvest brought safely in and did not think too much about the winter ahead.

It is easy to be critical of subsistence farming. Robertson, looking back half a century from 1799, was more understanding. *With all our boasted improvements, if we were under the necessity of - - -* (farming in these conditions with their knowledge and resources) *- - - dire necessity would have compelled us to act just as our fathers did, and to be exactly such farmers as they were.*[153]

As late as 1760 no one in Dalgirdy could guess how everything was going to change in the next sixty years.

11. THE KIRK

The Reformation: the dangerous birth of the modern world[154]

By the sixteenth century the church was in a state of decay. *The church was very largely at the mercy of unspiritual laymen, its foundations corrupt and worldly, its parish churches empty and ruined, its bishops a byword for immorality, and its congregations often contemptuous of its services.* [155]

Martin Luther sparked off the Reformation in 1517 with the radical idea that the Bible rather than the Church should be the basis of religion. The Bible is *The Word of God*. Salvation is through faith in Christ alone rather than by the sacraments of the church. You do not need a priest or saints to intercede on your behalf. We all have a direct line to God. It was to be *the priesthood of all believers.*

Up to that time the Latin Bible had been *the church's best-kept secret.* Now it was translated into everyday language and the printing press would make it available to all. Everyone had the right and the duty to read the Bible for himself. It was up to you to save your own soul through faith and by leading a good life.

The work of the church was now to teach and exhort. Images, ritual and ceremonies were unnecessary and distracting from the Word. This was religion stripped down to the bare essentials, appealing to the intellect rather than the senses.

The Reformation was slow to come to Britain and took a different course north and south of the border. In England change came in fits and starts between 1527 and 1553, amidst great religious and political turmoil. It was led from the top, driven by Henry VIII's need for an heir, and the King remained head of the church. The new Anglican Church was a careful compromise that kept the hierarchy and much of the rich liturgy of the Catholic Church.

In Scotland the reformers tapped into common feelings about the state of the Catholic Church, antagonism to the

French Regent Queen Mary of Guise, and Scottish nationalism. They won the support of ordinary people, burgesses, many lairds and even some nobles. This was a bottom-up revolt *against* the monarch.

And there was no false modesty here but a Biblical sense of purpose. *Scotland was a poor and seemingly insignificant nation. But, like Israel, God had chosen it to play a leading role in His plans for the establishment of true religion and the betterment of mankind.* [156]

John Knox hijacked the Scottish Reformation and stamped it with his genius. He was a self-styled prophet and a fiery preacher, a rebel and a firebrand, with the light of glory in his eye. It is also worth remembering that he wrote the history of the Scottish Reformation and his own part in it!

Knox had a university education and trained as a priest although he never had a parish. Instead, he became a lawyer and tutor to sons of the gentry. He joined the early protestant movement and after a rebellion at St Andrews was condemned as a galley slave in the French Navy where he spent 19 months. This would have killed many lesser men and forged him in steel. He then spent time at the English Court and was an Anglophile for the rest of his life. But when the catholic Mary Tudor became queen he had to flee and joined Calvin in Geneva.

After a long, slow start, the Reformation exploded in Scotland in 1559-60 when Knox came home. Within a year the Reformed Kirk was national policy, approved by Parliament. Yet unlike England and parts of Europe, where thousands died, Scotland only had a handful of martyrs on both sides.

The new Kirk rejected the authority of the Pope and his bishops and was to be truly democratic, even if it was still dominated by lairds, ministers and elders. It threw out the rich imagery of the Catholic Church and there was much wanton destruction of precious religious art. Some well-loved traditions were lost. No more Saints' Days in Scotland! The focus was now on the Word of God in the Bible and the sermon. This was a hard and demanding religion that did not offer much easy comfort. It was austere and at worst puritanical. Sometimes it seemed to drain all joy from the world by calling it sin. And if everyone reads the Bible for himself, there is a terrible tendency for the Kirk to fly apart in sectarian disputes.

Somehow it seems poetic justice that Knox's grave is now lost beneath a car park at the back of St Giles Cathedral in Edinburgh.

The Scottish Reformation had a powerful sense of the local community and its practical concerns were about *the common weal*. Knox's *First Book of Discipline* was a utopian blueprint for a better society. [157]

- Every parish should have a minister, who should ideally be elected by the congregation.

- The Kirk Session should consist of elected elders, who would assist the minister with enforcing spiritual discipline and managing church affairs.

- For everyone to be able to read the bible for him or herself, and to provide enough ministers, there must be a system of education for all. Each parish kirk should provide a school.

- Funding would come from redistributing the wealth of the old church.

The focus was now on the living. No more praying for the dead! There was deep concern for the position of the poor and downtrodden members of society. These were radical and utopian ideas. They were noble but unrealistic. Inevitably, they were watered down and took more than a hundred years to come to fruition. But the goal was set.

The early Kirk could not overcome the power of the lairds and nobility, who had already grabbed much of the land and wealth of the old church. And they were not going to hand them back. So lack of money set limits to what the Kirk could do. Schools were slow to spread as it sought funding from different sources. Social care suffered most. Poor relief was limited to funds from church collections, fines for spiritual offences and the odd charity from the wealthy.

For all that, society began to change, however slowly. The parish became the framework for pastoral and spiritual care and would remain so until the twentieth century. There was a new and pervasive culture, not just in worship but also in personal behaviour. In the Catholic Church, confession was confidential. In the reformed Kirk, sin and penance were on public display. Kirk Sessions practised social control and those who did not toe the party line were ostracized.

At best, Kirk Sessions were compassionate and caring, and built a strong sense of community and mutual support. The family was a basic part of the social fabric and Sessions did their best to keep it in good repair. At worst, they gave licence to nosy busybodies. *Calvinists disapproved of sex standing up because it might lead to dancing.* Or was that the other way round? For better and worse, the Kirk came to have a profound influence on Scottish society and daily life.

Yet we must judge this in the context of the time. Modern ideas of privacy and individual freedom date from the eighteenth century at earliest. And individual behaviour does have wider social consequences. Adultery, for example, led to very real social problems that the community must deal with. And the Kirk was not alone. The courts and most people condemned it too.

So what happened in a rural area like Killin? In practice, of course, no one could live up to Knox's high ideals. Some of the early ministers were a colourful lot.

William Ramsay was the Earl of Breadalbane's chaplain at Finlarig in 1555. He was Roman Catholic curate at Killin in 1557. Then, in May 1561, the Earl made him the first minister of the Reformed Kirk in Kenmore. This was a common pattern. Perhaps a third of former priests moved over to the new Kirk.

The first recorded minister in Killin was John McCorcadill in 1567 and he was still there in 1583. We do not know anything else about him.

William Menzies was minister of Killin from 1618 to 1636 and then moved to Kenmore. He was *the first minister to organise the congregation.* When in Kenmore, he *set himself with courage and marked ability to improve the religious and moral condition of his people. - - - The parish was divided into districts, each of which was placed under the oversight of an elder, who had to report to the session any matter demanding attention. Attendance at Communion and at the minister's round of examination was made compulsory, and fines imposed upon persons who were absent without cause. Those who were ignorant of the Creed and the Ten Commandments were also punished - - - The elders were exhorted to be diligent themselves in the observance of family worship and to encourage others to follow their example. The collections taken in the church and fines imposed upon delinquents were applied to the relief of the poor. The Kirk session granted loans to persons requiring temporary financial help, but always upon the security of some man of good standing.*[158]

The Kirk took over the old parish system but for historical reasons parts of Glen Lochay were detached portions of Kenmore and Weem Parishes, many miles away. Even so, everyone living in Glen Lochay was meant to get pastoral care from Killin, but this did not always happen. When Church Commissioners visited Dull in 1627, they reported that *the inhabitants never, or seldom, repair to the parish Kirk except on necessity of receiving the Lord's Supper and baptism and marriage; and great ignorance abounds in the land, and neglect of discipline, to the great grief of many of the inhabitants and to the minister's great grief and trouble.*[159] That would be just as true of Glen Lochay.

The Kirk had difficulty getting enough ministers who could speak Gaelic, and many parishes lay vacant at times or had to share ministers. In 1712, the church at Weem took action against their minister at the General Assembly *mainly on account of his not speaking the 'Irish' language.*

Robert Stewart was minister of Killin from 1680-1729. *His Gaelic nickname was 'Curam an t-saoghail' (Care of the World) because he was always preaching on that subject while gathering all the worldly wealth he could lay his hands on.*[160] In 1727 the

Presbytery found the parish *much neglected.* Stewart had a dispute with his assistant and successor over his refusal to hand over the Poor's box. At the end of the day, he had managed to amass enough wealth to leave estates to each of his four sons!

The minister of Weem preached at Duncroisk in Glen Lochay nine times between 1741 and 1776. Nine services in thirty-five years! That was an average lifetime.

Up to the middle of the eighteenth century, the grip of the Kirk on upper Glen Lochay was tenuous, at best. Legend says that when the minister was spotted coming up the glen the nine children in Dalgirdy ran up the hill to hide!

About that time the Kenmore Kirk Session *had frequent complaints from the Elders in the west end of the Parish, that the Kirk Session of Killin do not take care of the poor, particularly of the Invalids, or the poor objects that are confined to beds and unable to travel, in the west end of this Parish, - - - as they ought by agreement between the two Sessions - - - to take the same care of our poor in that end as they do of their own.*[161]

The Right Reverend James Stuart was minister of Killin from 1737-1779. He translated the New Testament into Scottish Gaelic in 1767 and his son later did the same for the Old Testament. The famous Samuel Johnson wrote a letter of support after his travels through Breadalbane. As you might expect from such a distinguished man of letters, it is in beautiful flowing English, written in a bold hand. It ends: *You will be pleased, Sir, to assure the worthy man who is employed in the new translation that he has my wishes for his success; and if here, or at Oxford, I can be of any use, that I shall think it more than honour to promote his undertaking.*

Estate records were about land and farms and money. The Kirk records tell us more about ordinary people, with revealing glimpses into their lives.

Old Parish Records include baptisms, marriage bans and burials. We only have Killin OPR from 1727 and they tell us most about births.[162] Marriage bans only give names, with no detail. There are no records of burials. *Owing to the number of places of internment, no register of deaths has ever been kept in the parish.* We do not know where these old burial grounds were in Glen Lochay.

Babies must have been born in Dalgirdy from time immemorial, but the first baby we know by name was in 1729.

30 Aug 1729 Malcolm McUrachter and Margaret McLean in Dalgirdy had a legitimate daughter baptised called Margaret.

There were three more babies from Dalgirdy in 1730, one in 1736 and three in 1738. So it continues. They were a fertile lot! From 1741, children born in wedlock were described as *lawful*.

5 June 1738 Ewan McCallum and Christian McDiermed in Dalgirdey had their legitimate daughter baptised called Christian.

12 Jan 1741 Ewan McCallum and Christian McDiermed in Dalgirdey had their lawful daughter baptised called Christian.

Sadly, it seems the first little girl died and they gave the next baby the same name. That was quite common.

We can also spot a few second wives. Mortality was high and many women died in childbirth.

Patrick McVean and his first wife Jean McCail in Dalgirdy had three children between 1774 and 1781. In 1785 the Kirk Session hired out the mort cloth for Jean McCail's burial, though we do not know her cause of death. In 1789 Patrick McVean and his second wife Kat Campbell had a son called Duncan. That baby died and another son called Duncan was born two years later. They had two more children by 1799.

We know of two sets of twins in Dalgirdy and, curiously, they were only two years apart.

12 Apr 1767 John Fletcher and ___ McCallum in Dalgirdy had their lawful twins baptised called Margaret and Christian.

7 Mar 1769 Duncan McMartine and Christian Clerk in Dalgirdy had their child in adultery baptised called Archibald.

28 May 1769 Mal McMartine and Eliz McGrigor in Dalgirdy had their natural twins baptised called Donald & Katharine.

139

Ninety-five per cent of babies were lawful, which is perhaps surprising in days before effective contraception. Did many couples simply get married when the girl proved she was fertile? 'Natural' was a euphemism for illegitimate. Fornication was sex between a man and woman who were not married. Adultery was when one of them was married to someone else. 1768 must have been a year of shenanigans in Dalgirdy!

The Kirk Session Records give more detail about what people got up to. Kenmore is earliest and shows the struggle to impose spiritual discipline.[163]

1 August 1652 *The Act anent the breaking of the Sabbath was announced because of persons that went to the woods to gather nuts.*

1 May 1653 *The elders were exhorted to go among their quarters to urge familie worship, and to see if there be Swearers, Drunkards, and Sabbath breakers.*

11 July 1660 *The Session taking into consideration the great abuse of the Sabbath by many, especially in tyme of divine service that many lie about without the Church, and will not come in to hear sermon, ordain two of their number to go out each day in tyme of service and take notice of the transgressors of that nature that they may be accordinglie punished.*

18 July 1697 *It was enacted this day that the poor should attend sermon and catechising, otherwise their names where absent their-selves are to be cancelled out of the Roll of the Poor.*

3 July 1752 *The Session in order to prevent Sturdy Beggars belonging to this paroch from imposing on the Country, have resolved that none be allowed to begg through the Country save such as have Badges or testificates to certify their being in Indigent circumstances; and further resolve that none get charity out of the Box but such as will dispone to the Kirk box a right to all their goods and effects of everie kind at the hour of their Death. - - - The Chamberlain of Breadalbane was present and concurred with both the said Resolutions.*

By 1771 the Kirk had a much tighter grip. The Killin Kirk Session Records then tell us about the people in Dalgirdy. [164]

Given out to: (lists, including:) *Duncan Campbell, Dalgirdy*

6.1.1771	*£0-3-0*
12.8.1771	*£0-3-0*
26.1.1772	*£0-3-0*
21.6.1772	*£0-2-0*
18.1.1773	*£0-2-6*
3.2.1774	*£0-1-6*

Janet McNaughton in Dalgirdy got similar amounts eight times from 1771-73.

From 1772-78, Neil McNaughton in Dalgirdy paid in five shillings a year *as the interest in his heinds* (cattle).

June 8th 1777 This day compeared before the Session Eliz. Robertson, daughter to the deceased Duncan Robertson late in dale of Ardchyle, acknowledging herself with child by uncleanliness to Peter Campbell son to Duncan Campbell in Dalgirdy and confessed so on the fifteenth day of January last as the time of their criminal Commerce. The Minister laid before her the heinousness of her sin, rebuked her for it and seriously exhorted her to repentance, she promised all due submission.[165]

From 1778-92, *Chris McGrigor, Dalegirdy* got between one and two shillings two or three times a year. On 3rd March 1783 she got five shillings. The list on that date was headed: *The Right Hon. The Earl of Breadalbane has been pleased to allow the poor of this parish Fifteen pounds fifteen shillings which was distributed as follows.*[166]

Nov 24th 1782 Of mort cloth money for Dun McNaughtan Dalgirdy   *£0-1-6*[167]

The mort cloth belonged to the church and was hired out for burials. It was hired again for Jas McVean on Aug 3rd 1783 and Jean McCail on Mar 6th 1785 but the fee was now £0-2-6.

Another *Dun McNaughtan* in Dalgirdy was paid from the Poors Fund from 1787-93 and *That. McVurich* from 1794-1802.

April 19th 1790 This day it was represented to the Session that many of those guilty of Fornication wished to pay a pecuniary fine for the benefit of the poor, if they were excused from public rebuke before the Congregation. The Session, after taking the above Representation into their Serious Consideration, are unanimously of opinion, that it should be left optional to all delinquents of the above description to pay one pound ten shillings and a rebuke before the Session or to stand publicly before the Congregation and to be exempted from this fine.[168]

Apr 29th 1804 This day compeared before the Session Christian McNaughtan Daughter to Niel McNaughtan in Dalegirdy, acknowledging that she is with child by uncleanliness and gave up Colin Campbell son to Dun. Campbell in Dalegirdy as the father of her pregnancy. She confessed as one of the Times of their criminal commerce on about the 1st of October last.[169]

Mar 17th 1805 Compeared Chris McNaughtan in Dalgirdy and was for the first time rebuked for fornication with Colin Campbell late there.[170]

June 1st 1806 This day compeared before the Session Christian McNaughtan in Dalegirdy, acknowledging that she is with child by uncleanliness and gave up Hugh McGregor in Achlyne as the father of her pregnancy. She condescended on about 6th of January last as the only time of their criminal congress. The Minister laid before her the Heiniousness of her Sin, rebuked her for it, and seriously exhorted her to repent of the same. The Elder from the Quarter was ordered to summon the said Hugh to compeer here against this Day Eight Days.[171]

Oct 14th 1806 Hugh McGregor Achlyne & Christian McNaughtan Dalgirdy, a natural son baptised called Donald.[172]

Oct 14th 1806 This day Hugh McGregor in Achlyne and son to Alexander McGregor in Botourniemore and Niel McNaughtan in Dalegirdy came to the following agreement respecting the Child brought forth in fornication by Christian McNaaughtan daughter to the said Niel to the foresaid Hugh McGregor. That is to say the said Hugh promises to pay to the said Christian Seven Pounds Sterling in name of Damages and to take the whole charge of nursing and upbringing the said Child till it shall be able to do for itself. He likewise promises all due submission to Church Discipline and to pay his fine. The said Alex McGregor his father becomes his Cautioner to the foregoing effect. The said Christian considering that the said Hugh has thus voluntarily taken upon himself the said whole charge, and accepts of the said seven pounds, and renounces any other claim she might have by law against the said Hugh and has delivered him his child. She promises all due submission to Church Discipline and to pay her fine and the said Niel her father becomes her Cautioner to the foregoing effect.[173]

Feb 7th 1808 Paid by Christian McNaughtan Dalgirdy as her fine for a relapse in fornication with H McGregor £1-0-0[174]

July 9th 1814 This being a public thanksgiving on the restoration of peace to the nations of Europe.   Collected   £0-6-7
(Napoleon defeated – for the first time.)

July 20th 1856 Compeared Duncan McDiarmid, Mason, Dalgirdy, with Catherine Henderson his wife, to undergo Church Discipline for the sin of antenuptial fornication. The Moderator reported that he had previously conversed with McDiarmid in private. The Parties were then rebuked and admonished, and having exhibited signs of penitence were absolved from the scandal according to the rules of the Church.[175]

At times, the Sessions seemed to be obsessed with sex and perhaps that is true. But when a baby appeared there was no denying the sin! And this was also a very practical matter. This was about the welfare of the child and who was going to support it.

The following entries are not about people in Dalgirdy, but

show some other aspects of welfare.

1811 To four articles to a poor stranger object subject to convulsions who was burnt by falling into the fire at Duncrosk £0-16-6[176]

1824 For 1 cart of peats for Geo McFarland's children £0-2-6[177]

1826	*To a coffin for a poor object from Caithness*	*£0-8-0*
	Two pints whisky	*£0-7-0*
	1 peck meal	*£0-1-6*
	To 3 yards muslin	*£0-1-9*
	1lb candles & 2 lb sope	*£0-2-1*
		£1-0-4[178]

Note the two pints of whisky, for the wake, not the poor object!

Sept 2nd 1833 Mr McIntyre Glendochart appeared on behalf of Ann McNab and stated that she has been for the space of three years in a state of mental imbecility and quite unable to support herself by any description of labour and destitute of means by which she could support without labour.

The Session having considered her case allowed Mr McIntyre to put in a written statement of the same as a foundation for an application to the Heritors in her behalf.[179]

Sept 2nd 1833 By cash to Widow McIntyre for Irene McIntosh's child £3-0-0

Widow McIntyre agrees to nurse the said child at the rate of Six Pound Sterling per annum.[180]

May 12th 1834 The Session proceeded - - to balance their Accounts for the last half year. - - - The balance in hand from Collections made at the Church since November last including the sum of £2-12-0 of Mrs Brown's donation not then distributed is £7-6-11 Sterling.

The Session then finding they cannot meet the exigencies of the Poor under their charge without applying a part of the money apportioned for improving the Cottages of the Poor and a part of the money apportioned for purchasing Blankets, for the general purpose of meeting the urgent cases of distress of all the Poor under their charge.

The sums at their disposal this day are as follows. Viz. the sum of £7-6-11 as above; the sum of £2-3-8 from the balance of the Meall money. The sum of £7 appropriated for the Cottages, and the sum of £3 from the money assigned for Blankets.

They then distributed £20-2-7.[181]

The old Scottish Poor Law was *a regulated and legalized scheme of begging, supplemented by voluntary assessments and church charity.* By the 1830s, Kirk Sessions were struggling to meet the demand. The state took over welfare in the 1845 Poor Law (Scotland) Amendment Act. Relief was still at a parish level but was now run by a Parochial Board and funded by taxation.[182]

The Atholl, Weem & Breadalbane Poorhouse opened at Logierait in 1859. No name from Dalgirdy appears in the Register of Inmates.[183]

The Free Church was the largest Protestant sect, which split from the Church of Scotland in the Disruption of 1843.[184] It was stricter and more Calvinist but its Kirk Session Records show similar human failings.

August 24ᵗʰ 1887 Compeared before the Session Mrs Margaret McFarland and Mrs Isabella McNab, lower Glen Lochay, with reference to the charge of defamation of character brought by the latter against the former. Mrs McFarlane on being interrogated said that she had nothing to say against the character of Mrs McNab or her friends and further expressed regret if in the heat of quarrel she had said anything hurtful to Mrs McNab. Mrs McNab on her part declared that she had nothing to say against the character of Mrs McFarlane or her family and expressed regret for any hasty words she may have used hurtful to Mrs McFarlane. Having declared their

145

satisfaction with each other's statement they were affectionately admonished to abstain from further dispute and to conduct themselves like good neighbours and members of a Christian Church and having formally shaken hands with one another they were dismissed.[185]

June 25th 1891 The Session discussed rumours that the lay Precentor (who led the services) had been seen several times the worse for drink. He had previously been accused of fornication but that charge was not proven. Soon after this they asked him to resign.[186]

After long delays the shock waves of the Reformation spread far beyond religion. The idea that people should think for themselves paved the way for today's individualism and democracy, and perhaps even capitalism. If all men are equal before God, what does that say about the balance of power between the three estates? It undermined the divine authority of kings and helped to transfer power from kings to parliament.

Before the Reformation the Church held at least a quarter of the land. Today it owns 0.03%. Before the Reformation about 10% of the population were clergy of one kind or another, who lived off the labour of the other two estates. Today that figure is less than 0.1%.

Today the influence of the Kirk has waned and many of us no longer go to church. Yet the Scottish character, so far as there is such a thing, still bears the imprint of the Reformation.

Scotland shares, and helped to shape, America's belief that all men are born equal. In Scotland, anyone really can become First Minister and we each should make the most of our talents. Sober, frugal, hard-working and ambitious to *make good*.

In Scotland we do not judge worth or success only or even mainly in money terms. We are very conscious of the duties of our social position. And our strong sense of community says that if everyone is equal, no one should think they are better than anyone else. So we Scots do our utmost to prove our individual worth but can be uncomfortable with success. We do not like pomp or flattery or ostentatious wealth. *Stubborn and disputatious: an inimitable mix of truculence, defiance, courage and sheer cussed independence.* That is actually Reid's description of John Knox but it is true of many Scots.

Hoots, mon! Wha's like us? Here's tae us, wi' knobs on!

Perhaps that all says more about how we would like the world to see us than how we really are. And you may dispute every word of it. But it contains a kernel of truth. It is difficult to escape completely from our peculiar religious heritage.

12. THE EARLS OF BREADALBANE

*The curse: The Earldom will not descend
more than two generations in one line*[187]

The eleventh Laird of Glenorchy was yet another driving and ruthless man who would become the first Earl of Breadalbane.[188]

Lord Macaulay summed him up. *John, Earl of Breadalbane, ranked high among the petty princes of the mountains. - - - In truth he cared for no government and no religion. He seems to have united two different sets of vices, of two different regions, and of two different stages in the progress of society. In his castle among the hills he had learned the barbarian pride and savage ferocity of a Highland Chief. In the Council Chambers of Edinburgh he had contracted the deep taint of treachery and corruption.*[189] Another who knew him well said that he was *cunning as a fox, wise as a serpent, and slippery as an eel. - - - No Government can trust him but where his own private interest is in view.* [190] His nickname was 'Slippery John'. Family traits ran true!

As a young man he managed to snare a beautiful heiress in London, who came with a dowry of £10,000. That is £750,000 in today's money. The tale goes that he had two Highland ponies brought down to London. He mounted one with his wife behind him, loaded his gold on the other, and set off for Lochtayside with two armed Highlanders trotting alongside. Alongside the pony with the gold!

He gradually took over the running of the estate, long before his father's death in 1686.

He also played politics in Edinburgh and was in the Privy Council of Scotland. One of his commissions from the Council was to put down a rebellion in Sutherland. There he discovered that the Earl of Caithness was badly in debt so he befriended him and soon became his main creditor. The Earl could not pay his debts so signed over his estate and title to Sir John and then died without issue. Sir John promptly installed himself as Earl of Caithness. The Sinclair family protested that he had got the title *upon gross and false representations.* The King agreed, revoked the title, and gave it to the rightful heir. But Sir John continued to lay claim to the estates. He invaded Caithness and fought one of the last private clan battles in Scotland with the Sinclairs in 1680. Later, after his wife died, he even married the Earl's widow to avoid paying her a pension! Never daunted, he managed to extract rent and gold from Caithness until his death.

To compensate for losing the Earldom of Caithness, Charles II made him Earl of Breadalbane in 1681. He also got the unique power to choose which son would succeed him, which would prove to be real handy.

During and after the Civil War he played both sides against the middle. There was *no end to the turns and doubling of his course.* Later, once he was sure which way the wind was blowing, he shifted his support to William and Mary. By that time it was in his interest to promote order so he became the crown's most loyal lieutenant. The government charged him to deal with the defeated Highland chiefs and gave him a budget of £12,000 to settle the peace but the chiefs and the government soon accused him of double-dealing. When asked to account for the money, Slippery John had a ready reply. *The money's spent, the Highlands are at peace, and this is the only way of accounting among friends.*[191] He faced trial for treason and was imprisoned in Edinburgh Castle but his friends got the King to drop the charges.

Then, in 1692, his kinsman Robert Campbell of Glen Lyon carried out the infamous Massacre of Glencoe. Many thought Sir John had a hand in that affair but an official inquiry ruled there was no proof. They simply accepted his sworn statement that he had nothing to do with it! But after Tony Blair and the Iraq War, we all know that the findings of government inquiries are not always worth the paper they are written on.

Sir John kept aloof from the Scottish parliament that agreed the Union in 1707. In the dissatisfaction that followed, he supported the 1715 Jacobite Rising. He was called to Edinburgh to answer charges but his doctor and minister certified that he was too old and infirm to leave his bed. Then the very next day he made a miraculous recovery and was able to visit the Jacobite camp in Atholl to give his support. Others said the real reason he went was *to trick others, not to be trickt, and to obtain a share of the French subsidies.* He got funding for 1200 men but only sent 3-400 under his eldest son Duncan.

After the Rising failed, Duncan was briefly imprisoned in Edinburgh, and Sir John would have been too but for his frailty. He died within a year.

However, like other nobles, the wily old Earl had hedged his bets. While Duncan fought with the Jacobites, his younger son John was a staunch Hanoverian. Tricky to the end, once the Earl saw how things turned out he made use of his right to choose his successor. He passed over Duncan on the supposed grounds that he was feeble-minded. Instead, he left the estate and the Earldom to John so that the government would not confiscate them.

The second Earl of Breadalbane was laird from 1717 to 1752. Critics dismissed him as *remarkable only for his longevity, dying in this ninetieth year.* I beg to differ. After the unhappy experience of his father's turbulent politics and the 1715 Rising, it seems to me that his goals were peace and prosperity rather than drama and glory. For the estate and its people, he was a successful laird who achieved these goals.

Times were changing and lords had to adapt. The old ways would no longer do. His forebears and even his father were feudal lords who led their men in battle. He and his descendants were members of the British landed aristocracy, with a vested interest in law and order. Never again would an Earl of Breadalbane lead his men in battle. The future would rest on how well they could exploit political, legal and social change rather than the crude use of force.

When the second Earl took over in 1717 the estate was once again in debt. After the '15 there was a government garrison in Breadalbane and for some years the country was in a state of lawlessness and unrest.

The second Earl saw the need to prove his loyalty to the government and did all he could to stop his tenants joining the Jacobite cause. In contrast to 1715, he kept Breadalbane out of the 1745 Jacobite Rising. Thanks to *the cautious administration of the 2nd Earl & his counsellors - - - peace prevailed and there was a considerable measure of security for both life and property. The district had an opportunity of recovering somewhat from the disastrous effects of the civil war and turmoil of the previous century.*[192]

By this time a Factor dealt with most of the estate management. The Factor had great power and the Earl depended on him to keep the estate running smoothly. He drew up contracts, collected rents, and kept the accounts. He dealt with grievances and settled disputes. The peace and prosperity of the estate and the tenants rested to a large extent on the Factor. The Earl was lucky to have his kinsmen John Campbell of Achallader and his son as Factors from 1710 to the 1780s. Both were skilled and wise administrators, trusted by Earl and tenants alike.

From the late seventeenth century the estate had also appointed local 'birley-men'. These were sworn appraisers who gave an impartial valuation in contracts or small disputes. The duties of the birley-men were:

1. Valuations for tenants leaving.

2. To deal with anyone whose animals destroyed their neighbours' crops.

3. *That the birley-men determine in all cases betwixt tenant and tenant and master and tenant within their Division not exceeding six pounds Scots.*

4. *That they report all persons who keep above their Soumes on their Grass.* (The number of livestock the farm was reckoned to support adequately.)

5. That they make intimation of their haile Tenants within their divisions that all Masters are to be liable for their subtenants and cottars as well concerning the woods as for thefts.[193]

Duncan McVean in Dalgirdy was a *Sworn Birlayman and Appraiser.*[194]

Any straying beasts were kept in a *poindfold* until a fine was paid. *It is statute and ordanit that thair be - - - on Bottnornay Moir, Bottnornay Beg and Dalgardy ane pind fauld, Coline Campbell & Donald Oig McVane.*[195] They got a small payment from the estate to act as poindfold managers.

The second Earl paid off his father's debts and made the family solvent again. He and his Factors made a start to Improvements on the estate. They built roads and bridges. They continued the forestry planting started by his ancestor, the seventh laird. In 1725 they introduced flax. In 1739 they started lead mining at Tyndrum.

The third Earl of Breadalbane (1752-1782) was a brilliant young man who was sent to Oxford University and groomed to take over the estate. He cut his political teeth as a Member of Parliament for an English seat and became a friend of the Prime Minister. He served as a British Ambassador and Lord of the Admiralty. But by 1745 his father was getting old and he came home.

As heir apparent he helped his father to keep Breadalbane out of the '45. With his social standing and political background, he was able to advise the king and the government on the Rising. It was mainly due to his efforts that Breadalbane was spared the misery that befell other parts of the Highlands after the Rising was put down.

The third Earl knew of modern farming practice in England and continued his father's policy of improving the estate. In 1769 he arranged surveys of the Breadalbane estates. From 1771 he gave longer improving leases and helped pay for inclosing. He introduced commercial sheep farming. Spinning and weaving became a thriving business.

He built the model village of Kenmore that stands today. He took pride in Taymouth Castle and its grounds, which became well known on the early tourist circuit of the Highlands. Back in the seventeenth century, Scottish barons had lived in castles. Black Duncan had re-built Finlarig Castle in 1609 with an eye to defence. It had thick walls, a small well-barred door, high windows, an armoury and gun ports. By the eighteenth century the Earls felt secure enough to live in mansions with thin walls, large windows and gardens.

When the third Earl died in 1782, his two sons were already dead. Up to this time the line had been unbroken for three hundred and fifty years from the first Laird of Glenorchy. But in the time of the first Earl, the Lady of Lawers had laid a curse on the family. *The Earldom will not descend more than two generations in one line.* The third Earl was that second generation and the estates and the Earldom now passed to his distant cousin. The curse would hold true from now on.

The fourth Earl held the estate from 1782-1834 during the main period of Improvement. He sent the sons of tenants to Norfolk and Leicestershire to learn new farming methods. Farms were combined into larger units and sheep runs established.

He also continued to improve roads and bridges, schools and support for 'the deserving poor'.

When war broke out between Britain and France in 1793, the Earl rushed to raise a Battalion of Fencibles. The arrangement was that they would only serve in Scotland, to release regular forces to fight overseas. The Earl, of course, took command of the Battalion. Each volunteer got three guineas when he enlisted and there were soon enough men for a second battalion.

However, there were sticks as well as carrots. The estate drew up lists of all men they thought suited to service. Tenants with no sons to offer could show their loyalty by finding a suitable recruit and paying his bounty. Some tenants objected and did not cooperate but they were seen as troublemakers and most of them were turned off the estate after 1795.

These two battalions served in various parts of Scotland until they were disbanded in 1797. A third battalion was raised in 1794 and its range of service extended to include Ireland, where it continued to serve until 1802. On their return, loyal recruits got preference on the estate.

Over this time the fourth Earl also had a successful career in politics. He was made the first Marquis of Breadalbane, just eighteen months before his death.

Between 1799 and 1805 the fourth Earl built a grand new stately mansion at Taymouth. To fund this he needed more income from the estate, which was of course the driving force behind the Improvements. But the loyal Rev Gillies had no such doubts.

The mourning for this good and worthy Scottish nobleman was deep and genuine. He had been an enlightened and considerate landlord, having always at heart the good of his tenants, and the improvement of his vast estates. He was in a very true sense the father of his people, who were always ready to recognise his worth.[196]

The changes may have been inevitable in a changing world, but petitions from the tenants show they also caused much social disturbance and anger. From a modern perspective, we may question if the Earl was quite as benevolent as Gillies makes out.

The fifth Earl was educated at Eton and followed family tradition to become an English Member of Parliament. These were still the days – just – when a local patron could control the election. Then, when he succeeded his father, he moved to the House of Lords.

The fifth Earl spent much of his life in London and abroad, perhaps fortunately leaving most of the running of the estate to his Factor. He tried to bring industry to Breadalbane but his attempts were quite unrealistic and met with little success.

The highlight of his time was when Queen Victoria and Prince Albert visited Taymouth in September 1842. This was part of her 'Royal Progress' in the Highlands and Gillies waxed lyrical. *There was intense excitement and joy in Breadalbane and throughout all Perthshire - - - and the outburst of loyalty and patriotism was simply amazing.*[197]

The Earl spared no expense. Himself led the 'Breadalbane Highlanders' with many of his kinsmen as officers. He chose two hundred of the finest looking men on his estate to act as the Queen's bodyguard. He clad a hundred gillies in shepherd tartan for Albert's grouse and deer drive, which bagged 20 roe deer, 4½ brace of black grouse, 2 brace of red grouse, 1 brace of capercailzie, 1 partridge, 1 wood pigeon, 12 hares and 7 rabbits.

The Queen, meanwhile, visited the dairy where she tried her hand at a butter churn, sipped some fresh milk and tasted an oatcake. Greatly daring! That evening there was a grand ball in the hall of Taymouth Castle. The next day, eight local stalwarts rowed the Queen the length of Loch Tay in a royal barge built for the occasion. To serenade her on her way, thousands of locals lined the shore and sang the National Anthem.

The Queen's diary shows that the royal couple were suitably impressed. She called dark Glen Ogle *the Kyber Pass of the Highlands. - - - Our reception, by dear Lord Breadalbane in a princely style, not to be equalled for grandeur and poetic effect. - - - It seemed as if a great chieftain in old feudal times was receiving his sovereign*[198]. She also visited Lord Breadalbane's 'cottage' – the twenty-room mansion of Auchmore!

Perhaps that episode best sums him up.

The fifth Earl died without issue in 1862, again fulfilling the curse. Under Scots law, the estate and the earldom would pass to his closest male heir, but that was no simple matter. It took five years of legal dispute about family lines, marriage status and legitimacy across two centuries before the case was settled. The ultimate winner was a seventh generation descendant of the ninth Laird of Glenorchy.

The seventh Earl of Breadalbane held the title from 1871-1922 and was the third Marquis of Breadalbane. He had one of the greatest feudal land-holdings ever known in Britain, stretching a hundred miles from Aberfeldy to the west coast. The Rev Gillies, dealing with the recent past, was at his most loyal. *He played the part of a territorial magnate with great popularity. He gave much attention to the development and management of his estates. He was always kind and considerate towards his tenants.*[199]

Others were more critical. A later writer described him as *a wealthy but rather eccentric chap, who, some may say, had far more money than sense.*[200]

And social change was stirring, with a 1903 satire in Punch.

In Braid Albyn

Frae Kenmore tae Ben More   (Ben More on Mull,
The land is a' the Marquis's;   not at Crianlarich.)
The mossy howes, the heathery knowes
An' ilka bonnie park is his;
The bearded goats, the towsie stots,
An' a' the braxie carcases;
Ilk crofter's rent, ilk tinkler's tent,
An ilka collie's bark is his;
The muir-cock's craw, the piper's blaw,
The ghillie's hard day's wark is his;
Frae Kenmore tae Ben More
The warld is a' the Marquis's.

The fish that swim, the birds that skim,
The fir, the ash, the birk is his;
The Castle ha' sae big and braw,
Yon diamond-crusted dirk is his;
The roofless hame, a burning shame,
The factor's dirty wark is his;
The poor folk vexed, the lawyer's text,
Yon smirking legal shark is his;
Frae Kenmore tae Ben More
The warld is a' the Marquis's.

But near, mair near, God's voice we hear -
The dawn as weel's the dark is His;
The poet's dream, the patriot's theme,
The fire that lights the mirk is His.
They clearly show God's mills are slow
But sure the handiwork is His;
And in His grace our hope we place;
Fair Freedom's sheltering ark is His.
The men that toil should own the soil -
A note as clear's the lark is this -
Breadalbane's land - the fair, the grand -
Will no' be aye the Marquis's.[201]

Gillies only gave the first verse!

After WWI, the economy and agriculture were in a depressed state. The family began to sell off the estate piece by piece to cover taxes, death duties, extravagance and debt. And her Ladyship helped by running up massive gambling debts on the gaming tables at Monte Carlo. In the early 1920s they sold Taymouth and 50,000 acres at the east end of the estate. This was the beginning of the end prophesied by the Lady of Lawers way back in the mid-seventeenth century.[202]

In time the estates of Balloch that were put together in hides will be torn asunder in lace.

In time the estates of Balloch will yield only one rent and then none at all.

The last laird will pass over Glen Ogle with a grey pony leaving nothing behind at all.

The seventh Earl died in 1922, again without issue, and trustees ran the estate for the next twelve years until the death of his widow. During the 1920s, to meet death duties and other taxes, they sold off many western parts of the estate.

In due course the Earldom passed to Charles William Campbell of Boreland in Glen Lochay, who became ninth Earl from 1923-59. But it was not until the Marchioness died in 1935 that he finally took possession of what was left of the estate.

Much had gone but much remained. So, with gay abandon, he set about expensive renovations of all the big estate houses including Boreland Lodge in Glen Lochay. But this was the Great Depression, agriculture was in a bad way, and his financial straits grew dire. So he continued to sell off parts of the estate to meet his debts.

In 1942 he sold Boreland Estate in Glen Lochay to the Stroyan family. After five hundred years the Campbells no longer held Dalgirdy.

In 1948 he sold the final remaining land of Kinnell House and farm back to the twenty-second chief of Macnab. The last Laird of Glenorchy then left Breadalbane by train over Glen Ogle, with his little grey pony in the cattle wagon. And so the Lady of Lawers' prophecy came to pass.

When the ninth Earl died in 1959, his only son John became the tenth and last Earl of Breadalbane. But there was no estate and no money. He was estranged from his father and never married. He lived in a small flat in London and worked at various jobs including playing the bagpipes and as a laboratory cleaner, where his work mates knew him as plain Jock Campbell.

Since Jock died in 1995, the Earldom has been dormant.

Why did the Campbells of Breadalbane die out when their kinsmen in Atholl and Argyll kept their estates and their positions? For all their success, the lairds of Glenorchy never quite made it to the top rung of the aristocracy. They were always the cadet branch of Clan Campbell and played second fiddle to the Dukes of Argyll.

From the eighteenth century the family lost its genetic vigour. A lack of strong sons spelled their doom.

More prosaically, their estate, power and wealth were all in the Highlands. Their land holding was great but it was poor land that could not support the lifestyle they aspired to. Unlike many Scottish nobles, they never had any better land in England or the Lowlands. They never developed any income apart from agriculture nor got lasting benefit from the Industrial

Revolution. The later Earls were not businessmen. Unlike their forebears, they failed to adapt to changing times and taxes.

In the end, perhaps they simply did not have the will or the drive or the ability to *keepit conquessit*. Nor deserve to.

13. LAW AND ORDER

One law for all

We need law and order so that people can live in peace with as little trouble and interference as possible. Look at Afghanistan or Somalia to see what happens without law and order. Yet when we criticize such places we often forget that we have only achieved it ourselves in the past few hundred years.

In early societies, people literally had to take the law into their own hands. That does not mean there was anarchy. All groups had to maintain order and in a small group that was done mainly by social pressure. Custom - that unwritten law. Most families still manage this pretty well most of the time.

Christianity helped. Before you could make peace with God, you must be at peace with your neighbour. Part of the ritual of the early church was *kissing the paxboard,* which was the congregation's kiss of peace. The parish priest helped to settle minor disputes.

But once people settled they had to defend their land. If their lives or livelihood were under threat they **must** respond. Hopefully, they could deal with the threat and restore peace. Too often, however, this led to feuds, which seem to be common in all primitive societies. The blood feud or vendetta is a long-running fight between rival families or clans. A feud begins when one side feels, rightly or wrongly, that it has been attacked, insulted or wronged. It seeks revenge and that makes the other side react in kind. This leads to a cycle of tit for tat. Like any civil war, it can lead to extreme acts of violence. It draws in family members and supporters and the feud can go on for generations. It gets harder and harder to reach a peaceful solution. The Mafia is a good example.

Early lords were first and foremost military leaders but they also imposed order. The lord's hall was the seat of justice. The lord or his deputy passed judgement on disputes and crimes in his land and among his people. The problem, of course, was that when there was no written law each lord could do what he chose. Most would stick with custom, most of the time. But the lord was the highest power in the neighbourhood and looked after his own interests first. Only a brave or foolish man would seek justice against his lord in the lord's own hall.

Men were bound to their lords and lords to kings by their oaths. If there were no oaths there could be no lords or kings and no law and order either. In the *bond of manrent*, men gave their bond to a lord and became his 'followers'. In return, the lord became the protector of those who entered his 'friendship'. Earlier bonds put equal stress on the lord's and the men's obligations. Later bonds stressed the man's duty to assist the laird in any of his actions and causes, usually *save only against the king*. The lord's duties were taken for granted. As late as the sixteenth century the Lairds of Glen Orchy made more use of bonds of manrent than anyone in the Highlands.

Bond of manrent and calf granted by Donald McKissag in Dalgardie and John Dow Mukissag in the Moir of Glenlyon to Sir Duncan Campbell of Breadalbane. Dated at Finlarig 1ˢᵗ March 1592.[203]

As kingdoms developed, kings strove to establish royal justice throughout the realm. In 1180, King William the Lion reserved four pleas to the Crown – rape, robbery, arson & murder. He set up Sheriff Courts and appointed Sheriffs to try these cases, like Mortimer in Perth. But royal authority and the Sheriff Courts made little inroads into the Highlands.

At the end of the fourteenth century *the highlanders - - - are a savage and untamed nation, rude and independent, given to rapine.*[204] Feuding was common. Cattle raiding was seen as - - - *the principal source of all their barbarity, cruelty, cunning and revenge* (which) *trains them up to the use of arms, love of plunder, thirst for revenge - - -.*[205] Legend and poetry show that raiding was one of the main Highland pursuits - 'the Highland sport'.

Real progress on law and order did not come until James VI, who saw the problem clearly and advised his son: *Rest not, untill ye roote out these barbarous feides.* [206]

Parliament passed an Act in 1587 *For the quieting and keping in obedience of the disorderit subjectis inhabitantis of the Bordouris, Hielandis, and Ilis.*[207] All landlords in the kingdom were held responsible for the good behaviour of their tenants and followers. The Appendix to the Act was a *roll of the names of the landislordis and baillies of landis in the hielandis, quhair broken men hes duelt and presentlie duellis.* The list included *The Laird of Glenorquhy* and many of his neighbours. The 'Roll of Broken Clans' included *Clangregour - - - And als many brokin men of the surnames of - - - M'Nabbis.*

After the Union of 1603, James had the greater power of the British Crown behind him. He knew Scottish needs and practices well and was a skilled politician. He did much to organize the Scottish courts and legal profession and got support from the reformed Kirk. But he showed his cunning best in dealing with the nobility, where he was expert at getting the key players to work with him. Most important in our area were the Campbell Earls of Argyll and Breadalbane. Their land formed a buffer zone between the peaceful Lowlands and the wild Northwest Highlands. They were also half Lowland in outlook. So James enlisted their aid, giving them government tasks that strengthened their position and at the same time met his aims. Dealing with the MacGregors was a good example.

For many centuries kings had to rely on local barons to administer justice. Baron Baillie Courts began in the twelfth century[208] and were most important in the Highlands where there were no Sheriffs.

The baron had responsibility to **administer** the king's justice within his barony. Yet that did not mean he was judge and jury. The baron was responsible for running the court and he appointed the court officials who dealt with minor cases. But for major cases, his tenants and vassals made up a jury and gave judgement.

The Baron Court had the right of *pit and gallows*. You can still see the pit at the ruins of Finlarig castle. Tradition says this was a beheading pit for people of gentle birth, while common people were hanged on the gallows tree. However, some charters suggest that *pit and gallows* was actually the right to hang men and drown women. That would mean it was a drowning pit. It all sounds barbaric but the death sentence could only be used under strict conditions. And such major cases were rare.

1623 *Trial of Gillechrist M'Intaillour* who was accused of a series of thefts including two sheep, one sheep, a cow, a goat, and various goods. Also of Marie N'Gregour for aiding and abetting M'Intaillour and resetting stolen goods. The jury of 15 men included *Coline Campbell in Dalgardy*. The jury reached a unanimous verdict of guilty and decreed that *the said Gillechrist M'Intallour to be instantly hangit be his craig upone ane gibet or gallows quhill he be deid and the lyf out of his bodie, - - - and that the said Marie Nik-Gregour to be schurgit and banest the countrey.* (Scourged and banished from Breadalbane.)[209] Sentence was carried out immediately. No delays for second thoughts or appeals or any other such nonsense!

Most of the time the court dealt with estate matters. It drew up regulations, gave out fines and settled disputes. The court was then looking after the interests of the laird and it is no surprise that the Campbells kept a close eye on court proceedings. This gave the baron enormous power. And there was no appeal or redress against any miscarriage of justice. Some lairds took full advantage, though there is little evidence that the Campbells made any gross abuse of their power. One Breadalbane tenant did sue the laird in 1627 for a crop of straw and the court awarded half his claim.

The Baron Baillie Courts of Glenorchy had some of the best records in the country, going back to 1573.[210] There would be earlier courts but these are the earliest records that survive. The court was like a small version of the royal parliament and passed local laws with *the advice and consent of the whole commons and tenants.* Most of the regulations were about social order and the running of the estate.[211]

- First and most important was that all lairds and tenants were responsible for their cottars and sub-tenants. No vagabonds should be allowed to settle.

- Next came rules about woodland. Wood was a scarce and valuable resource that was the laird's property though largely for the community's use. The main concern was to prevent unlawful cutting or grazing.

- Every tenant, crofter and cottar should have his own kailyard.

- Everyone should use the peat bank they were given, with rules about when and how to cut peat.

- There were rules for the burning of heather that had to be done in March. If near woods, *six honest neighbours* had to supervise and stand by to quench the fire if necessary.

- There were rules about grazing and the number of 'soums' of cattle and sheep that each farm could carry. There were rules about head dykes and use of the shielings. From the early seventeenth century there was concern about over-grazing.

- Tenants had to use the estate smithies and mills. The court set prices for smiths, for grinding corn and for weaving cloth. Tenants had to help keep smithies and mills water-tight, and help the miller bring in millstones.

- Ale could only be brewed under licence from the laird. It must meet a certain standard and alehouses had regular inspections. The alehouse must provide service to those who sought it but was not allowed to serve ale before the church service on Sundays. Drunkenness was an offence, for which the court imposed a fine while the kirk set *public repentance on the stuill.* The court controlled the production, sale and drinking of whisky.

- Game was the laird's and protected by the court under heavy fines. No one should shelter a poacher. Every tenant had to help deal with vermin like wolves, foxes and crows.

Fines were a good source of income for the estate and were set in money terms. In earlier times there was little money in circulation, so fines were often paid in kind. A fine of 25 merks could be paid by a cow or ox fattened and salted for winter use.

Entries in the Court Books cast another light on life in Dalgirdy.

1595 *The accused thief* (not named) *riding at night to Donald McVain's house in Dalgirdy in the month of October last, 1595, and taking away plaid and cheese.*[212]

1597 *The following are wanting of a kaleyard:*
Johne McFinlay McOlean in Dalgirdy for the holding of Donald Dow, his brother, and Gillespik McCansk his cottar.[213]

1615 *Donald McGillechreist in Dalgirdy is a court official/juror.*[214]

1616 *Duncane McDonald Aird in Dalgirdy pursued Donald Dow McGillegariv there for striking him on his head with a dirk last harvest.*[215]

1618 List of persons convicted for not taking *thak* (thatch) to Finlarig includes: *Donald Dow McGillegarive in Dalgirdy, two threave* (a measure of cut grain or thatching material).[216]

1625 *Coline Campbell pursued the tenants of Dalgirdy for not building the head dyke.*[217]

1633 *Jon McPhatrik Vain in Dalgirdy - fined for cutting peats.*[218] (Probably the wrong time or place or method.)

1647 *Dalgirdy:*
Alaster Dow McDougall convicted for pealing timber.

Duncan McNecaird convicted for killing a deer.[219]

1671 Gilchrist McIllguie pursued Molldonich McIllchrist in Dalgirdy for taking a cow and a firlot of meal.[220]

1683 Persons appointed to be foresters. List includes: *For the woods of Tullich, Tirai and Dalgirdy, Patrick McKainish alias Campbell in Tirai.*[221]

Duncan Roy McMartine held the tack of Dalgirdy from 1725-1731, though he actually lived in Kenknock.

1725 Complaint by Alexander Stewart in Kenknock and his spouse Margaret Stewart and also at the instance of James Campbell in Craig Procurator Fiscal of Court for his interest against Duncan Roy McMartine in Kenknock.

That the said Duncan Roy McMartine, having shaken off the fear of God and without regard to the laws of the Kingdom, did upon Monday the 3rd of May come to the house of the said Alexander and thereafter entering the house in a very rude manner asked the said Margaret where was that dog her husband. That if he had him he would make a riddle of his hide before they parted. Whereupon she immediately for her husband's safety ran to the door of the room where he happened to be and secured the same by locking it.

McMartine was fined 100 merks; to beg Mrs Stewart's pardon on his knees before two witnesses, and to post bail for his keeping the peace.[222] McMartine also appeared in several other legal disputes. A violent, litigious man!

1727 The Baily fined and armerciates Finlay McNaughtan in Dalgirdy in Ten Pounds Scots for beating Robert Campbell there because it appeared from the Defender's own confession but absolved him from any damages claimed by the pursuers.[223]

1728 Complaint by Malcolm McVain in Dachuil against Findlay McNaughtan in Dalgirdy about baggage lost in Glen Lochay. - - - *Search made by James Campbell Officer found in the* house of the said Finlay McNaughtan upon the 23rd of October and the following items had been taken out of it viz. *four pounds wool worth three merks Scots, a napkin and a Silver hart worth eighteen shillings Scots, a knife worth three shilling Scots and two shilling Scots of money.*

Decreed to return to Malcolm McVain these items or to pay their value thereof and pay Twenty Pounds Scots of damages plus expenses of searching.

The Defender admitted that he had kept the baggage - - - *for no other reason than that he thought whatever he found should belong to himself. - - -* Damages were reduced to twelve pounds plus expenses.[224]

1731 The Baily decreed John Dow McKechrist in Botuarniebeg to pay to Patrick Campbell son to Robert Campbell in Dalgirdy twelve pounds twelve shillings Scots for intrometting (interfering) *with and clipping the hair of a filly which was pasturing in the hill above Boruarniebeg about Lamass last year - - - Because the defender compeared and acknowledged his clipping the filly as lybelled.*[225]

1731 John McIlechreist in Botuarniebeg pursued Patrick Campbell in Dalgirdy for twelve merks Scots, for grazing a mare for four years and two pounds Scots for a years grass to two cows. - - -Baily absolved Patrick from the claim because - - - he acknowledged that he gave the pursuer an ease of his fee when he engaged his servant.

McIlechreist appeared in a number of claims and counter-claims against different people about this time.[226]

1732 Finlay McNaughtan in Dalgirdy pursued Robert Campbell there for three pound Scots as the hyre of a bull for four years, as also Meg More, John McNaughton and John Roy McMartine all in Dalgirdy for four merks as a year's hyre of the said bull preceding harvest last. The Bailly absolved the Defenders because they compeared and alleged that the Pursuer's bull was insufficient and the pursuer refused to Dispone upon oath how far he was aware of the Bull's insufficiency.[227]

What is an *insufficient* bull? Did he fail to perform? Or did he prove to be infertile?

1732 Hugh McCallum in Dalgirdy and the procurator fiscal for his interest pursued Alexander Docharlach in Dalgirdy for breaking through his house when said Hugh and his family were at the Sheallings - - -. Said Alexander or his wife- - - carried away upwards of (blank) pecks of Meall. - - -His wife thereafter offered payment if it should be kept quiet. As also the said Alexander's wife stole a silver heart from the said Hugh's wife in the latter end of harvest last upon a Sunday. Compeared Isobel McGrigor the defender's spouse and judicially confessed the stealing of the meall out of the pursuer McCallum's house.[228]

1733 Petition by Robert Campbell in Dalgirdy that in summer 1730 two quays which were *calved and brought up together in the said town of Dalgirdy* were stolen or strayed to Glenlyon. The Court decided against Campbell.[229]

1733 *Procurator Fiscal of court entered a complaint of following persons, who are guilty of cutting and destroying the Earl of Breadalbane' their Master's wood at their own hands and without paying for the said woods conforming to the Regulations and Acts of Court.* A long list of farms in Glen Lochay includes:

Dalgirdy:

Hugh McCallum	*Negative*
John McNaughtane	*Negative*
Rbt Campbell	*Confessed a doz & a half of alder with the Birlymen's liberty*
Patrick Campbell	*His son*
Alex Dochartach	*Confessed 4 or 5 alder Fined 12/- Scots*
Angus McDiarmid	*Cottar sick and excused*

Baily absolved those marked negative or excused.[230]

1734 A claim in which a witness stated that Alexander Dochardich, sometime in Dalgirdy, was a debtor. However, he had *deserted the country for misdoe manners so that the pursuer cannot have diligence against him - - - .*[231]

1746 *Summons pursued at the instance of Gilbert McLaren, foxhunter in High Botaurnie against the following persons. Making mention of - - -* (list includes) *Hew McCallum in Dalgirdy fifteen shillings and eight pence of old Rests. Duncan McDiarmid there fifteen shillings and two pence old rests all for a year and a half's foxhunting due preceding Christmas last.*

Hew McCallum alleged he killed these foxes himself but could not prove it. The Baillie decided for McLaren.[232]

1746 *Summons by Patrick McNab at Milnmore against Hew McCallum in Dalgirdy in pursuit of the sum of Eight Pounds Four Shilling Scots as the remains of the price of a horse sold and delivered to him payable at Matinmas last.*[233]

1746 *Ewen McCallum in Dalgirdy being personally summoned to compear is decreed to make payment to Alexander Robertson Esq waker* (fuller of cloth) *in Killin of the sum of Two pounds eighteen shilling Scots remaining of Twenty pounds Scots in arrears since March 1744 - - - contained in his accepted Bill with half a Crown of expenses of plea.*[234]

Let me hasten to say that Dalgirdy was not unusual. Most *bailes* had a similar crop of cases over the course of a hundred and fifty years.

The government abolished Baron Baillie Courts in 1748 as part of the crackdown on Highland chiefs after the '45. Those who had supported the government felt ill-treated but London insisted on one law for all. Lairds lost the income from fines. The Earl of Breadalbane claimed £6,000 in compensation but only got £1,000.

County Sheriff Courts took over and answered to central government. The law was now uniform across the country and everyone – lairds, tenants and cottars alike – was equal before the law. No one was above the law. Lairds could no longer behave like tyrants over their tenants.

Cattle raiding remained a problem until the eighteenth century.

Late autumn was the season for raiding, once the harvest was safely in but before the winter snows. *They go out in Parties from Ten to Thirty Men, traverse large Tracts of Mountains till they arrive at the Lowlands where they Design to Commit Depreciations, which they chose to do in places distant from the Clans where they Inhabit. They drive the Stolen Cattle in the Night time - - - and take the first occasion to sell them at the Fairs or Markets that are held in many parts of the Country.* [235]

They raided from the Highland glens into the rich straths of Lennox and Strathearn, and from Badenoch and Atholl down the Angus glens. *The clans in the Highlands, the most addicted to rapine and plunder* (include) - - - *the McDonells of Keppoch, the Broadalbin men and the Macgregors on the borders of Argyleshire.*[236] Kenmore was *a very frequent and beaten pass for driving stolen cattle from Perthshire, Stirlingshire, Kinross and Clackmannan into Glenlyon, Rannoch, Breadalbane, Glencoe, Appin and Lorn.*[237] As late as 1749 the army commander at Tummel Bridge kept a watch for cattle thieves at the head of Glen Lyon.[238]

For several years after the '15 Rising there was turmoil in Breadalbane. *The country was in a lawless condition.*[239]

Two years after the Rising, the Factor was in despair. *The state of the Highlands will soon be rendered desperate by stealing, for companies of armed men are seen in the hills, who cross this country to Strathearn and the braes of Menteith, and take cows and horses in small droves of ten or a dozen. When the night turns longer, and the cows stronger for driving it will be much worse, for a dozen armed men may rob and plunder the whole side of a country, since there is no arms to oppose them, which these loose fellows know very well. The garrisons of regular troops are no ways fit to curb them.*[240]

A month later he wrote again. *They begin to steal horses, particularly on the sides of the Loch. Those I suspect most are the people of Rannoch and Glenlyon, and some within ourselves.*[241]

The second Earl worked with the government to put down unrest and restore law and order. His Factor set up a watch to catch the thieves. *I have appointed a watch of 18 men of the loose fellows in the country, John Macnab to command the one half, and Duncan Roy the other. They are to carry arms with the permission of the governor of Finlarig, and to be paid every month.* [242] Within a year the Factor was able to report that only one cow had been stolen since the watch was set up.

After the Union of Parliaments in 1707, London had ultimate responsibility for law and order. This was strong central government with greater resources and higher expectations. After 1715 they placed major garrisons at Fort William, Fort Augustus and Fort George in Inverness. After 1745 there were also smaller garrisons at Callander and Kinloch Rannoch. New military roads let troops move quickly about the country.

But the British Army did not have enough men to maintain law and order across the Highlands. So, in 1725, General Wade raised a militia to keep a watch for Jacobites and cattle raiders alike. Three of the six companies came from Clan Campbell. They were known as the 'Black Watch' and later became a famous regiment in the British Army.[243]

But it was only after the '45 that the government was finally able to impose law and order across the whole of the Highlands. At last there was peace. Law and order would prevail from now on. Never again would Breadalbane suffer the ravages of war, raiding or lawlessness. Ten years later the Factor reported proudly. *There have been no thefts here or depradations committed on this Barony since 1748 except once. The thief was Banished to the Plantations, and the Factor recovered payment to the Tenants from whom the goods were stolen, out of his effects. - - - No persons suspected to be thieves or of resetting them live in this Barony.*[244]

As the eighteenth century wore on, many of the more barbaric punishments of Scots law ended. There was no more pinning and cutting of ears, branding, public flogging of women or banishment. Sins such as breaking the Sabbath or swearing became matters for the Kirk alone.

But as so often, the army was slow to change. It continued flogging until the 1870s.

The Navy used the cat-o'-nine-tails and 250-500 lashes usually killed the victim. The Army used a lighter cat made from a drumstick with nine thongs of cotton cord each with three knots. The British Army flogged about a thousand soldiers each year. The whole point was *pour encourager les autres* so flogging was on parade, with the man's Regiment standing at attention to witness punishment.

On 1 December 1794 the Breadalbane Fencibles were posted in Glasgow. The army arrested several men for a minor offence, but their comrades felt this was unfair and broke them out of jail. There was no violence and no one was hurt but the army considered this to be mutiny.

Gillies says that the ringleaders gave themselves up and Major Colin Campbell had to march them to Edinburgh for trial. One of the prisoners was a man called John McMartin. He wanted to attend to some personal business before his trial so he asked the major for permission and gave his word that he would re-join the party before it reached Edinburgh. Major Campbell knew and trusted McMartin so he let him go. The party marched on, as slowly as they could, but McMartin was delayed. Major Campbell was at Edinburgh Castle, handing over his prisoners, when McMartin rushed up and took his place in line. His main concern was that the major should not get into trouble.[245]

The story became a shining example of the honour and trustworthiness of the Highlander. In view of what happened next, that may seem hypocritical.

6th Jan 1795 General Court Martial held at Edinburgh
Six private soldiers in the 1st Battalion were tried and found guilty of the crime of mutiny. Three were sentenced to death and three to flogging.

John McMartin - - - is thereby judged to receive 1,000 Lashes in the usual manner; but the Court recommended him to Mercy. [246]

Next month, the sentences were suspended. The soldiers then got pardons, if they agreed to enlist in other Regiments serving abroad. McMartin would go to North America. But for some unknown reason the pardons were not exercised and McMartin and a man called Scrimgeour had their sentences carried out.

27 June 1795

Account of disbursements by Donald Mackerrachar Invalid at Edinburgh Castle on account of the prisoners confined in the said castle.

Bread & milk to make poultices six days	
for John McMartine at 4d per day	£0-2-0
Ditto one day for J Scrimigor	£0-0-6
Wine the day they were punished	£0-3-6
Attendance left to your generosity	£0-6-0
	£0-12-0 [247]

There was a man called John McMartin in Dalgirdy in the early 1790s. [248] Was this the very same man?

It is hard to imagine the cruelty of a flogging. The victim was tied in a crucified position and the lash applied to his bared upper back. Drummers wielded the lash, working in relays as their arms tired. A thousand lashes took at least three-quarters of an hour.

Dr Ferguson gave an eyewitness account from 1799.

He was sentenced to receive a thousand lashes. When brought up for punishment, he stripped as if in scorn, and presented as fine a model of compact form, hard muscle, and dark thick skin, as ever I beheld. The drummers were well-grown sturdy lads, who had always performed their duty well, and to them, after the punishment began, he particularly directed his abuse, daring them to do their worst, for they would never extract a single groan from him. Seven hundred and seventy-five lashes were most severely inflicted, when, perceiving from his countenance alone that nature was giving way, I had him taken down and carried to the hospital. In a few weeks he was reported cured, and the commanding officer declared that the sentence should be inflicted to the utmost lash. He was accordingly brought out again. It was winter, and the snow was on the ground. He was tied up with his back to the wind, and the punishment began. At the first lash the newly-organised skin gave way, the blood streamed down his back, and he who, on the first infliction, was all defiance, now writhed and cried out. As the flogging proceeded the lash became clogged with blood, which at every wave of the drummer's arm was driven in showers by the wind over the snow-covered ground; his cries became actual yells, and the integuments of his newly-cicatrized back were cut literally in pieces. I stopped the punishment when he had received sixty lashes; but his second cure was now a very different affair. Healthy suppuration could not be established after such reiterated injury, and sloughing and deep-seated abscesses were formed amongst the great muscles of the back. When I left the regiment some months afterwards, he was still in the hospital, a poor hectic wretch, utterly broken down from the terrible effect of the second flogging.

This was Dr Ferguson's evidence to the UK Parliament, which did not finally put an end to flogging in the British Army till 1881.[249]

Law and order came at a heavy price, but it was an essential first step to building a better and more prosperous society.

14. ROADS AND BRIDGES

A highway to the world

Roads are rights of way that join places and people together.

A modern road takes the easiest route. It has a smooth, hard surface – leaving aside our current rash of potholes! It is well-drained to prevent floods and mud. The whole point is to make travel as easy as possible, whether on foot or horse or wheels.

But ease of travel does much more. It opens up our world. It lets us see other places and meet other people. It improves communication and the spread of ideas. It makes transport possible, of people, livestock and goods. It provides access to markets and economic development, to shops and services.

After law and order, roads are the essential next step towards joining the modern world. That is why the Romans put so much effort into building roads. Roads carry the lifeblood of civilization.

Up to the eighteenth century there were no roads in rural areas. Tracks up and down the glen and between the *bailes* were simply beaten by the feet of people and animals over the years. They had no bottoming or surface or drainage. They zigzagged up and down steep hills and meandered around rocks and bogs.

These tracks were only suitable for people on feet or hardy ponies. Even in good weather they were impossible for wheeled transport of any kind. In bad weather they could become impassable even to horses. Rain turned flat ground into puddles studded with big stones. In long wet spells and winter they were nothing but muddy quagmires, churned up by animal hooves. Slopes became torrents. Frost turned them into sheets of ice. Over moorland there was nothing to see but bleak, featureless

175

waste and when the snow drifted or the mist came down it was hard to follow any track.

There were no bridges, so rivers and burns in spate became dangerous or impassable. You can skip across the Allt Ghaordaidh in dry weather without getting your feet wet. In spate it is a torrent of brown water and white froth. Fast-flowing water only needs to be knee-deep to whip you off your feet, batter you against the rocks, and kill you. And that is only a burn. You would not risk crossing the River Lochay in spate, even with a boat.

So, many tracks were unusable in winter months. It is difficult for us to imagine today. Killin is the nearest village and it is only five miles from Dalgirdy and ten minutes by car. But for much of the winter it might as well have been on the other side of the moon. On a really bad day you could not even get to the next *baile*.

Drove 'roads' were not really roads at all but simply stretches of easier going across the hills. They kept to higher, drier ground so they were not much use for ordinary traffic.[250]

People walked or went on horseback. Most people did not travel far except for raiding and war. When Montrose looked for guides in 1644 he found that most locals were *scarce acquainted with a place but six miles from their own habitations.*[251] Though perhaps we were playing dumber than we looked!

People transported goods on their own backs or on horseback. Small items went into panniers or baskets. Larger objects were tied to wooden hurdles fixed on each side of the horse.

Bulky loads like hay and dung and peat were moved short distances on a sled. This was simply two saplings tied either side of the horse's collar like shafts, their ends trailing on the ground behind with crossbars to carry the load. Primitive sleds of a forked tree and a few rough planks served to drag large stones from the fields. Sleds could work wherever there was fairly clear ground and were still in use in some inaccessible parts of the Highlands into the twentieth century.[252]

Nothing isolated people and preserved the old ways of life

so much as difficult travel. Lack of access to the big wide world held back every kind of progress. Better communication between town and country and between farm and markets would be an essential first step to Improvement.

Black Duncan, the seventh Laird of Glen Orchy, built the first Bridge of Lochay. *In the yeir of God 1627 - - - he causit big ane brig over the water of Lochay, to the great contentment and weal of the countrie.*[253] This made it easier for the people of Dalgirdy to get to Killin except when the burns were in spate. By 1684 *the Bridge of Lochay is decayed and it was ordained by the court that it shall be put up again.*[254] Then they had to rebuild it yet again. By 1741 they had had enough and built a proper stone bridge.

1741. *Contract between Achallader on one part, and James Robertson and Thomas Clark, masons in Dunkeld, on the other part, whereby the latter are to build a stone bridge across water of Lochay a little below where the last bridge stood, the arch to consist of 52 foot between land breasts, 15 foot broad, 12 foot thereof to the clear, 'topt with hewin stone in the ludgeings and puckt up and causewayd from end to end', to stand for seven years. For sum of £111-16 Sterling, in instalments at fixed points.*[255]

That bridge still carries the modern road and its keystone proudly proclaims 1741. The cottage at the north end of the bridge was the tollhouse.

He who controls the roads rules the land.

Kings and Parliament made many attempts to improve roads and bridges from 1553, but with little success outwith the main towns and highways. It was not until 1719 that there was an effective Act for Statute Labour Roads. Landlords became responsible for the roads on their land. All able-bodied men had to give six day's labour each year to improve the highways in their parish. Justices had to report each year on the state of the local roads. In many places this did not amount to more than a few days' grudging work on 'Parish road day' but it does seem to have worked in Breadalbane. The estate list shows 52 tenants, 8 crofters and 9 cottars liable for statute labour in Glen Lochay.[256]

The Jacobite Risings added to the pressure for better roads across the Highlands. The prime purpose was law and order, which linked to 'civilizing' and economic development. *As the opening of a communication and rendering the access quick and easy through a country full of Disaffection and Barbarity is a principal step towards civilizing them, some roads would be proper which might in case of a Rebellion establish an easy and quick communication to his Majesty's Troops thro' the several parts of that country.*[257]

Between 1724 and 1740, General Wade built two hundred and forty miles of roads and thirty major bridges.[258] Some are still in use today, like the line of the A9 through Drumochter Pass or the bridge over the Tay at Aberfeldy. The military road from Stirling to Fort William came over Glen Ogle to Lix Toll, along Glen Dochart to Tyndrum and up the west side of Rannoch Moor to Glencoe. You can still see what it was like when you walk this part of the West Highland Way.

From Lix Toll a road ran down Glen Dochart and along the north side of Loch Tay to Aberfeldy. Pennant described it in 1769.

On the North side of this lake is a most excellent road, which runs the whole length of it, leading to Tiendrum and Inveraray - - The whole road was made at the sole expense of the present Lord Breadalbane, who, to facilitate the travelling, also erected thirty-two stone bridges over the torrents that rush from the mountains into the lake. - - -(I) find the whole country excels in roads, partly military, partly done by statute labour, and much by the munificence of the great men.[259]

These were what we would now call trunk roads. But minor roads up the glens came early in our area.

1726 *Minutes of a meeting of the Commissioners of the Breadalbane Estate, Edinburgh.*

That the bridges either were entirely wanting or if in some places they had them, they were scarce of use but for foot travellers and the timber employed in building these bridges occasioned a great and almost constant waste of the Earl's woods both in the making and keeping them in repair. - - - That the tax of 20 shillings Scots on the Merkland formerly levied and applied for guarding the country from Theft and Depredation - - (shall continue to be collected but will be used instead) - - the one half for building stone bridges of breadth sufficient for a sledge and no more over the waters on both sides of the loch and in the glens, beginning at the East where there's most people. (And the other half for schools.)[260]

In 1733 the Dalgirdy rent of £104-16-8 Scots included £6 *Poor & Bridge Money.*[261]

Breadalbane Estate built a sled road up Glen Lochay in 1731-33.

1731 *Account due to Patrick McCartor for blasting the rocks of the Coolige to make a sledge road to Glenlochay, begun in August 1731. Total* £95-2-4
Paid 29 December 1731.[262]

1732 *Stated account of building three bridges in Glenlochy, summer last 1731. Paid to Duncan McEwen and James Toshach, masons, 23 October 1731.*
Materials (itemised) £64-7-10
To the masons for building the three bridges, each arch being fourteen feet wide. £120-0-0
Total £184-7-10[263]
(One of these was the Dalgirdy Bridge.)

1732 *Discharged Accounts to James Toshach Masson for Bridges 1732*
To winning stones and building the Bridge of Duncrosk consisting of three arches, one of thirteen, another of fourteen and the third of eight foot diameter. £166-13-4[264]

1732 *Account due to Patrick McCarter for himself and others for blasting of rocks and levelling the highways in Glenlochay* Total £145-10-10[265]

1732 *Receipt by James Toshach and Duncan McEwan, Massons, for 26 pounds Scots being 10 shillings per day to each of us for 26 days work performed by us causying and making syrds(?) in that part of the road in Glenlochy called Collige which could not be done by common tenancy.   31 October 1732[266]*

This was originally a sled road and would be five or six feet wide. It seems that most of the work was done by local statute labour, while the estate brought in contractors to blast the road through the Coilig and stonemasons to do the skilled work on the bridges.

Dalgirdy bridge was built in summer 1731 and still stands today although it is no longer in use. It is the only bridge in the glen that remains in its original state because the Hydro built their new bridge beside it. There are three other old bridges in the glen, but they are now encased beneath the concrete of the new Hydro bridges.

Dalgirdy bridge is typical eighteenth century construction. It is a single stone arch, fourteen feet one inch wide at its base. It seems to have been built in two stages. The first bridge, on the downstream side, is nine feet wide overall. The carriageway would be about six feet wide between the parapets. It was then widened by a further six feet. This second stage is very similar but is not as well built. It was probably added early on though I have not been able to find any record.

When we got Dalgirdy in the early 1980s the old bridge was still in fair condition. It gave the only access to the small field in front of the cottage and the farmer drove his tractor over it. We parked cars on it without a worry. Over the past thirty years the second stage of the bridge has deteriorated. The base of the arch is starting to slip and there is a hole in the roadway between the two sections. Stirling Council wanted to demolish it for safety ten years ago but the farmer refused. That would have been a terrible loss of history. But none of us would drive over it today!

This was the first real road up Glen Lochay. It meant that you could always get to Killin in an hour or two, summer or winter. It could take a sled to transport goods and very soon a wheeled cart or carriage.

For all they seem primitive, these early roads served their

purpose. The Statistical Account of 1791 gave a glowing account. *The district of Breadalbane, in general, is well supplied both with roads and bridges. The military road from Stirling to Fort William passes through a great part of this parish, and the improvements made lately on that line of road, with the great order in which it is now kept, serve to render the communication of this country with the south of Scotland and the west and north-west Highlands, easy and agreeable. The country roads through the parish were originally made, and are still kept in repair, by the statute labour, which is exacted in kind.*[267]

In 1845, Tullich farm was advertised as having *the advantage of good roads.*[268]

At the end of the eighteenth century there was a track down the west end of the Dal to a ford across the River Lochay.[269] There was also a set of stepping-stones. The ford is made of large flat stones up to six feet across, wedged against a rock sill so that they do not wash away. It has withstood spates for two hundred years and is still as good as new. When the river is low, you can walk across in rubber boots. The track then zigzags half-a-mile up the opposite hillside. In places the track has disappeared into the bog, but there are short stretches where you could still drive a 4X4. It was probably an old peat road.

There were also four footbridges across the Allt Ghaordaidh, which again probably date from the late eighteenth century. There is one just above the river Lochay, one at the old head dyke and two higher up the hill. All that is left are the stone buttresses on either bank. The three lower ones would be simple wooden bridges. The top bridge was made of three large flat stones, which now lie in the burn below. One stood on edge in the middle of the burn. The other two spanned across from each buttress to that central support. These bridges would be essential when Dalgirdy farm worked both banks of the burn.

We know of at least four men in Dalgirdy who worked on the roads.

Whit 1835-Whit 1836

John McDiarmid Repair and uphold of the road from the
Bridge of Lochay to Kenknock Gate in Glenlochay   £10 – 1 - 3

Labourers for improving and repairing the road at the head
of Glenlochay   £9 – 4 - 7[270]

John McDiarmid lived in Dalgirdy Longhouse and was listed in the Census as a labourer.

John Ferguson lived in Dalgirdy Cottage in the 1880s, when the Census said he was employed as a *road surfaceman*. His son John lived in Dalgirdy until 1922 and the Census described him as a *road contractor (employer)*.

Robert Wright, who was in Dalgirdy in 1922-23, was also a roadman.[271]

There is still a fascinating set of quarry scoops on Dalgirdy. These are man-made hollows, three to six yards across, where gravel has been dug out of moraine hillocks. Most of them are on the upper side of the road where it could be shovelled straight into a barrow.

There are ten of these scoops on Dalgirdy, in less than a mile. That compares with a few scoops higher up the glen, none on Tullich, and a couple in the lower glen. Was this where the roadman in Dalgirdy loaded up his barrow in the morning before setting off to repair the road?

Thomas Telford was a famous Scottish civil engineer who is buried in Westminster Abbey. In 1801 he prepared a master plan to improve roads, bridges and harbours in the Highlands. He saw this as the way to develop trade, create employment and stop emigration and called it *one of the noblest projects ever laid before a Nation*. The government appointed him chief engineer and over the next two decades he built 920 miles of roads and 1200 bridges, and improved a further 280 miles of military roads. He also built the Caledonian Canal from Fort William to Inverness.[272]

As part of this project, in 1811 he commissioned a survey of a new road from Fort William to Stirling. The old military road and today's A82 ran up the west side of Rannoch Moor.

Telford's proposed New Rannoch Road would have run down the east side of the Moor into the head of Glen Lyon. From there - - - *a moderate rise carries the Line to a Pass called Larig-na-Loone, at the head of Glen Lochay, down the North side of which the Road may be carried along comparatively favourable ground, and at a descent not exceeding one in thirty to Killin.* This would have saved fifteen miles compared with the old road. The estimated cost was £17,283-4-0.[273]

The Perthshire Highway Commissioners thought it was a great idea. *Report by Telford on proposed road from Kyle Rheu to Killin by Rannoch Moor. The committee are of the opinion that the opening of such a road of Communication would be of considerable importance to the County at large and to certain individual Proprietors in the County of Perth, but that the meeting as a body possess no funds from which a contribution can be made.*[274] No one else was willing to pay for it. Telford was bitterly disappointed and thought the project failed because *the personal convenience of the proprietors is not immediately concerned.*[275]

From a selfish point of view it was a lucky escape. If this had become the main road to Fort William and the West Highlands, it would have destroyed the peace and tranquillity of Glen Lochay. Dalgirdy would probably not be here.

Glen Lochay road must have stayed much the same until the twentieth century. Then there was new traffic for which the road was never designed, and that was met with shock and horror.

In 1880-89 the Road Commissioners had long debate about Steam Locomotive Traction Engines on the road because of its *narrowness, inclination and imperfect construction, and the bridges on the same are not adapted for the traffic of locomotives.*[276] They finally dealt with the problem in a By-Law.

1889 Bye-Laws for Locomotives on Roads.

Applicable to the following Highways, which from narrowness, inclination or imperfect construction, require special regulations.

1. No locomotive or any loaded wagons attached thereto shall be permitted to stop on any bridge or culvert on any of said roads or highways for the purpose of drawing water from the streams or ditches passing under said bridges or culverts or for any other purposes whatsoever.

2. If any locomotive shall damage any of said highways, or the bridges, culverts, side-ditches or fences so as to render the same dangerous for ordinary traffic, or to public safety, the owner or persons in charge of such locomotive shall give immediate notice thereof to the nearest surfaceman and to the surveyor and place a watchman, with the necessary day or night signals, to warn parties using the highway, and to assist them in passing with their cattle, horses or other bestial, carts, carriages or other vehicles.

4. The Wagons or Carriages for the conveyance of merchandise drawn by any locomotive shall be constructed so that the wheels shall not follow in the same track, and no Locomotive shall pass along the same track as that made by the previous locomotive which has passed along the same Highway.

5. Owners of locomotives remain liable for expenses in respect of the passing of excessive weight or extraordinary traffic along any of said highways.

The list of highways covered by these By-Laws included:

17. The road from the Bridge of Lochay near Killin to the head of Glenlochay, including portion of road in the south side at the foot of Glenlochay.[277]

That stopped Locomotives using the road! But then the motorcar arrived.

1906 *Car traffic in Killin District.* The Commissioners considered a Petition - - *by ratepayers and inhabitants of the Parish of Killin, urging that the Secretary for Scotland be asked to issue an order prohibiting Motor Traffic on the following roads: (1) the Road from Glenlochy Lodge to Kenknock on the north side of the River Lochay* (and others - - -).

It is stated in the petition that these Roads are very narrow, being only from 7 to 8 feet in width, full of sharp and steep gradients, and quite unsuitable for Motor Car Traffic; they are not through roads in any sense, and there would be no hardship to motorists in having them closed. Further, the Petitioners urge that the speed of Motors through the village of Killin is restricted to 10 miles an hour.[278]

This time it was a losing battle. No one was going to stop the motorcar and the march of progress!

The Glen Lochay road stayed much the same until the Hydro came. In preparation for the Scheme, civil engineers, surveyors and transport officials inspected the road.

1953 August 20 *Record of a meeting held in Glen Lochay to record the condition of the roads there. After inspection the conditions of the roads were agreed as follows:*

North Lochay Road

a) Bridge of Lochay to 1.9 miles west, near Falls of Lochay. Tarmacadam road, cold sprayed and chipped in 1951. Average width 8'6". Condition very good. Verges sound.

b) Falls of Lochay to Ben Challum estate boundary (the west march of Dalgirdy), distance 3.3 miles. Gravel road with tarmacadam tracks, sprayed in parts. Raised crown in places. Average width 7'6". Condition fair.

c) Estate boundary to Kenknock. 1.9 miles. Gravel road with tarmacadam tracks only. Average width 7'6". Condition fair.

d) Kenknock to beginning of New Hill Road, 0.4 miles. Average width 7'6". Gravel road, condition poor.

Bridges on the above road were agreed as follows:

1) Duncroisk Bridge. 3.25 miles west of Bridge of Lochay. Two span masonry arch with stone parapets. Some open joints in abutments and ring. Condition fair.

2) Dalgirdy Bridge. 4.4 miles west of Bridge of Lochay.

Masonry arch. Condition poor.

*3) Allt Lebhain Bridge. 5.2 miles west of Bridge of Lochay.
Masonry arch. Condition poor.*

*4) Allt Gharbh Bridge. 6.35 miles west of Bridge of Lochay.
Masonry arch. Condition very poor.*[279]

At that time the road was still mostly unfenced and passed through the fields. You had to stop every few hundred yards to open and close the field gates. Cattle and sheep wandered across the road, so you had to wait until they got out of the way and try to drive round the worst of their mess.

You can still see what that road must have been like if you go up to the head of the glen. Beyond Kennock, it is a narrow Land Rover track that is still a private estate road. It is a gravel road with good bottoming but no tarred surface. It is well drained with culverts over the small burns, though you have to ford the larger burns. There are no fences and it runs across the open hillside.

The Hydro would rebuild a modern tarred road with concrete bridges and fences, and then the Local Authority took it over. But that is another story.

15. IMPROVEMENT

The Agricultural Revolution

There was a revolution in Dalgirdy. A farming revolution.

Between 1770 and 1825, in a single lifetime, we went from subsistence farming to modern commercial farming. In 1770 the glen looked much as it had since medieval times. By 1825 it looked much like today. Change had been coming before 1770 and would continue after 1825 but these fifty-five years saw the greatest change.

Many forces for change came together about 1750-60. Better social and living conditions led to population growth that put pressure on the land. There was peace, law and order, and freedom from raiding. People could at last be sure of reaping the rewards of their labour. Better roads, transport and the Union with England opened up markets. Glen Lochay was now in the grip of economic forces that would prove irresistible. Landowner and tenant alike wanted a better return from the land, but this took capital investment and radical change in farming practice.

This was the time of the Scottish Enlightenment and one of the key ideas was *improvement*.[280] Tradition was no longer enough. We should unleash the power of human reason and progress would come from our own efforts. Nowhere was there more scope and zeal for improvement than in farming and many of the leading figures of the Enlightenment were also improvers on their own land.

The Industrial Revolution and the Agricultural Revolution went hand in hand. You could not have one without the other. Improved farming gave higher yields and could support more people. Yet it did this with fewer people working on the land, so many were freed to go and work in industry. In return, the Industrial Revolution gave the tools that made new farming methods possible.

The Industrial Revolution really got going in Scotland from about 1780 and this was a turning point in history. Before, social progress was slow and gradual. From now on, progress would mean rapid and never-ending growth.

The world of the Highlanders was about to be shattered by forces over which they had little control. And there would be great disruption before their descendants reaped the benefits in full.

By the late sixteenth century the lairds of Glenorchy were making the first efforts to improve agriculture. Finlarig was the estate farm. By the early seventeenth century it had large enclosed fields for the stock paid in as rent. It became an experimental farm to try out and demonstrate good practice. At the same time, we have seen that the Baron Baillie Court was laying down the first rules about how the tenants should work the farms. [281]

In the 1750s and 60s the Highlands began to supply cattle to meet the growing demand of Lowland and English markets. The British Army and Navy became major customers. Cattle became the mainstay of the Highland economy.

Droving became part of the Highland way of life.[282] Each year, drovers gathered thousands of cattle from across the Highlands and Islands. They came down the drove roads from Rannoch, by Glen Lyon and over to Glen Lochay on their way to the cattle markets. Bawling cattle, shouting drovers, barking dogs and buzzing flies all headed for the Crieff Tryst in October.

Drovers were independent men. They wore vivid plaids and blue bonnets and had ever-ready snuff mills. The plaid was garment, blanket and bedding all in one. Their staple diet was oatmeal, shared with their dogs. These were hardy men, able to stand the weather and live without shelter for weeks on end. And they were men of honour. Some bought and sold on their own account. Others acted as agents for people with capital who left the dirty end of the business to the drovers. They took responsibility for the cattle on the long walk south, getting them to the sales on time while keeping them in good condition on the way.

In 1712 there were ten drovers listed in Glen Lochay though none of them was in Dalgirdy.[283] The only drover we know of in Dalgirdy was John McNaughton in 1836, though there were probably others.[284]

Droving went on until the nineteenth century. The end of the Napoleonic wars brought a drop in demand. New cattle breeds were less suitable for driving long distances. In the 1830s cattle began to be shipped by steamship and in the 1880s by rail.

Early people had probably always used some manure for crops. Yet Earls from the seventeenth to the nineteenth centuries felt the need to preach about the proper use of manure.

*The keystone to a Farmer's prosperity is the art of creating a sufficiency of Manure, possessing qualities not only to raise his green crops but also to enrich permanently his soil; and all the arrangements which he makes ought to be of such a nature as to increase in quantity and quality his manure heap. He will, in fact, regard his dung-pit as his bank, and will lose no opportunity of adding to the account kept there. - - - With the judicious use of enriching manure, a farmer will accomplish much - without it, he can do little, for it is his mainstay – and its application to the soil the only means he has of **paying back** what he has taken from his fields in the way of crops. - - - No Farmer should forget that the various crops which he raises extract from the soil the greater proportion of the materials of which they are composed; and that, unless these are supplied in the shape of manure, no land, however fertile it may be, will continue long to yield good crops.[285]*

The problem was how to get enough manure and to apply it. There was only a small amount of re-cycled straw and thatch. They could dig turf into the arable ground but that stripped other areas. Animal dung was by far the best natural manure. The simplest method was to let stock graze on the arable land until the seed was sown and then keep them off it. But that required some kind of dyke or enclosure to keep them in and out. And it was difficult to apply to small terraces. Or they could keep the animals penned, gather their dung, and spread it where they needed it, but that took more labour. It was only once they kept animals indoors over the winter that it became a large-scale process. Then they had to strike a balance between the number of animals, the amount of dung they produced, the area under crops and the quantity of winter feed they could grow.

There is a band of limestone across Breadalbane and lime was used from the mid-seventeenth century. It helped to neutralize acid soil and gave a modest increase in crop yields. As early as 1670, the Baron Baillie court listed the *Names of those deprived of bringing home lime: Tenants in Dalgirdy deprived of lime except Maldonich McIllchrist.*[286]

At first, making lime was a cottage industry and the main limit was fuel. *The farmers, after breaking it to the size of a turkey's eggs, burn it frequently with peats and timber. - - - In many instances the kilns made by country people to be used for burning limestone on their own farms are very awkward.*

It was only in the late eighteenth century that lime became more widely used.

In 1799 *Limestone has been discovered early and much used in many parts of this county, especially towards the Highland districts. - - (but) its general use in this respect is within the remembrance of people still alive. - - - The quantity laid - - on light land with a gravely subsoil - - - is 30-35 bolls per acre.*[287] That was about two tons per acre.

There is an old limekiln on the Dal, just below the road. It is a large mound of stones about eighteen feet across and six feet high. There is a central bowl about six feet across, lined with stone, and fifty years ago a boy could climb down inside. There is a faint platform on the north side, next to the road. The south side has collapsed and you can no longer make out the flue.[288]

Although flax was grown on Loch Tay side from 1725 it does not seem to have been a cash crop on Dalgirdy. *The culture of flax is universal - - -. The farmers in (most) places grow some for their own use.*[289]

Peas came to this area some time before the middle of the eighteenth century. Peas add nitrogen to the soil and have the great advantage that they can be dried and stored all winter. Dry weight, they are about a quarter protein.

The potato was brought to Europe from North America before the end of the sixteenth century, but only became common in Breadalbane about the middle of the eighteenth century. At first, people viewed it with suspicion but hunger soon overcame any doubts. Lix in Glen Dochart was *sowing some potatoes and flax seed* by 1755.[290] In 1780, Dalgirdy planted three bolls of potatoes – about four hundredweights.[291]

By 1799 *Potatoes have become a principal food of the common people, especially in winter; and are considered as the greatest blessing that modern times have bestowed on the country; in having, it is probable, more than once saved it from the miseries of famine etc.*[292]

The culture of potatoes is carried to a great extent in this county, especially in the Highlands. In a rainy climate and on a light soil, no species of crop promises equal return to the husbandman or equal utility to the public. When new ground is to be reclaimed by a potato crop, they are planted with the spade in what are called lazy beds - - -. In arable ground potatoes are planted for the most part with the plough.

Of all roots this is the most valuable. It grows on the poorest soil, is in season at least nine months of the year, affords an excellent food for man when properly dressed, pays neither kiln nor mill dues, is soon brought from the field to the table, supplies the place of a fallow by pulverising the ground and clearing it of weeds, and yields more sustenance per acre that any plant we know - - -.[293]

Potatoes produced three times more calories per acre than any other crop. But this meant that they drained the soil of nutrients, so needed a lot of manure. They were vulnerable to weather, with poor crops in 1807 and 1836. And if potatoes were grown year after year in the same ground, they were liable to blight and other diseases, like the crop failures in 1795 and 1848.

Improvement really took off in 1770 with the Entail Improvement Act. This encouraged longer leases that made it worth a tenant's time to improve his land. It encouraged enclosure, drainage, building and planting. Most important, it offered a mechanism for landlords and tenants to share the costs and benefits. If the tenant made improvements, the laird paid at least part of the cost. Higher yields gave the tenant more income so he could pay a higher rent and the laird also got a return on his investment. It was a win-win situation. Over the next thirty years Breadalbane Estate paid out £9,000 and rents increased eight-fold.

In preparation for Improvement, the third Earl got professional surveys of his estates in 1769. Superb maps of both sides of Loch Tay still survive.[294] Tragically, the maps of Glen Lochay have been lost. They could have given us so much more information about Dalgirdy land.

Breadalbane started to give 'improving leases' in 1771. These were for at least fifteen years. Each tenant had to reside on his land and stock it with his own animals. There were to be no sub-lets. The estate tried to put up the rents and the tenants made a plaintive plea that they could not afford to pay. A lament echoed by farmers everywhere to this day!

1770 Memorial for the Tenants in that part of Glenlochy lying above the Coilig.

The difficulty which the Memorialists found in producing their former rent from the product of their farms convinces them of the impracticality of paying the rent now proposed to be asked of them, for the following reasons among many more that might be advanced. In the first place, the price of cattle has fallen very considerably from what it was for several years back, as has also the price of grain of all kinds. The wages of servants are exorbitantly high, the price of victuals is also, and for several years back, the growth and produce of corn diminished greatly in that part of the Glen aforementioned, not withstanding the Memorialists utmost care and attention to improve their land. Among those who signed were Duncan McMartine and John McVean in Dalgirdy. This is one of the first mentions of efforts *to improve their land.*[295]

Improvement was usually driven by the landowner. At first, *there is a reluctance among the lower ranks of men, to change old customs or to relinquish habits which have acquired the sanction of time and are established by the authority of ages.*[296] By 1770 tenants were well aware of the benefits but also of the practical difficulties. Improvement was costly and took an immense amount of hard work that not all could manage. Returns could be slow. And it broke up traditional communities and support systems. Yet Glen Lochay seems to have changed faster than many other parts of Breadalbane.

By 1799 the people of this county seem in general to have a spirit for improvement, but - - it is greater in some places than others. The highlands in general are behind most of the districts in the lowland provinces in the knowledge of farming. That country is less adapted to an arable system. The principal attention of the inhabitants is directed more to their cattle and flocks than to agriculture. - - The acuteness of the people has nevertheless, in a great measure, surmounted these difficulties; and in many instances their ground is cultivated in the highest style of farming that can be adapted to their climate and soil.[297]

The first and most important step was to enclose the land, which gave the fields and dykes that we see today.[298] It kept animals and crops apart and gave the farmer much greater control over land use.

The benefits were clear but the costs were high. It takes a ton of stone for each yard of dyke and a good man to build six yards a day. And more work to gather and carry the stones before you even start.

By the late 1760s, Duncan McMartin in Dalgirdy had already *made improvements upon it in clearing the ground and making enclosures by building a head dyke at his own expense.*[299]

In 1770-73 the tenants of Dalgirdy got five payments for their march-dykes and for field dykes, which added up to two years' rent. One example is enough.

1773 Advances for inclosing:
To the tenants of Botourniebeg and Dalgirdy for a March

Dyke between them: a double stone dyke consisting of 41½ roods
@ 3s4p/rood being four foot high £6-18-4
    To the tenants of Dalgirdy for an enclosure £1-15-0
    To the tenants of Dalgirdy & W Tullich for a March Dyke
between them £4-13-4[300]

A rood was about six yards.

The Dalgirdy lease in 1776 spelled out the arrangements.

It is contracted and agreed upon between John Earl of Breadalbane - - & Duncan & Patrick McVean & Neil McNaughton all in Dalgirdy - - -. The said Noble Earl hereby - - - letts to the said Duncan and Patrick McVean and Neil McNaughton equally between them their heirs and successors (excluding assignees and subtenants without the special advice and consent of the said Earl) All and whole the farm and lands of Dalgirdy consisting of a three merkland - - - with the houses, biggings (buildings), yeards, grazings, shealings, mosses, muirs, meadows and whole pertinents thereof - - - and that for the span of full twenty one years. - - - With power to them during the continuance of this tack (but under the breaches after mentioned) to occupy, labour and manure the said lands with the pertinents (all that goes with the land) freely & quietly without any impediment.

(The tenants) bind and oblige them and their heirs executors successors and inheritors - - - to pay to the said Noble Earl and to his heirs and successors, for the time being the sum of Twenty six pounds four Shillings and sixpence halfpenny Sterling money in name of yearly tack duty, including therein land tax, Minister's stipend, Schoolmaster's salary and all other public burdens due and payable out of the said lands

(The tenants) bind and oblige them - - - to labour and manure the said lands duly and properly, and to have a fifth part of the arable land yearly in fallow or under turnip, pease, clover or such like green crop, and to consume thereon the whole straw and hay growing on the premises, and to lay out the manure arising therefrom upon the same.

- - - And to inclose all the low grounds of the said farm viz.

the corn and meadow grounds thereof with a stone dyke four feet high, or where the ground will not admit of a stone dyke with a ditch ten feet wide and five feet deep, and to build twenty Roods thereof at least yearly till the whole is finished, his Lordship advancing them money for defraying the charges thereof for which the said Duncan and Patrick McVean and Neil McNaughton are to pay at the rate of 7½% yearly of additional rent from the time of such respective advances.

In 1779-80 there were several further payments for march-, head and field dykes.[301] The head dyke that still runs east from the Allt Ghaordaidh all the way to Tirai carries a stone with the name *J McVean 1782*. This is the best dyke on the hillside, five foot high and more than a mile long. Unlike the march-dykes, it is clearly a sheep dyke with 'sheep creeps' that can be opened or blocked off as required. By 1782 Dalgirdy probably had most of the dykes and fields that we see today. That ended the old infield-outfield and runrig systems.[302]

Two of Duncan McVean's older sons got the neighbouring farm of Innischoarach in 1785 and set about improving it. They built 288 roods of head dyke, a sheep fank and tup park, two houses, two barns and a corn kiln. They enclosed the pasture and built a bulwark to stop flooding from the burn.[303]

Enclosure was only part of the story. Enclosure, clearing stones, drainage and ploughing all worked together to improve the soil. Even in the early stages this raised yields by at least 20%.[304]

Drainage was the only way to make the meadows usable for crops. Draining and enclosure often went hand in hand. Early stone drains gave some increase in water run-off, but really good field drainage did not come until after 1820. By the 1840s, commercial tile works were producing cheap drain-tiles and Drainage Acts gave low-interest loans. If you dig on the Dal today you can still find old stone drains and early tile drains.[305]

Ploughing was also essential to break up the soil and one of the most important tools of improvement was the modern plough. James Small made his first plough in 1765, with a curved iron blade that cut the turf more efficiently and turned the soil over to give the kind of furrow we see today. This was such a great improvement that it came into widespread use very quickly and may have reached Glen Lochay by the early 1780s. From the mid-1780s *the modern plough team (of two, larger horses introduced from the lowlands) has been in use in Breadalbane.*[306] Yet it was not until the 1830s that James Smith invented the subsoil plough that could break up hard impervious clay to a depth of sixteen inches. Deep ploughing and better drains made the soil much more fertile.

At the same time they cleared large stones from the fields. At one time Breadalbane had a full-time blaster. Ploughing, clearing stones and using the stones to build dykes, all went together. Weeding was best done by hand and even the children had to help.

By 1780 the *Sowing and Holding of Dalgirdy*[307] was:

Oats	7 Bolls	2 Firlots
Bear	3 Bolls	
Peas		3 Pecks
Potatoes	3 Bolls	
Lintseed		8 Pecks

A Boll was 140 pounds, a Firlot 35 pounds and a Peck 9 pounds. That would be enough to sow ten to twelve acres, which is the size of the Dal. With the improvements, it might give a return of 30 Bolls of oats and 15 Bolls of barley.

Better strains of corn and barley had larger, heavier heads and gave higher yields. Drainage and ploughing let sweet meadow grass replace rushes and coarse grass. Farmers began to sow rye grass and clover. Hay became a major source of winter feed for the livestock.

Turnips only became common in west Perthshire at the end of the eighteenth century. The Dalgirdy lease of 1776 mentioned turnips but they were not sown in 1780. They were still not common in 1795 when the potato crop failed from blight. But by 1799 *large fields of turnips are cultivated in almost every part of this county - - -* including the glens, *the wildest and highest inhabited land in the whole shire.*[308] Turnips were another valuable winter feed for livestock.

By the end of the century crop rotation was standard. John Malloch put in a petition to keep his farm in 1798.

In case your Lordship should be pleased to allow me to continue in Tomore I do promise to make the said farm in five Divisions - one for sowing corn - one for sowing bear - one for pease, potatoes and turnips - one of Clover and raigrass - one for Pasture - and the Midows where it is requisite to Drain and Dry them in order to be fit for sowing corn or bear in the same and any Barren ground there shall lime and plough it until it is natural ground for Sowing. Any other improvements that your Lordship will think proper I am willing to do them Etc[309]. The Factor made a note in the margin: *Malloch the Improver.*

For all the improvement in soil and yields, upper Glen Lochay would always be limited by the small amount of arable ground and the climate. Most of Dalgirdy was only fit for grazing and livestock would always be its main produce.

Larger Lowland cattle replaced the old Highland breed to give more milk and carry more beef. By 1795 *In Rannoch, Glen Lyon, Glen Lochay, Struthfillan and some other places, the Argyllshire breed prevails.*[310]

But the real change came with the sheep. 'Southern' breeds like the Blackface and the Cheviot came to Glen Lochay in the 1770s. These were larger than the old Highland sheep and gave much higher yields of wool and mutton. They were also much hardier. To many farmers' surprise they could winter outdoors, which meant that a farm could keep many more. And no more smearing of their coats!

Sheep are the most profitable, the most useful and the most inoffensive browsing animals known in this part of the world. Upon any given extent of pasture, their returns are almost one third more than that of any other flock.[311]

With the Lowland sheep came the sheepdog. The modern Border collie was bred in the Scottish Borders in the late nineteenth century. I admit that I am biased but they are the most intelligent dogs in the world. They win most sheepdog trials, agility and other dog sports.

Let me digress for a moment. Wiston Cap was the most famous Border collie who ever lived and is on the badge of the International Sheep Dog Society. He was not only World Sheepdog Champion but in the next ten years sired three Supreme Champions and was grandsire to three more. A busy dog at stud! I was once lucky enough to share my life with - not own! - one of his great-granddaughters. Misty is now passed on to the great dog heaven in the sky and buried on the hillside behind Dalgirdy. But my grandson says she will love it there because heaven is full of bones!

We saw that in 1769 Dalgirdy had 72 cattle, 4 horses, and the column for sheep was left blank. A year or two later it had 44 cattle and 80 sheep. By 1780 it had 330 sheep, 20 cattle and 6 horses.[312] Dalgirdy was now a sheep farm and that is roughly the number of sheep its land carries today.

The shielings probably fell out of use in the 1770s.

And vermin were under control. Between 1782 and 1797, John Sinclair was paid £15-11-0 for killing 151 polecats, 50 martins, 15 wildcats, 45 weasels and 37 badgers about Taymouth.[313] Most of the wildcats were in the earlier years and by the end of this period there were few left. By 1799 *Eagles carry off lambs - - - but by the vigilance of the shepherds they are much reduced in numbers. - - - Crows - - are a continuing problem. - - - The fox-hunters have regular districts of the country committed to their care, for which they levy annual assessments on the several farms - - -. Wolves* (have been) *- - exterminated.*[314] They had a rather different definition of vermin in these days!

Dalgirdy was now a profitable sheep farm. We saw that the rent stayed much the same up to 1770. It doubled in the 1770s, doubled again by 1796 and doubled yet again by the turn of the century.

That was only possible because farming was booming. The price of cattle rose 300% between the 1740s and the 1790s. The price of wool also rose. The introduction of potatoes meant less meal needed to be bought in. So the balance of trade moved in favour of the Highlands. Improvement really was paying off. This was a time of optimism and great expectations in the Highlands, which sadly outran reality.

At the height of the boom the Earl tried to push things even further. After all, he had a new mansion to pay for!

In 1797 he appointed a surveyor, Mr Robertson, to advise how to improve the farms.[315] By now it was clear that sheep were by far the most profitable use of this land. Many of the farms were too small to be viable and there could be economies of scale. The farms were also split between too many tenants and there were too many crofters with small portions of land.

The following year, the Earl laid down an ultimatum.

- - - *the Lett of Glenlochy which I have now resolved shall take place at Whitsunday next, and as I have already obtained pretty accurate knowledge of the value of the farms out of lease as well as received offers for some of them, it will be but fair in publishing the arrangement of the present Tenants to desire them to give in immediate offers of the rent they are willing to give on a lease of 9 years, at the same time to inform them that a great augmentation is expected. Summons of Removing must be issued immediately to all the Tenants in Glenlochy and Glendochart whose farms are out of lease, but let it be understood that the legal warning will not be taken advantage of in case we agree about the rent. - - - All the present Tenants should be preferred on equal terms, but I can see no good reason for letting my lands under its value to people who have already enriched themselves by it. - - - I am ready to do justice to them at the same time that I do it to myself.*[316]

Many of the tenants in Glen Lochay were unable or unwilling to pay the higher rents. For all their nice words, the Earl and his Factor were ruthless. Despite all that Duncan McVean and Neil McNaughton had done to improve Dalgirdy, their lease was not renewed.

Dalgirdy was instead let to Duncan Campbell and Donald

McTavish who made a higher bid. Campbell tried to argue that he should get the whole farm but the laird had already promised McTavish a third.

That as the rent now laid upon the said farm cannot be made up but by giving it to one Tenant and keeping sheep in place of half of the number of black cattle formerly on the premises, the Memorialist hopes - - - that your Lordship will allow him to enter then to the possession of the whole Farm, which with very little assistance he can occupy by his own Children, if laid out in the manner above proposed. He therefore craves an answer, so as he may without loss of time purchase sheep etc.[317]

Subsequent events showed that they over-bid. They struggled to cope and fell into arrears with their rent.

In 1810 the surveyor reported on the state of the farms in Glen Lochay.

Dalgirdy: Will maintain rather more Stock than Wester Tullich but at present not fully stocked, and both cattle and sheep under the 2nd Class or rather approaching to the 3rd. Management of the 3rd rate. Present rent may do, especially if the Cottar were confined to the arable on the west side of the burn with one Cow. It was intended that the farm and Wester Tullich should have a joint stock of sheep, but the tenants do not agree upon this point. The Tenant of Wester Tullich complains of Duncan Campbell as a bad neighbour, & from what I could learn, I am inclined to think there is some ground for the Complaint.[318]

By this time the estate was doing all it could to combine farms into larger units. It cut the numbers of crofters holding small bits of land and moved tradesmen into the villages.

Economic pressures grew. After the end of the Napoleonic Wars in 1815 the UK fell into a recession. Cattle prices fell and Highland farms could not compete with more efficient Lowland producers. The economic state of the Highlands was grim. The only Highland product that stayed profitable was sheep and the only answer was to move to large-scale sheep farming.[319]

Despite the Earl's great expectations, rents fell. Allowing for inflation, they would never again reach the levels of 1800.

At Whit 1825, Dalgirdy, Wester and Easter Tullich and Tirai were combined into the single farm now known as Tullich, which was held by two tenants. Twenty years later Tullich was advertised as: *A very fine safe farm - - - produces stock of excellent quality. Keeps nearly 2000 sheep and 50 or 60 cattle - - - almost entirely grazing. The hogs are all sent out to wintering.* (It has) *the advantage of good roads. Steadings thatched.*[320]

The tenants would continue to improve the land with better drainage, ploughing and manure. They would sow grass and improve crop rotations. They would improve sheep facilities on the farm. But to all intents and purposes the revolution was complete. Dalgirdy had been absorbed into the modern farm of Tullich.

In 1650 just 3% of Scots lived in towns but by 1841 that had risen to 30%. In 1841, 25% of Scots still worked on farms but that fell to 10% by 1911 and just 1% today.

So what happened to the people who lived in Dalgirdy?

16. DALGIRDY PEOPLE

For people make places

We only have patchy information about people in Dalgirdy before the eighteenth century.

The first person we can identify who actually lived in Dalgirdy was Duncan McCarbre in 1536.[321]

We know the name of a cottar called *Gillespik McCansk* as early as 1597. He was found to be *wanting of a kailyard* but we do not know anything else about him.[322]

Many people moved about a lot. Alexander Campbell was in Dalgirdy between 1743 and 1746. His wife was Christian McArthur and their sons John and James were born there.[323] They moved down to Corrycharmaig in 1747, up to Botourniemor in 1753 and then to Botourniebeg by 1755.[324] They had four more children - Isabel, twins Margery and Anne, and Archibald. Then we lose track of them. Alexander's name does not appear in any of the rental lists, so he was not a tenant. A crofter would hold on to his croft and not move about so much. So he was probably a cottar or farm labourer. In the 1740s his family would still live like medieval peasants in a cottar's hovel.

Patrick and Duncan McMartine held the lease on Dalgirdy from the early 1750s until at least 1771.[325] But the lease may only have been for a year or two at a time, so they did not have much security. Patrick's wife was also a McMartine. So were they brothers, in-laws, cousins or distant kin? Were they related to Duncan Roy McMartin who held the tack in 1725? We know that John McVean was a third tenant in 1770-73, but he may have been there longer. These three began to improve the land, clearing stones and building dykes, but they did not stay to get much benefit.[326]

Duncan and Patrick McVean and Neil McNaughton are key figures in the Dalgirdy story. They held the lease from 1776 to 1797 and did most to improve the farm.

The McVeans were a Sept of Clan Macnab who lived in upper Glen Lochay from at least 1550.[327] *The tribe of the Clan McVeans whereof the petitioner descended had been inhabitants in Glenlochay during many generations back.*[328]

Duncan McVean seems to have been the leading tenant and was about sixty when they got the lease.[329] He and his wife Christie McMartin had ten children. One died young but the other nine survived. His first and fourth sons would get the farm of Innischoarach on the other side of the river. His fifth son Duncan was born about 1757 and would take over his father's share of Dalgirdy.

Patrick McVean was also known as Peter. He was Duncan's brother but 17 years younger. An earlier Peter McVean was *of a roving nature and a not very honest disposition and his brother put him out of his house. - - - (He had) a flourishing family.* Our Patrick/Peter seems to have been a chip off the old block. He had already been 'removed' from his previous farm.[330] He had six children by his first wife, Jean McCail, and three of them were born in Dalgirdy. Jean died in 1785. He then married Katherine Campbell, by whom he had another six children.[331] As far as we know, all but one survived.

So of twenty-two McVean cousins in Dalgirdy, twenty lived to adulthood. What a change from a century earlier!

Patrick's family were an unruly lot. He himself said they were *not subject to the father's control, especially they being the production of a first marriage by a mother then dead, and the petitioner having a new family by a second wife all under age and un-provided for.*[332] When he remarried, *the children of the first marriage how soon they came of age to earn their bread left his family after insisting upon getting payment of their mother's share of his effects.*[333]

The third tenant was Neil McNaughton, who could also claim that his *forbears have been tenants upon the estate for several generations back.*[334] When Neil started in Dalgirdy he had a loan from the kirk to buy cattle.[335] His wife Catherine McVean may have been Duncan's cousin's daughter. They had three or four children, which was *a small family* in these days. One of his daughters, born in Dalgirdy in 1780, grew up to be the promiscuous Christian.

There was also a crofter called Angus McNaughtan, though we do not know if he was related to Neil. He had a wife and four children. A widow had another croft and there was a cottar, though we do not know if he had any family.

So by 1793-95, Dalgirdy *baile* had six households with something like eleven adults and seventeen children still at home.[336]

Duncan Junior was an enterprising man who was about 19 years of age when his father got Dalgirdy. His wife's father had the Inn at Luib in Glen Dochart, so he managed to marry the proverbial alewife. By 1791 he said that his *constant employment for 24 years and upwards was an Undertaker of Building Farmhouses & parks to which he was often called upon by your Lordship's principal tenants and others, and that by these industrious means he acquired a Capital sufficient to stock a farm of Fifty Pounds Sterling or thereby.*[337] He then applied for the vacant farm and inn at Luib and offered to build *a proper house for the accommodation of the public, consisting of five apartments in the lower flat and three bedrooms in the garret, besides a garden and offices.* He would *carry out the whole work at his own charges* and sought a long-term lease.[338] Perhaps fortunately for Dalgirdy, his offer was turned down.

He subsequently said that on Dalgirdy he had *built a good house with stone and lime and made a good room in one end with a chimney therein.*[339] There was another note. *The tenant of Dalgirdy upon consideration of having built a good house to be exempted from the payment of the timber.*[340] The Stobie map of 1783 was the first to show a building on the west side of the burn.[341] So Duncan McVean Junior built our Dalgirdy Cottage some time in the early 1780s.

Shortly after that, his brothers built two similar houses on

Innischoarach. These were valued at £100 but the estate disputed that figure. *The two steadings which they built are only ordinary ones, thatched houses of one storey high containing a room and kitchen. - - - When good houses are built in place of bad ones it is customary indeed, but optional, to encourage tenants by giving them the timber gratis, which was done in the present case, but building fine houses is often more from a spirit of vanity and emulation than a real improvement.*[342]

Most of the other remaining ruins on Dalgirdy also date from about that time. There was a Longhouse with two small windows and a barn just above the road on the east side of the burn. There was a single-roomed Bothy with a small window at the east end of the bridge. And there were two more longhouses with barns on the Dal, beside the track down to the ford. These all had simple dry-stone walls and were not nearly as well built as our cottage.

Auchindrain in Argyll gives some idea of what the *baile* was like. It was one of the last surviving 'primitive villages' when Queen Victoria visited it in 1875 and is now a historic centre, rebuilt to show what it would have been like.[343] So it is about a hundred years later than Dalgirdy *baile*. It is larger than Dalgirdy and has a dozen houses with their byres, barns and sheds. The largest houses were better and more modern than Dalgirdy cottage with two good rooms and small bedrooms upstairs. The cottars' houses were still one room, dirt-floored bothies. There were kailyards and small enclosures. People got water from a burn winding through the *baile*. There were narrow, gravel 'roads' and paths between the buildings with ditches and footbridges. There was a blacksmith and a weaver and some people worked on the estate as birleymen and roadsmen. There was even a bothy where the community supported a poor disabled woman.

As Duncan McVean grew old, Duncan Junior took over his share of the farm and the lease. He then lived in Dalgirdy cottage with his wife and small family and his old father who stayed with them.

The Dalgirdy lease expired in 1797 and there was a fierce bidding war for the new lease. Background events would help to decide the outcome.

When the Earl raised the Fencibles in 1793, Duncan McVean Senior gave one of his sons. Patrick, Neil McNaughton and Duncan Junior each arranged a Highlander and paid their bounty. Neil and Duncan did not have any suitable sons, so that was fair enough. But Patrick did have several sons and the estate would never forgive him when none of them joined. He made desperate attempts to explain his failure.

It may be pledged by some one or more of the petitioner's evil wishers that he might easily present your Lordship with one of his own sons in place of a stranger. This the petitioner was exceedingly willing to do, and used his utmost endeavour to accomplish it, but in vain - - -.[344]

That the Memorialist willing to show his attachment to your Lordship, used all his influence with each of his sons to enlist with your Lordship, and being unsuccessful they having absolutely refused to obey him, he procured and presented another Recruit equally good with any of them.[345]

Other bidders made the most of this and Patrick got little sympathy.

The tenants had a long-running dispute with the crofter Angus McNaughtan. In 1786 he petitioned the laird for more land. His main complaint was about Duncan McVean. *Some years ago, the foresaid croft was wholly conferred by the late Factor, upon the said Duncan MacVean, who since enjoys the benefits of the said Croft over and above an equal Division of the rest of the Farm with the other two Tenants & he further enjoys exclusively, the benefits and use of the Biggings above annexed to the said Croft.* Angus wanted that land but he also got little sympathy. *The petitioner has got a Cow's Grass and therefore may be contented.* [346] In 1795 the constables had to be called in when Angus's cattle strayed on to the tenants' land.[347]

By this time the tenants were rebelling against doing service for the laird and Dalgirdy got special mention.

1794 August 27 Report from James Campbell, Ground

Officer, Killin.

The Tenants did not go so regular out this year for the Coals being mistrusted with the Oak Bark that they were ordered to carry to Crieff. Dalgirdy was mistrusted by carriers and theirs is not carried yet being eight bolls.[348]

1794 September 8 Report from James Campbell, Ground Officer, Killin.

Tenants in Deshoir and Glenlochy west of the Coilig were refusing to go out for carriages of the wood lying above Finlarig to Edinample, despite being warned twice. - - - I do not know what to do with them.[349]

The final nail in Patrick's coffin was when he was accused of wood stealing. He put up a desperate defence. First he tried to blame his son, who had conveniently left the country. *That one of the petitioner's sons of his first marriage returned home to Glenlochy, and he in an unwarrantable and foolish manner went without the Petitioner's knowledge, and cut three small ash sticks or trees in the wood of Wester Tullich, which he carried home upon his shoulders and deposited in an outhouse belonging to the petitioner. - - - altogether unknown to the Petitioner - - - who* only found them *a few days thereafter upon going to the said outhouse.*[350] At first he stuck to this story. But then he rather spoiled it by claiming he *had ample proof* that it was the new tenant McTavish who had stolen the timber![351] The Earl and his Factor did not believe him. *The wood stealer to be removed.*[352]

Meantime, Duncan Junior and Neil McNaughton applied for the farm between them. Then Neil died and Duncan tried to get the farm alone. He pointed out once more that he had *improved my possession of the farm very much besides which built a good house - -, therefore I will be sorry at heart if another shall enjoy the sweets of my labour after having your good Lordships promise to enlarge my Possession at the first opportunity that would occur.*[353]

The estate surveyor supported his claim. *Duncan McVean - - - with his children's assistance has improved the farm very much.*[354] *Tenants and others recommended by Mr Robertson for having been zealous in procuring the value of the farms in*

Glenlochy. List includes: *McVean in Dalgirdy*[355]

But the most rent Duncan could offer was £80, with vague talk of £90. It was not enough.

Patrick fought to the bitter end. He delayed his removal by legal action.[356] He pled that he *had no other possession allowed to him - - - and asked- - - that he remain in Dalgirdy with his second wife and small family to continue his profession, as if deprived of his profession he will be left destitute.*[357]

In May 1798 he came to the last throw of his dice.

That as nothing he could say or do to convince his innocence of the aforesaid crime, and that he was warned to remove from his possession, and is still destitute of any possession or residence wherewith to support himself and young family he hopes that your Lordship will deem it reasonable to allow him the money he gave to said recruit being £17 Sterling, and that your Lordship will give Directions for paying that soon to him, in order for assisting him to bring himself & family to America, herein he is now found in the above Manner to go as soon as he can get an opportunity.[358]

We do not know if he got his money but it seems unlikely. The Earl could not afford to set a precedent.

Patrick emigrated to America where he was known as Peter. He died in 1810 and is buried in Mumford, Montgomery County, New York.[359] The nineteenth century village lies just outside Rochester and is one of the largest living history museums in the US.

He followed many other McVeans of Glen Lochay who had emigrated since 1774.[360] Today there are more McVeans in the United States and Canada than in Scotland. There is not a single McVean in the Killin phone book.

Dalgirdy was instead let to two new tenants, Duncan Campbell and Donald McTavish, who gave the highest bid of £95. But they had other advantages. Campbell seems to have been one of the *tenants of superior claims have got the preference* because his eldest son Archibald was a Lieutenant in the Fencibles.[361] McTavish worked for Mr Robertson, the surveyor.[362]

But they outbid themselves. By the end of 1799, *Duncan Campbell the Tenant of Dalgirdy is a Bankrupt and cannot succeed.*[363] By February, *Duncan Campbell in Dalgirdy is at last so sensible of his inability for the farm that he lately called a meeting of his creditors.*[364] By March the Factor advised that Campbell should be removed.[365] Somehow, he was allowed to struggle on.

From 1807 both Campbell and McTavish were in arrears with their rent. McTavish gave up his lease and Duncan's younger son Peter came in to share the lease. They continued to struggle. Duncan Campbell died at Killin in 1818 and his son Peter shortly after him.

By 1825, James Campbell (no relation) took over the modern farm of Tullich, at first sharing it with another tenant. His sons and grandson would farm there until 1935.

The Agricultural Revolution had enormous social impact. Communal rural life changed to individual farming. Enclosure let the new breed of farmer improve his soil and crops and livestock, without interference from his neighbours.

Tenant farmers in 1770 were peasants who lived and worked with their cottars. By 1825, James Campbell was a professional farmer and businessman. He made enough profit to build up his capital, improve his standard of living, and pay a good rent. He lived a life of middle class affluence, separate from his farm labourers. In 1770 the social divide was between laird and peasants. In 1825 it was between the capitalist farmer and his labourers.

Large farms in the hands of a few tenants meant that most people became a landless labour force. Economic forces made peasants redundant. The farm labourer might resent his loss of land but in material terms he was better off than he had ever been. The main price of progress was loss of the traditional way of life. Whatever the faults of subsistence farming, the old *baile* had a real sense of community. It kept families together, working around the home and on the land. The new farms were more efficient and profitable but the human price was that they were more 'business-like'.

Housing now reflected social status. The farmstead at Tullich stood isolated and aloof with a courtyard surrounded by farm buildings. That is still the heart of the working farm and you see farms like it all over Scotland. The farmer, his family and house servants lived in a modern, stone-built, slate-roofed farmhouse. Other farm workers lived in the farmstead or in separate cottages.

In the 1851 Census,[366] John Campbell described himself as a *grazier employing five servants*. His wife, two daughters and his sister lived in the farmhouse. There was also a house servant, a seamstress and her daughter, a dairymaid, a farm labourer, a cowherd and a shepherd.

Dalgirdy was now housing for the workers.

The first detailed national Census was in 1841, when three houses were still occupied - Dalgirdy Cottage, the Longhouse and the Bridge Bothy.[367] The Bothy fell vacant some time in the mid-1870s and the Longhouse in 1888, after which Dalgirdy Cottage was on its own.[368]

Depopulation of the glen ran apace. In 1793-95, Dalgirdy *baile* had some eleven adults and seventeen children. In the 1841 Census there were nine adults but they were getting older and there were only three children. By the 1870s there were two families and after 1888 there was only one family left.

The Bothy was occupied in 1841 by a crofter and his unmarried sister, and they were still there in 1851. Ten years later they had been replaced by a retired domestic servant. Then, in 1871, the Census showed that the Glen Lochay schoolteacher was living in Dalgirdy. When I first saw this I assumed the teacher would be in the Cottage but he was actually in the single-roomed Bothy with his wife and young stepson.

John McDiarmid lived in the Longhouse from 1835 until his death in 1888. He worked as a labourer, a road surfaceman and a crofter. However, even today it is common for men around Killin to have more than one job, some of them part-time. In 1841 he was living in the Longhouse with his wife, two sons aged 20 and 15 who were also farm labourers, and two young daughters. His first wife died and by 1861 his daughter was listed as his housekeeper with her three young sons. John then remarried and had another son and daughter by his second wife. In 1881 his 16-year-old son and 14-year-old daughter were still at home and there was also an 11-month-old grandson named *William Little*, though I cannot find any record of his birth. John died at Dalgirdy on 13 June 1888 aged ninety-two years of *senile decay*.[369] His family then moved away and the Longhouse fell out of use.

Dalgirdy Cottage, meantime, was occupied by a succession of farm workers.

In 1841 it was home to a farm labourer, his wife, a lodger who worked as a tailor, and a one-year-old whose name was listed intriguingly as *not known*.

Ten years later there was a different farm labourer and his 40-year-old sister, who also worked as a farm labourer.

Ten more years and there was an 81-year-old retired shepherd with his 78-year-old brother who was still working as a farm labourer, his 75-year-old sister, and a boarder. On the night of the Census they also had a visitor.

By 1871 there was a different shepherd in the cottage, with his wife and two young lodgers who were pupils at Glen Lochay School. He died at Dalgirdy in 1876 at the age of seventy from an abscess of the testicle.[370]

John Ferguson and his family came to Dalgirdy cottage about 1880. John had been born in 1826, when his father was a farmer in Duncroisk but by 1841 the family had moved to Corrycharmaig. John stayed at home and worked with his father, taking over the lease of Corrycharmaig when he died in 1868. Three years later John married Margaret McPhail, who was 18 years younger, in a Free Church service held at Bridge of Lochay. Their first three children, John (Jock), Peter and Mary, were born in Corrycharmaig. Donald (known to the family as Dan) and James were born in Dalgirdy and James was the last baby born there in 1883. As head of the household after his

211

father died, John also took in his sister's illegitimate baby and raised her as his own. All the family spoke Gaelic and English.[371]

We do not know why John left Corrycharmaig in 1880 at the age of 53, though farming hit bad times in the '80s. He then lived as a *sub-tenant* in Dalgirdy and worked as a road surface-man. However, his older sister was married to John Campbell, farmer in Tullich, and another sister to John McDiarmid in Dalgirdy longhouse. So it looks as if his powerful Campbell brother-in-law looked after him and Dalgirdy became a family affair.[372]

John Ferguson died at Dalgirdy in 1895 at the age of sixty-eight, of sub-acute meningitis. His widow took over as sub-tenant in Dalgirdy until she died in 1916. Most of the family grew up and left home, but their eldest son Jock never married and stayed at home with his mother. In 1891, at the age of seventeen, he was an *agricultural labourer* but by 1901 he described himself as a *road contractor (self-employed)*. He took over the sub-tenancy from his mother and stayed in Dalgirdy until he moved away in 1922.[373]

The Fergusons were the last family for whom Dalgirdy was really home.

James seems to have been the brightest of the family. By the age of 17 he had left home and was working as a ploughman for his cousin in Tullich. He then got a small-holding further up Loch Tay. When he married in 1929 he became a tenant farmer near Inverness and by hard work built this up to three farms. Jock, Dan and Mary never married and went to work on James' farm. Jock was *a cheery man who loved life*. Dan was *as strong as a horse* though perhaps *more brawn than brain*. Sadly, James' wife was seriously ill after the birth of their last child and medical care was expensive. This was the Great Depression and James lost the farm. At the time of his death aged fifty-one in 1935 he was working as a farm labourer.[374]

Between 1922 and 1933, a series of shepherds and estate workers lived in Dalgirdy. Two are worthy of mention. Robert Wright and his family were there in 1922-23 and their son Jim will re-appear again. Hugh McLean was a shepherd who lived in Dalgirdy with his wife and three sons in 1930-31. Hugh's grandson is Dougie McLean, the well-known Scottish singer and songwriter. Dougie says that his grandfather was the inspiration for his best-known ballad Caledonia and its memories of a lost land and time. *Caledonia you're calling me. And now I'm going home.*[375]

In 1933, Dalgirdy Cottage fell vacant.

But it still got intermittent use.

Dr James Campbell was a grandson of the Campbell family in Tullich Farm. He and his family stayed in Dalgirdy cottage for their summer holidays when he was a boy in the 1930s.

Jock Ferguson came back to Dalgirdy in 1937 after James died. He ran it as a small croft and had the small field across the road. There was a fenced front garden with fruit bushes and a rhubarb patch. There was a henhouse and pig shed at the back, and the large shed on the west end was a cowshed. He also worked at times on Tullich farm. Jock was found dead in his field at Dalgirdy in 1939. There were no suspicious circumstances and it was recorded as a *Sudden Death* due to *Heart Failure.*[376]

Soon after we got the cottage, a lady stopped and came in to tell us that she had stayed there as a girl. She came from a family called Prentice who lived in Stirling and her father had been an insurance agent who covered the Killin area. During World War II he rented Dalgirdy cottage from Tullich Farm for £7 a year and his wife and children lived there for seven or eight weeks during the school summer holidays. At that time the small back room was still a built-in box-bed. There were two brass beds in the 'ben' for all the kids. They did not use 'upstairs' as it was *filthy and full of Highland ghosts*. The children had names for each part of the burn – *the bathing pool, the crystal pool and the giant falls.*[377]

In the 1950s half-a-dozen Irish bracken cutters stayed in Dalgirdy for a few weeks each summer while working in Glen Lochay. In 1955 a cigarette set fire to Dalgirdy in the middle of night and they had to waken the farmer for help and got an axe to cut out the smouldering thatch. Early the next morning the fire re-ignited but this time they managed to put the fire out properly and Dalgirdy was saved. There was no fire brigade in these days.[378]

About 1969-70, Edinburgh University Outdoor Centre on Loch Tay used Dalgirdy to stay overnight when pony trekking. Their ponies were in the small paddock across the road.[379]

In the 1970s local shepherds and stalkers held parties in 'Dalgirdy Inn' when the weather was too bad to work![380]

There is a final postscript. Jim Wright was an old shepherd on Tullich Farm, who lived in upper Glen Lochay all his life. As we have already noted, his parents were in Dalgirdy before they moved to Innischoarach in 1923. Jim was born in 1924 and may well have been the last baby conceived in Dalgirdy. He was one of the last pupils in Glen Lochay School. In his working days he frequented Dalgirdy Inn. After he retired, he lived in a caravan just down the road so he was also the last person to live on the old Dalgirdy *baile* until he died in 2001.

Young people left to seek better opportunities elsewhere. Old people were more likely to stay but slowly died off. There was population shift from the farms to the village. Many people went to towns and cities in the Lowlands as industrial workers. Some went abroad, sometimes to even more primitive conditions. Patrick/Peter McVean's son John lost three children on 26 June 1805, in an epidemic of dysentery in Johnstown, Montgomery County, NY, where they were buried together in a single grave. *They were lovely in their lives, and at their death were not divided.*[381]

Despite the number leaving, the population of the district rose slightly in the second half of the eighteenth century.[382] In 1791 there were 2360 people in the Parish of Killin, of whom 150 were in the village. But *within these 60 years, by the union of farms and the number of sheep introduced - - - the number of the people has decreased considerably in the higher parts of the parish. - - - But, so far as the population of the parish is to be judged from the session records, it may be concluded that it has increased in the lower parts thereof, and particularly in the village of Killin, with the district that surrounds it, nearly in the same proportion in which it has decreased in the higher parts*[383]. The population of the parish fell slightly to 2002 people in 1831, but then more sharply to 1277 people in 1881. Today it is back up to 1600 people but 90% live in the villages.

Duncan Ban McIntyre was a famous Gaelic poet of nature, who lived at the top of Glen Lochay. He expressed what many felt.

Song to the foxes.[384]

On the foxes be my blessing,
For they the silly sheep are chasing.
Is it the sheep with brindled head
That through the world confusion spread?
Our land put out of cultivation,
And raised the rent to ruination?
Place for tenant there is none.
His gain and occupation gone:
Quitting and leaving he must be
The place where lived his ancestry:
The townships and the sheilings round.
Where warmth and welcome both were found.
No houses but the ruined remains,
No cultivation on the plains.
Every way of use and wont is
Altered in the Highland counties.

There is one snag to that story: it is not Glen Lochay. Duncan Ban left in 1767, before the sheep came, to live and work as a policeman in Edinburgh for the rest of his life. He wrote his poem many years later at the peak of Edinburgh society's fury at the Clearances in Sutherland.

The Highland Clearances still evoke raw emotion and a deep sadness for a lost past. But we must distinguish myth from reality. A Clearance was *an enforced simultaneous eviction of all families living in a defined area such as an entire glen* and some of them were undoubtedly brutal. But most were in the North-West Highlands and Islands. There never was a 'Clearance' in Glen Lochay. Depopulation did take place, and there was some bitterness and resentment, but the process was much more gradual.

The Earl looked back in 1803. *By enlarging the Farms I might have increased my Revenue very considerably but the immediate consequence would have been an Emigration to a great extent. My Object however was to retain the people, and at the same time to make them instrumental in the Improvement of the Country.*[385] Even so, this was a time of great social upheaval. And, whatever the rights and wrongs, it left behind a sense of grievance.

The hard reality is that this marginal land could never support the previous number of people to a tolerable standard of living. Subsistence farming has not survived anywhere in the developed world. Everywhere, despite every effort, Improvement has led to rural depopulation.

Although there were no Clearances in Glen Lochay, the end result was just the same. It is easy to blame greedy lairds but the Earls of Breadalbane were better than most. No one could stop the march of progress. Economic and social forces were irresistible. And expectations rose. Most often, people were attracted away by better prospects elsewhere. No one ever chose to go back to subsistence farming and peasant life.

The future was elsewhere and left Dalgirdy behind. The question was what should happen to it now?

17. TRADE AND INDUSTRY

Money, money, money - - -

Perth has always been the economic heart of Perthshire.

The River Tay was the life-blood of Perth. The river stretches from the mountains of Drumalbin to the North Sea and is a barrier to land travel up the east side of Scotland. It was also a vital waterway into the southern Highlands. Until Victorian times, Perth was the lowest bridgeable point on the river and also the highest point that sea-going boats could reach.

People have lived around Perth since the Stone Age and the name comes from a Pictish word for a wood or copse. It was always a centre of power and an ancient royal seat. King William the Lion made Perth a Royal Burgh in 1210 and by that time it was already an important port. Trade with England, France, the Baltic and especially the Low Countries made it one of the richest towns in Scotland.

James I made Perth his main residence, so for a time it was the first city of Scotland. But after he was murdered there in 1437, his son James II moved the royal seat to Edinburgh. Perth lost its city status and has been trying to get it back ever since. It finally succeeded in 2012, as part of Queen Elizabeth II's Diamond Jubilee celebrations.

Up to 1700, Perth was the largest town in Scotland apart from the four main cities. By 1800 it combined the best of Glasgow and Edinburgh. On the one hand, it had a 'new town', academies and high society. On the other, it had a linen industry, cotton mills, paper mills and printing works. It exported salmon packed on ice for the London markets. This was a golden age of small-town life.

From the fourteenth century, commerce gave burghs like Perth an importance out of all proportion to their size. Scotland exported raw materials and imported manufactured goods and luxury items. The main exports were wool and hides. Imports were much more varied. One Scottish ship captured by the English in 1394 carried red leather, woollen and linen cloth, canvas, linen thread, dyes, wax, wine, salt, pepper, saffron, ginger, brass pots and plates, dishes, basins, bitumen, iron, Flemish belts, hose, caps, hoods, gloves, saddles, bridles, spurs, boots, weavers' shuttles, paper, parchment, candelabra, a helmet, swords, locks and keys. The value of the cargo was £170 while the ship itself was only worth £13-6-8.[386]

Most of these imports were for wealthy people in the burghs and the aristocracy. We have already seen that by 1583 the sixth Laird of Glenorchy lived in a lavish style with house and board full of imports.

Up to the fifteenth century, rural peasants had no money and were largely self-sufficient. They ate the produce of their land, spun their own wool, made their own clothing and did their own leatherwork. They made their wooden furniture and household furnishings. The only outside supply they really had to get was salt. In 1624 the Baron Baillie Court set a special toll for the pedlar who carried salt.

It is statute and ordanit that ilk strainger cadger sail pey aucht penneyis at the brig of Killin for every lead of salt that they carey athrocht the bridges.[387]

David I issued the first Scots coins in the twelfth century, at parity with the English pound. Wool and hide exports boomed in the thirteenth and fourteenth centuries. But around 1400, Europe fell into a recession. After Marco Polo discovered China we began to import silk and exotic spices from the Far East and soon ran up a trade deficit. Europe ran short of silver. Scotland's export market collapsed and there was very little domestic manufacture or trade to fall back on. The Scottish economy was in dire straits. From 1367 the pound Scots began to devalue against the English pound and by 1470 the exchange rate was only four to one. There was inflation and the price of grain rose. Sound familiar? There really is nothing new under the sun.

On the good side, the collapse of foreign trade stimulated

domestic manufacture and trade. But progress was slow and mainly in the Lowlands and the burghs.

It was probably not until the mid-sixteenth century that Highland farmers began to sell a few cattle and earn a little cash. But much of that went to pay the rent. So trade in the Highlands was still very limited, though there was a petty trader on the north side of Loch Tay by the mid-sixteenth century. Mallcolme Gait's inventory in 1576 showed that even a successful tenant farmer still had very few manufactured goods. Most cottars would have none apart from a pot and a few knives.

Smiths and millers were the earliest rural trades. Iron was essential for weapons and tools, so the blacksmith was a man of consequence from early times.

There are two bloomery mounds on Tullich, one of them just over the march from Dalgirdy. The bloomery itself is a large mound on raised ground, more than 20 feet across at the top and standing 15 feet high overall. The bowl is 12 feet in diameter and lined with stone. It is now 4 feet deep though it is full of earth and leaves and must have been much deeper when in use. There appears to be a flue on the windward, west side and a working opening on the opposite side. On the east side there is a raised working area measuring 30X10 yards.[388]

There are bloomery mounds like this all over the Highlands. These were crude iron furnaces and date from the fifteenth century or earlier. They used local bog iron and excavations show charcoal, slag and small pellets of pig iron.[389]

As early as 1440 the first Laird of Glenorchy brought a family of smiths called Macnab to Dalmally. Their job was *to manufacture arms and armour, as well as to perform other necessary parts of the smiths work.* The same family still had a smithy there in 1800.[390]

By the early seventeenth century the Baron Baillie Court of Disher & Toyer set rules for blacksmiths. Tenants had to help keep the smithy watertight. The court set prices. But tenants were also forced to use the laird's smithy under penalty of a fine.

1617 *Johne Roy McCarbrie is accused for non-payment of*

the duty of the blacksmith of Dalgirdy or else the tack to expire.[391]

Estate mills probably date from at least the fifteenth century. We know for sure that there was a mill in upper Glen Lochay by the end of the sixteenth or early seventeenth century.

1592 Donald McPatrik Roy in Tirai pursued Patrik Beg McAlby there for a boll of meal delivered by the said Patrick.[392]

1617 Jon McOleane in Tirai pursued Donald Sinclare for payment by him for thirty three shillings as the price of two dozen white bread received by him at midsummer.[393]

1619 Donald McNokard at the Mill of Glen Lochay pursued Johne Roy McNeving In Moreinch for the sum of £10-12-3 - - -.[394]

You can still see the remains of the mill at Tirai, a mile down the road from Dalgirdy. There were four buildings with a cobbled track between them. The mill building measures 6 X 8 yards with a wheel-pit built onto the west wall. The laid runs 125 yards from the river to the wheel-pit, and is about two feet wide and lined with stones. Its water intake is cut fifteen yards through the solid rock of the riverbank. At the mill, the laid runs onto an artificial bank about six feet high. That ends above and three yards short of the wheel-pit, which suggests that the wheel was fed from above by a sluice. Inside the west wall of the mill, beside the wheel-pit, is a raised platform for the mill machinery.[395]

The mill was an important source of income for the laird and the Baron Baillie Court again set the rules. The miller paid a high rent to the laird and was responsible for keeping the mill in good repair, with help from the tenants.

1615 Corriecharmaig – Patrik McGrasich (miller in Killin) pursued the cottars Gillemartene, Ewen McEan McDonald and Duncane McNokard for not coming to help with the mending of the mill in Killin according to the Laird's command.[396]

Every tenant was *thirled* to the mill for his area and one of the terms of the lease was that he had to take his grain there. The court set the miller's fees, which were between one-tenth and one-twelfth of the grain ground.

1641 *Item it is statute and ordained that quarnes be brokine,
and ilk tennent and cottar to goe with thair grindable cornes to
the milnes, quhairto they ar thirled, under the paine of x lib toties
quoties.*[397]

There was obvious scope for exploitation and *thirlage*
caused a lot of resentment. Robertson condemned the practice
in 1799. *Thirlage is a grievous burden; and its pernicious
influence on the improvement of the country is severely felt. - - -
This servitude was no doubt introduced originally as a
compensation for building and upholding a mill, and for paying
the wages of a miller: and we can suppose a stage of society, in
which the culture of the land was wretched, that the price was no
more than enough; but these circumstances no longer exist. - - - It
is an odious tax, because it is in every sense a tax upon
industry.*[398]

Robertson felt it was an *Obstacle to Improvement* and
argued for free market competition. Yet there was still *thirlage*
in Breadalbane as late as 1838:

*Articles & Conditions of Leases of Farms on the Estates of
the Marquis of Breadalbane:*

*Seventh: The Tenants shall carry all their grains to the Mill
to which the Lands are respectively thirled, and their Smith work
to the Proprietor's Smithy, and shall pay to the Miller and Smith
such dues as the Proprietor shall, from time to time, establish for
the different Mills and Smithies on the Property, and they shall
perform their share of necessary services and carriages to the
Mills, Mill-Dams, Water-Leads and Smithies, and other services
of the like nature that are useful on the Estate, according to use
and wont.*[399]

The modern villages began to develop about the sixteenth
century as trade spread out from Perth.

The 'Model Village' of Kenmore dates from the 1570s.
There had been earlier markets in the area but they moved to
Kenmore in 1575. There were eventually six markets each year,
held on the village green. The first hostelry at Kenmore was

built in 1572 and claims to be Scotland's oldest inn. However, the present square of English-style cottages was not built until 1760. *Lord Breadalbane permits the inhabitants of the village to live rent-free, on condition that they exercise some trade and keep their houses clean; so that by these terms he not only saves the expense of sending on every trifling occasion to Perth or Crief, but has got as good workmen, in common trades, as any in his Majesty's dominions.*[400]

The seeds for the future village of Killin were the fort of Dun Lochay, Finlarig castle and the early Christian church. These were in a strategic position at the south-west end of Loch Tay and the village still has the same advantages.

Centres of power and wealth have always attracted people. They offered protection and the prospect of work. To some, there was the chance of advancement or the scent of profit. So from early times there would be a small cluster of hovels around the fort. These were homes for servants and labourers who worked in the castle and on the laird's land. Again from early times, there might be a few basic tradesmen like stone, metal and leather workers. In the fifteenth or sixteenth centuries there was a mill and a smithy. By the seventeenth century the village was the centre of the community, with kirk, court, school and doctor. It was all coming together.

In 1694 Killin became a burgh of barony. This was a kind of second-class burgh that could hold markets and had certain trading rights, though few became true market towns. Killin held fairs from that time and this was, of course, yet another source of income for the laird.

From the mid-seventeenth century Killin was a stopping place for drovers on their way to Crief. It was the first village after coming over the moors of Rannoch and a place to stop overnight and, more important, have a drink. But it was only after roads improved in the 1720s and '30s that trade could really flourish. The Killin Hotel claims to be on the site of the *Street House*, which was a refreshment stop for the Aberfeldy to Tyndrum coach.

The Old Statistical Account described Killin in 1791. *The*

village itself is small, and formed on no regular plan. It contains only about 150 souls, but the district that surrounds it is for several miles closely inhabited. Most of the villagers are tradesmen who have an acre of ground, along with a house and garden, for each of which they pay rent to the Earl of Breadalbane. There are 6 fairs held here annually, at which a good number of cattle is ordinarily sold with a considerable quantity of woollen and linen yarn, besides a variety of other articles imported and exported out of the country.[401]

There were regulations for weavers and shoemakers in the late sixteenth and early seventeenth centuries. By 1791 Killin had four weavers, six tailors, eight shoemakers, three smiths, six wheelwrights, a mason and three merchants.[102] Another list about the same time showed two alehouses, a cooper, a miller and men doing various jobs in the lint mill.[403] Alcohol was clearly important and the minister gave his careful and considered opinion. *There are several houses in this parish in which ale and spirits are sold, but none that deserve to be termed inns except two. One of these is in the village of Killin and the other at Tyndrum. - - - A distillery, too, has been erected lately in the neighbourhood of the village of Killin, which is the only one in the parish.[404]* Somehow, he does not seem to disapprove!

At the same time Glen Lochay had nine weavers, two tailors, a shoemaker, two smiths, three wheelwrights and a merchant.[405] Many of these might be in the lower glen but we have already seen blacksmiths, millers, a builder and weavers in the upper glen.

We know very little about trade in Glen Lochay. Presumably, most people always went down to Killin. But there is a large rock beside the River Lochay up near the head of the glen that is still called the Herring Stone. Legend says that from the early seventeenth century, fishwives came from Loch Fyne to barter their herring for local flax, butter and cheese. Soon after we got the cottage, a travelling van called in to try to sell woollens though that was already dying out. But it may now be coming full circle, because some of the big super-markets are starting to deliver Internet orders up the glen!

The Industrial Revolution raised hopes that Breadalbane could join in and reap the profits. The Earls were most enthusiastic because they thought this could make their fortune. Some locals had more mixed feelings, just as with tourism today. They wanted the money and all that goes with it but did not want their old way of life to be disturbed.

The second Earl started flax growing in 1725 and brought wool-workers from England to teach the arts of spinning and weaving. By 1769, Pennant saw a thriving industry on Loch Tay side. *The country, within these thirty years, manufactures a great deal of thread. - - - They spin with rocks, which they do while they attend the cattle on the hills; and, at four fairs in the year, held at Kenmore, above sixteen hundred pounds worth of yarn is sold out of Breadalbane.*[406] But that picture was already out of date. By 1770 spinning wheels were in common use. The first lint mills in the Highlands had been built at Killin in 1748 and at Lawers in 1761. In 1770 the Killin mill dressed more than seven tons of flax.[407]

The introduction of southern sheep greatly increased wool production. There was a woollen mill near Kenmore before 1769, which could card and spin wool, and dress and dye cloth.[408]

But weaving of flax and wool into cloth was still done by hand. Many people did it as a part-time job. Angus McNaughtan was a crofter on Dalgirdy in 1786. He wanted more land because of *his having the Burden of a family of four young children all only to support upon his Industry and Labour as a weaver, which cannot be but inconsiderable, especially in so remote a corner of the country.*[409]

The flax industry collapsed in the 1820s because it could not compete with cheap imports from abroad. Factories in Dundee drove the local weavers out of business. Wool prices collapsed in the 1870s in the face of foreign competition and hill sheep farming has struggled ever since.

Breadalbane has rich geology and several Earls had bright hopes that the mineral wealth of the estate would make their fortune.

There was a silver mine at Tyndrum in 1428, when King James I was desperate for silver bullion during the European recession. But it was not until lead was found there in 1739 that mining began on an industrial scale. The mines on the hillside opposite the village spewed out vast amounts of poisonous spoil that pollute the land to this day. But they were dogged by the costs of transporting ore down Loch Lomond, bad debts and bankruptcy. Various companies tried off and on for the next fifty years and one even built a smelter on site to reduce transport costs. None was a lasting success.

The fourth Earl re-opened the mines in the 1820s, in the same old way, with the same old results. There were further attempts to mine lead, silver and gold at Tyndrum into the twentieth century, but always with limited success. Today the price of gold has risen to record levels and there are yet more plans to re-open the mine. Time will tell.

The fifth Earl was a keen amateur geologist and, despite all the setbacks, never gave up hope. Gillies said that he could often be seen wandering around the estate with his terrier dogs, chipping away at rocks with his wee hammer. Sadly, his amateur enthusiasm ran away with his business sense, to the despair of his Factor. The records show that he spent tens of thousands of pounds on mining 'experts'. They dug exploratory shafts all over the estate and Breadalbane is still riddled with holes like a rabbit warren. They wrote ever more optimistic reports, laying out the case for further development. They managed to set up a copper mine on the south side of Loch Tay, where they even built a chemical works to produce acid. But you can guess the outcome. Within a few years it lay derelict and the estate had to sell off the plant at a loss.[410]

There was a chromite mine in 1855-56 at Corrycharmaig in upper Glen Lochay. It raised fifty tons of ore but once again it was uneconomic. There was a report into the possibility of re-opening it in 1921 and even some trials but the costs of mining and transport ruled out any commercial venture. Yet Corrycharmaig is still listed on the British Geological Survey and appears every so often in the Scottish Journal of Geology. So there may be hope yet!

For all the hopes and enthusiasm, plans to industrialize Breadalbane were doomed from the outset. None of the minerals in Breadalbane were in sufficient quantity or concentration to be commercially viable. And the costs of transport to market have always been insurmountable.

By 1845 the population of Killin village had grown to four hundred. *It has a sub-office of the Central bank and also a savings bank. There are several shops where goods can be purchased at a reasonable rate. There is a daily post to and from the south, so that the Glasgow papers can be read at Killin at five or six o'clock on the day of publication. There is a post three times a week to and from Kenmore and Aberfeldy. - - - There is a weekly carrier to Stirling, etc. and one monthly to Glasgow via Dumbarton, also one monthly to Crief. In summer, there is a daily or thrice weekly coach running between Killin and Dunkeld, while a coach leaves Killin every morning for Loch Lomond to meet the steamer on that loch.*[411]

Killin changed forever in 1886 when the Iron Horse pulled into the village.

During the Victorian railway boom every great landowner wanted a railway. Aberfeldy already had a good rail link to Perth, which was drawing traffic and trade from the east end of Loch Tay. At the same time sheep and cattle prices were falling. Business in Killin was going downhill faster than a shepherd in an October blizzard. **Something** had to be done!

The Callander to Oban railway opened in 1880 and ran over Glen Ogle, within a few miles of Killin. The heaven-sent answer was a branch-line down to the village and on to the head of Loch Tay. None of the railway companies were interested. So the bold Marquis formed the Killin Railway Company, put up his own money, and talked the locals into buying shares. They got nine tenders for the work and in these days they were all from Scottish companies. After much consideration, like true

Scotsmen, they chose the cheapest bid from a builder in Skye. With the benefit of hindsight it was only a small firm and the price was suspiciously low. The line was only five miles over easy ground but it needed two major bridges over the Dochart and the Lochay. There were delays. Costs over-ran. Then the builder went bankrupt. But the Marquis was not a man to be discouraged and he soon found a new builder to take over.

The work was completed in three years at a cost of more than £30,000. The single-track line ran four miles down to Killin and a further mile to the head of Loch Tay. There were three stations. Killin Junction was on the main line on the north side of Glen Ogle. Killin Station had a small goods yard with sidings and a crane. Killin market, auction and holding pens were right next door. Loch Tay Station had an engine shed and a pier to link with steamers on the loch.

The line started with a small 'Pug' engine, of the kind usually used for dockyards. Locals soon got used to the noise of the engine chugging up the gradient to the Junction amidst billows of smoke and steam. And with its tall stovepipe chimney, it was nicknamed the Coffee Pot. But they soon realized that they needed a more powerful engine. For most of the line's life, a 0-4-4 engine pulled one or two carriages and in winter they were sometimes empty. At the peak of the summer tourist run it was a very different matter. On one glorious occasion two engines had to combine forces to pull twenty-one coaches full of tourists. I can still remember the width of the main street filled with a horde of six hundred tourists arriving for lunch in the local hotels.

The building of the railway brought work and money into the local economy for a time. The railway made travel and transport much easier and cheaper for ordinary people, long before the motorcar. It gave a good service for goods and supplies and deliveries for the village. It transported sheep and cattle to market, though the facilities were poor. But despite early hopes and enthusiasm, it did not bring any industrial development. And it always struggled financially. It made a small profit in its first year but never broke even again.

The Marquis also set up the Loch Tay Steamboat Company in 1882. The oak-built Lady of the Lake sailed between Killin and Kenmore, with stops at the loch-side villages. There were cargo boats for cattle, sheep and farm supplies. He hoped to improve transport and the economy of Loch Tayside but it was never a commercial success. Its greatest claim to fame was that it had the only boat ever to sink in Aberfeldy main street when the trailer bringing it to Kenmore collapsed into a drain. Passenger services ended in 1939 at the outbreak of WWII.

The railway, like the steamers, was never profitable. The Callander to Crianlarich line closed as part of the infamous Beeching cuts in 1965. It was due to close in November but fate dealt the final blow when a landslip in Glen Ogle ended services six weeks early.[412]

The rail track is now part of National Cycle Route #7 from Drymen to Pitlochry. Killin Station is a car park and council depot. The line down to Loch Tay is part of a circular village walk and Loch Tay Station is a private house.

Yet these efforts did produce a lasting legacy. Each advance in transport and trade improved access to the Lowlands and the world. They built up the infrastructure of the area, with major and lasting benefits for the local economy. They made it easier for people to come and live here but also to leave. They changed the quality of local life. Even more important, they changed rural attitudes in more subtle and fundamental ways. Killin was now part of that wider world, with all the benefits that brought.

And it opened the door to mass tourism. Killin was poised to become a Highland holiday resort.

Killin was now on the map.

18. MEDICINE

Keeping the patient amused while Nature cures

Peasant life was blighted by war, famine and disease. Starvation, poor housing and lack of hygiene meant that resistance was low. Wounds were slow to heal and turned septic. Lack of understanding meant there was little that anyone could do. No wonder rural health was poor.

Before the seventeenth century there was no access to any medical care in upper Glen Lochay.

People had used herbal medicines since the Stone Age and learned by trial and error which plants could help which symptoms. It was usually an old woman who had the knowledge, and it was passed down the generations. Wild garlic for its health-giving properties. Fennel for pain. Juniper for rheumatism and arthritis. A little foxglove for a weak heart. We know now that some of these remedies did work, even if they were not as effective as modern drugs. They had no effect on the underlying disease or the final outcome, though that is also true of much modern medicine. But they did give some relief, especially when accompanied by spells and charms. We should not dismiss the power of the placebo, which still accounts for up to 30% of the effect of many drugs.

The first doctors were called *leches* and some used this as a surname. So John the leche became John Leche. The name survives as Leitch.

The first leches were in the laird's household, and would treat his family and retainers. There may have been a leche in the Laird of Glenorchy's company as early as 1444. One had a bond of manrent in 1552.

JHOKE LECHE alias Campbell binds himself to Collin Campbell of Glenurchquay and his heirs, choosing them to be his chiefs, to serve them in Heland and Lawland on horss and on futt upon the saidis Collynis and his ayris expenssis quheneuer he be requirit, and also binds himself and his heirs to give the said Collin and his heirs their Calps; both parties being bound to each other under the penalty of one hundred merks Scots. Signed at the Isle of Lochtay before witnesses - - -.[413]

Then, from 1565 to 1571, there was Colin Leche.

Colin Campbell of Glenvrquhay granted to Colin Leiche of Craigintarif the third part of the four merklands of Ardorane Ovir, and of its woods and fishings, for the usual services, and a quart of aquavite at the Feast of the Nativity of our Lord.[414]

Rather different terms and conditions from the NHS today!

The Royal College of Surgeons of Edinburgh was founded in 1505, but only a few leading men were what we would call real surgeons and they were in the cities. Most were *barber surgeons* who also practised pharmacy. By the eighteenth century, country surgeons or *surgeon apothecaries* provided most health care in rural areas. They were the forerunners of today's family doctors.

The first barber surgeons were *a sort of body servant, providing a plethora of basic health maintenance services such as treating fractures and dislocations, wounds and infections, along with blood-letting, cupping, pulling teeth and even cutting hair.*[415]

The surgeon apothecary travelled round his practice with the tools of his trade in his saddlebags. He treated fractures and dislocations, wounds, infections, ulcers, burns, skin rashes and venereal disease. He helped at difficult births. He used a lancet to open infected swellings. He applied salves, plasters and poultices. When all else failed he applied a caustic or cautery with a hot iron to stop bleeding or burn out infection. But his treatment for almost every illness was blood-letting by lancing a vein or applying leeches, hence the name *leche*. And most of his income came from the herbal medicines that he made up himself using a mortar and pestle in his closet. Then at the end of the day he was the undertaker. Talk about burying your mistakes!

Despite the title, country surgeons did not do much surgery. Remember there were no anaesthetics before 1847. Yet on rare occasions some of them did perform heroic surgery. I was a surgeon and I cannot believe the courage of a family doctor tackling an operation like this, perhaps once in his career. And the patient! Desperation drives us to new heights.

In 1763 the Weem Kirk Session Poor Fund paid ten shillings *To John McKerchar from Glenlyon whose leg was cut off by Mr Lindsay Surgeon in Crief.*[416] He survived to go home and claim welfare.

1833 *To all whom it may concern* by Alexander McCalman, Surgeon:
I hereby certify that in capacity of medical attendant at the Netherlorn Slate quarries for nearly the last thirteen years past I have known Donald MacLugas who worked as a quarrier till summer 1832 when by a blast going off unexpectedly his left hand was so shattered to pieces and mangled that it became absolutely necessary to have it immediately removed by amputation above the wrist. He is now 33 to 34 years of age, was married about six years ago, and has three of a family. At ten years of age his father died when he was sent to work for the quarries being the oldest of the family. He continued to be the support of his widowed mother, a sister and two brothers till they could do for themselves - -. Since he recovered from the accident - - he has applied himself most diligently to improve himself with considerable success and is still persevering under charge of the Parish Teacher.[417]

Surgeon apothecaries trained by apprenticeship. A youth bound himself to serve his master for three years, to reveal no secrets of master or patient, and to commit no sins. He paid £50 sterling – a great sum of money in these days - in apprentice fees. In return, the master provided bed and board and bound himself to give full instruction in the arts of surgery and pharmacy. From the late seventeenth century students began to have more formal classes. Then exams were introduced at the end of their training. By 1858 this had evolved into a university degree and formal registration as a doctor.[418]

This letter from a student to his sponsor in Breadalbane gives some idea of how hard it must have been.

1755 Feb 12th John McIntyre Edinburgh to John Campbell Barcaldine.
- - - I have no money to carry on my education. Carwhin gave me ten guineas and Clacharnby a hundred merks, twelve guineas of which I paid for Medical College and three pounds to others I was indebted to since last year so that very little remained and though just now I have my boarding and accompt of books with other articles I know not to whom I can make application as my friends have done for me already so that I will of necessity be obliged to leave the town in a hidden manner or invent some method of getting money. But going on this way will be pernicious to my character and will hinder me from being recommended to Breadalbane after such behaviour and I think it a misfortune if now I must leave the Classes after being so far advanced. Therefore as you have always been my very good friend I hope your former generous disposition will induce you to take my case into consideration - - -.
P.S. Dr McFarlane thinks I might attend botany this summer and I know I will be quite deficient without the knowledge of herbs.[419]

The earliest records of treatment are for the laird's household, by surgeon apothecaries from Edinburgh or Perth.

21st June 1646 Receipt by John Talyeour, chirurgian, burgess of Perth, to Sir Robert Campbell of Glenorchy, kt, for 500 merks scots, for his pains in healing wounded men belonging to the lairds of Glenorchy, elder and younger, who were hurt at a conflict with a strong party of the rebels, 4 June last.
Receipt by John Talyeour, chirurgian, burgess of Perth, in name of Constantine Lawrie, apothecary there, to Sir Robert Campbell of Glenorchy, kt, of £69 8s 4d scots, for drugs and other necessaries furnished by said Constantine for healing the wounded men, hurt at a conflict on 4 June last, said men being tenants and servants to said Sir Robert.[420]

1663 *Account due to David Moray, apothecary.* It includes *a leech in a pot at £1.18s Scots, lemons and oranges, conserve of roses in a pot, Venice turpentine, cinnamon water, half an ounce of wormseed at 8s Scots, figs and a purging nodule for the laird.*[421]

1667 *Accounts due to David Moray, apothecary in Perth.* Items supplied included *clysters to the child that died [10 May 1661], marigold flowers to Duncan, a powder for worms for Duncan, a cerecloth for Lady Glenorchy in February 1666, wormseed and flower of brimstone, oil of 'speck' for the old lady's corpse in a glass [26 December 1667], to the chaplain a vomiter, sugar loaves, claret and powder of bettony.*[422] Note the claret! For the chaplain!!

1715 Account to the executors of Colin Campbell of Carwhin, deceased, by John Merry, chirurgien apothecary in Edinburgh. Carwhin had almost daily attendance from 7 Dec 1714 to 2 Feb. There is an itemized account for 106 prescriptions, of which these are typical examples:

Two drams liquid laudanum in a glass	£0-10-0
Aromatic herbs for his bath	£0-8-0
A dose of pacific pills (repeated)	£0-3-0
A purging Clyster	£1-7-0
A glass of balm of Gilead (repeated)	£0-9-0
Liquorice and althea roots (repeated)	£0-3-0
6 handfuls of chamomile for the bath	£0-6-0
6 leeches	£1-4-0
A large healing plaster to cover his haunches and part of his thigh	£0-6-0

As all too often, the list ends with:

A large cerecloth to wrap the body in	£66-13-0
Six pounds weight of aromatic powders	£9-0-0
Six ounces of aromatic oils for the corpse	£1-16-0
Total bill £150-11-0. Paid 5 April 1715.[423]	

1719 Account due by Breadalbane to Mr John McGill FRCSEd, surgeon apothecary.

Bill for £44-4-0 Sterling plus reminder of unpaid account.

Thirteen pages of items supplied included *balsam of tolu, medicines for Lady Hariot and Lady Mary, ointment for the kitchen maid and for the cook, syrup of blackthorn, frogspawn water for my lady, fine hiera picra, Jersey sage, Jesuit's bark, salt of vitriol, liquid laudanum, oriental bezoar, Virginia snakeroot, gentian, centaury, French lancets, chamomile flowers, Irish slate, powdered calcined hartshorn, oil of worms, syrup of chicory with rhubarb, Venice treacle, verdigrease, sassafras, tincture of myrrh, tincture for the teeth, melilot, Epsom salts, powdered aloe, rasped human skull, powdered dragon's blood.*[424] Really?!

By mid-century there were country surgeons in various parts of Breadalbane.

Charles Campbell, surgeon at Killin was witness to a marriage contract in 1755 but we do not know anything else about him.[425]

1769 *Received by me William Campbell surgeon in Lawers son of Colin Campbell tenant deceased in the Mains of Lawers from the Earl of Breadalbane ten pounds sterling as his Lordship's allowance to me for my exercising my said employment on his Lordship's estate for a year preceding this date.*[426]

1771 Receipt by John McIntyre in Morenish for £2 15s sterling *allowed by his lordship to help to buy a horse for me to ride about to see my patients.*[427] This might be the same John McIntyre who had begged support for his studies.

John McLagan was surgeon at Taymouth from 1777-96 and is the first doctor in the area that we know much about. He got an MD degree from Glasgow University in 1786 – half-way through his time at Taymouth - which was rare for a country doctor at that time.[428]

1778 *Taymouth March 20th Receipt for the sum of twenty five pounds sterling as my annual allowance from the Earl of Breadalbane from Whitsunday 1777 – Whit 1778.*

Received by me likewise £9-16-8 sterling as the value of the maintenance of a cow and horse.   John McLagan[429]

Much of his practice was still pharmacy.

1776-77 *Account due by Breadalbane to John McLagan, surgeon.* It included the usual remedies and also listed who was treated in the Earl's household. *To the princess a vial of hartshorn, two sweating powders for Tibby, Roman vitriol for the butcher, hiera picra for the smith, a glass of discussing mixture for the fowler, two doses of salts for the gardener, a glass of camphorated oil for Jenny Doer, quicksilver for the overseer, two doses of physic for the cook, etc.*[430]

In 1786 he had to deal with a difficult childbirth.

Memorial of Malcolm McPherson in Kyltirie, district of Deshoir, asking that quarrel between petitioner and relatives of deceased Janet McCallum in Croftvollich of Carwhin, who died in childbed of his child, over expenses of midwife, surgeon and funeral, should be settled without going to law.

That the Memorialist had the misfortune to begat Janet McCallum in Croftvollich of Carwhin with child. That on the 23rd June her childbed pains came upon the said Janet McCallum and after the Memorialist called for and brought the assistance of a regularly bred midwife, it was found the child could not be delivered without the aid of a Physician and Surgeon, and consequently Dr McLagan from Taymouth and Duncan Campbell surgeon in Killin were called and got, and by their joint skill and endeavour the Child was parted from the Mother but at the expense of both their lives which could not be prevented by skill or care.

That the Memorialist though a poor man, justly thought himself in part instrumentally concerned in the above melancholy events, and therefore meant and still inclines to bear such a share in proportion of the necessary expenses incurred on the said dismal occasion.

That the Memorialist is creditably informed that the said now deceased Janet McCallum died possessed of sufficient means to pay her Funeral Charges and the Physician and Surgeon's accounts.

But her family had the money and did not want to pay their

share![431]

Smallpox is one of the best examples of how medicine was changing about this time.

Smallpox starts with sudden onset of fever and flu-like symptoms. Two or three days later the fever breaks and the patient feels better. But then the rash appears, at first on the face, hands and forearms, and over a few days spreading to the whole body. Lesions appear in the nose and mouth, which break down into ulcers that release large amounts of virus. The patient is then highly infectious. The rash passes through various stages to pustules. After a week or two, if the patient survives, the pustules form scabs that heal to leave pale, depressed scars.

Thirty per cent of those who caught smallpox died. Sixty-five to eighty per cent of survivors were left with deep, pitted scars or 'pockmarks' on their faces.

There were two rare forms of smallpox. In the haemorrhagic form the lesions bled into the skin and body linings. It was always fatal. In the malignant form the lesions did not form proper pustules but stayed soft and flat. That meant the body's defences were giving up the battle and it was almost always fatal.

1757. *Doctor Clark's Directions in case the Laird's son should be seized with the smallpox at Taymouth.*

1. The best preparation for the smallpox, when they are in the country, is a low and cool diet. He ought therefore to abstain from all high seasoned dishes, strong soups, and everything that is salt. He should even eat sparingly of butcher meat or fish, and shun all violent exercise or anything that may overheat him. He may drink goat whey every morning, which may keep his belly open and contributes to cool his blood.

2. When the fever appears, it is usual to take blood the first day and Vomit the next, - - - (though) numbers recover without them. - - - As far as can be judged from appearances in the measles lately, it is not very probable that Mr Campbell will stand in great need of bleeding, nor indeed is it very necessary at any rate, unless the fever is very high. Because of this, it is not at all needful and by some is thought to do harm.

3. But it is certainly reasonable to give an Impeca-coaina Vomit before the eruption - - - and if the Vomit does not work downwards a milk Clyster (an enema) *is to be given that same evening.*

4. After the smallpox begins to appear, the fever in some degree continues for three days till the eruption is complete, during which nothing is needful but to drink plentifully of tea, water gruel, almond milk, barley water, or plain water boiled with a small part of milk.

5. Upon the fourth day the fever ordinarily ceases, - - - but restlessness hinders the smallpox to raise and fill. - - - (He) must be given a large spoonful of Syrup of white Poppies with six or seven drops of laudanum mixed with it, the same to be continued for three nights.

6. Upon the eighth day his drink is to be changed to sweet whey, which he may drink in plenty, and if it does not open his belly he must have a milk Clyster.

7. This is the regular course of the smallpox in the kindly distinct sort, and no other medicine is necessary, except that it is of use sometime to apply a poultice to the throat.

8. During the three days of eruption, if he feels cold and chilly with a low pulse and the smallpox not red enough (i.e. in shock), *plain jack whey is the best Cordial.*

9. If on the fifth day the pox still appear flat and small, that is, do not raise and are pale, (i.e. the malignant form) *a blistering plaster is to be applied between the shoulders.*

10. If the Vomit *is not effective, prescribe various other* purgatives.

11. In case the defluction (catarrh) *is troublesome and ill to expectorate* (i.e. chest complications), *which happens frequently upon the returning of the pox, give a spoonful of the squill mixture once in four or five hours, till it grows loose and easy. If the mixture provokes a puke, so much the better.*

12. About the seventh day, almost always a new fever begins, called the blacking or secondary fever - - -. This fever is slight and attended with no bad symptoms. - - - But sometimes (especially in

the confluent kind) it is accompanied with weight in the head,
extraordinary sleepiness, raving or difficulty of breathing. In any
of these appearances blood is to be taken immediately to seven or
eight ounces. If it cannot be got with a lancet, two leeches are to
be applied to each temple, and after they drop off the bleeding to
be promoted as long as possible with a linen cloth dipped in warm
water. A Clyster is likewise to be injected of half a mutchkin of
whey, with oxymel of squills and syrup of cuckthorn, of each a
spoonful. An infusion of Senna leaves with a little Cinnamon - - -
till his belly is open. The purging is to be kept up as long as these
symptoms continue.

13. The most dangerous symptoms are the red, purple or
black spots mixed with the smallpox and frequently attended with
bloody urine or some other bloody evacuation (i.e. the
haemorrhagic form). *Abstain from bleeding and blistering,*
though both commonly practised. Give no medicine but bark
mixture till the spots disappear and the urine is free of blood.

This shows much clinical experience and careful
observation of the course of the disease. Dr Clark's management
would help to keep the patient comfortable and discouraged
more harmful treatments like bleeding. Most of all, however, it
gave the illusion of 'doing something'.

But perhaps we should not be too critical. Even today there
is no cure for smallpox.

The breakthrough came with inoculation, for prevention is
always better than cure. Inoculation had been used in India for
centuries and was brought to England in 1718. But it used a live
strain of the smallpox virus, so there was a small risk and many
people were afraid to have it. It only became common in
Scotland after 1765. Jenner developed vaccination with the
cowpox virus in 1796 and because it was safer and more
effective it was soon used throughout Scotland.

Dr McLagan began to use inoculation in 1779.

You may remember that in October last, I happened to
mention the havoc that the natural smallpox was making in the
neighbourhood of the King's land in Rannoch. That in a village
where there were 14 or 15 children eight or nine were swept off

and those that survived much hurt in their eyesight. That it would soon spread over Rannoch if not speedily prevented by inoculation. The inhabitants were poor and ignorant and would never consent to have their children inoculated except it was done gratis. - - - The case could not admit of much delay, as the smallpox was then in the very next town to the Rannoch lands. I consulted you what was to be done and you without hesitation advised that I should inoculate without delay - - -.

This enclosed list will best show the number that was inoculated of poor people's children. - - - I inoculated in whole including both sides of Loch Rannoch 155 and every one of these did well and all except two or three took the infection nor do I imagine that half a dozen of these will be pock marked. You need not doubt that I had a vast deal of fatigue for many weeks attending such a number and some of them being 20 miles distant from the other. You know the country and the roads. Preparing them took up some time. I don't imagine that there were so many inoculated in Scotland in so short a space before this time.[432]

Dr McLagan got little credit. He was only paid £15 for his labour, despite his protest. *I am very sensible that it is thought un-genteel in our Profession to find fault with their payers and complain of their fees; but - I have been much disappointed -.*[433]

Then the neighbouring surgeon in Dunkeld added insult to injury. He supported inoculation, but the local people - - - *were resolved not to allow him, Mr McLagan, to inoculate their children, as four of those he had inoculated in Rannoch had died. I am very far from insinuating that he was to blame. But as you know the prejudices of the Country people are not easily removed and I am afraid that - - - (the programme) would be frustrated if he was employed.*[434]

The Minister of Killin, writing in the 1790s, had no such doubts. *The great mortality, occasioned in former years by the smallpox among the children, has been of late in a great measure prevented by the introduction of inoculation.*[435] By the turn of the century, vaccination ended the threat of smallpox.

Mr Duncan Campbell was surgeon in Killin between 1786

and 1804. His brother was Lieutenant Archibald Campbell so it seems likely that he was an older son of Duncan Campbell who was in Dalgirdy in 1800.[436]

1786 *Receipt for £5 sterling for a year's allowance from Breadalbane.*[437]

1804 Killin Kirk Session Records show that *Dr D Campbell in Killin* paid £2 in fines *for fornication with Margaret Campbell his late maid.* He also paid the maid's fine.[438]

The Rev Dr Hugh MacKenzie was minister of Killin Parish Church from 1828-34. He was born in Sutherland and trained in Aberdeen as a medical missionary. *He was an evangelical preacher, and always ready to give the benefit of his medical knowledge to the poor of the parish.*[439] He died when his horse threw him late one night coming home from preaching in Kenmore.[440]

The Poor Law Act came into force in 1845. Parish Boards now had to make sure that *all poor persons in need of medical relief must be duly and punctually attended by a competent medical practitioner.*[441]

Charles Alexander McDiarmid was Medical Officer to the Boards of Killin, Kenmore and Weem Parishes from 1846-54. He got his diploma from Edinburgh in 1831 at the age of eighteen. In the 1851 Census he described himself as *Licenciate of the Edinburgh College of Surgeons & General Practitioners.* There never was a College of that name, but it is a fair description and the earliest use in this area of the term 'General Practitioner'. He lived with his wife and three or four servants in *the Doctor's House in New Street.* It is a modest terrace house that still stands on Main Street and is called Birchbank.[442]

Soon after he took up his post he petitioned the Earl to improve his house. *The house is still very damp, and too confined, and there is a want of some small offices yet.* The Reporter agreed that it needed work costing £50-60 *to render these buildings sufficiently commodious and suitable for the accommodation of a respectable medical man, which the Killin District requires. - - - Dr McDiarmid's appointment to Killin has proved a most satisfactory one. As a practitioner, and as a Gentleman of excellent heart and character, he is very valuable in so remote a District. I consider him very deserving of encouragement, and would strongly recommend doing what is necessary to render his accommodation reasonably comfortable, so that he may not be easily induced to leave the place.*[443]

Sometime in the 1850s the Estate built Loch Tay Cottage further down Main Street and that is still the local doctor's house.

Charles' father died in 1854 leaving him a modest fortune and he promptly gave up medicine. He stayed in Killin for the rest of his life, living on the proceeds of his investments and giving his occupation as *Fund Holder*. He built a large Victorian mansion that is now the Dall Lodge guesthouse. He died in 1890, leaving £2,000,000 in today's money, yet he only had ten shillings cash in the house and £26-16-0 in his current account.[444]

Mr James Todd was surgeon in Killin from 1860 78. He came from Lancashire and trained in Glasgow. Before being appointed as the *Parochial Medical Officer and Vaccinator* he had been an Acting Assistant Surgeon on the staff of the British Army in the Crimean War.

In 1861, 1891 and 1901 the Killin surgeon was not at home on the night of the Census, which perhaps shows how much he had to travel to cover his district.

Dr Crerar came from a Killin family and his obituary in 1890 describes the life of a country doctor. *Alexander Crerar FRCSEd, JP Late medical officer of Rannoch who died recently. For 34 years he had efficiently discharged his duties over the extensive and sparsely peopled district of Rannoch, and it has been publicly stated that during that time he was never a week off duty. He is described as being a skilful and highly respected physician as well as a sincere and worthy man. He will be especially remembered for his kindness and attention to the poor.*

He was a justice of the peace for the County of Perth.[445] Dr Crerar was made a Fellow of the Royal College of Surgeons of Edinburgh in 1871, which was a rare honour for a country doctor at that time.

Dr Alexander Bryce was top of his year in Glasgow University. He was only Medical Officer in Killin for two years from 1892-94 before being tempted away to Birmingham where he went on to a distinguished academic career.[446]

Dr Alexander David Wilson was Medical Officer, Killin Parish from 1895 to 1926. He was a keen bowler and the bowling green is just across the road from the doctor's house. The story goes that the front porch of his house served as the waiting room. So when his surgery was due to start he could continue bowling until the porch was full and people were waiting outside. But others say the porch was not built until later, so the story can't be true – at least not of Dr Wilson!

The Highlands and Islands Medical Service was set up in 1913 to meet the special needs of health care in poor and sparsely populated areas.[447] It included the Highland District of Perthshire. This was the first comprehensive and free state health service in Britain and a prototype for the National Health Service thirty-five years later.

Dr William Stevenson was Medical Officer from 1927-36. He did not like going the twenty miles to Tyndrum so many patients there changed to the Dalmally practice.

At least one of these early doctors was *fond of the bottle* and many old stories start *and the doctor was so drunk - - -*. Years later an old man in Crianlarich told about his wife going into labour. He had to cycle the thirteen miles to Killin and wake the doctor, who put his head out the bedroom window to answer the call of duty. Once he heard the problem, he thought about what he would need. 'Have you a bottle?' he asked. 'No? Well, away up to Killin Hotel and get a bottle of whisky while I get out the horse and trap'. By the time they got to Crianlarich both were drunk, but the wife gave birth without their help! The doctor stayed in character to the end. When he died, the hearse taking him to be cremated in Glasgow broke down outside

242

Dumgoyne distillery. But despite any personal failings, everyone thought he was a very good doctor!

Dr Duncan McColl served Killin from 1937 until 1965. He was a native Gaelic speaker from Skye but Perthshire Gaelic is a distinct dialect and at first he had difficulty understanding some of the older locals. Dr McColl had served in the Royal Army Medical Corps in WWI. Before Killin he worked for the Highlands and Islands Medical Service in Dalmally and many of the Tyndrum patients moved back to the Killin practice with him.

In 1948 the practice became part of the new NHS. Up to that time a single doctor served the whole of the Killin district. During the Hydro Scheme, the number of patients rose to three to four thousand and Dr McColl took on a series of assistants. In 1956 his assistant left at short notice, so his wife phoned their daughter Dr Mairi McColl who had just completed her training. She never planned to work in Killin but agreed to came back to help her father out and *try it for a year.* Dr Duncan McColl retired in 1965 just about when the Hydro work came to an end. The number of patients fell and Killin went back to a single handed practice. Dr Mairi ran it until she retired in 1989 with an MBE *for medical services to the community.*

Each census from 1861 to 1901 showed three nurses in Killin. Yet there was no 'official' District Nurse until 1909, and she was funded at first by private charity. The Nursing Association provided a house for the resident nurse, which is still in use as the nurses' clinic.

Before that time the 'howdie' *helped with childbirth.* The howdie was *a midwife, formerly applied to an untrained woman who also performed other kinds of sick nursing.*[448] Women from Glen Lochay who were near to giving birth, particularly in winter, stayed in the howdie's house in the village so that the doctor would be nearby if required.[449]

Today Killin has three family doctors, who work from a

custom-built health centre. There are three community nurses and a part-time practice nurse. Midwives and health visitors come from Stirling. There are 1½ pharmacists. There is a practice manager and two secretaries. Dr Mairi thinks that today's doctors only work part-time!

There were no hospitals in rural areas. In 1627, in Killin parish: *As for hofpitalls we haid none.* In Kenmore Parish: *Thair is no hofpitall nether any foundatioune of ane hospital within the faid parochin.*[450]

The first hospital for Killin was Perth Infirmary, which was built in 1838. But very few patients from Glen Lochay would travel as far as Perth at that time.

From the 1890s until the early 1930s there was a small 'fever hospital' in Killin. This was a mile outside the village, to isolate infectious cases. In the 1920s it was last used for a scarlet fever outbreak.

Today the nearest hospital is at Stirling, thirty miles away. There is an ambulance stationed in Killin. At first this was manned by volunteers but it has had trained paramedics since 1975. In real emergencies, patients are now evacuated by helicopter.

It is all quite a change from health care in the seventeenth century.

19. SCHOOLS
The three Rs: Reading, Writing and 'Rithmetic

The Christian church brought education to Scotland. Young men who went into religious orders learned to read and write in abbeys and monasteries.

Lay education came much later. Some sons of feudal lords had private tutors and the first grammar schools in towns began in the twelfth century. But it was not until 1496 that James IV passed the first Education Act that decreed all sons of barons should attend grammar school. Progress was slow but by 1516, two hundred out of 216 barons could at least sign their name. Literacy was rising among the male elite even if they were still not a very erudite bunch.

St Adomnan's abbey at Dull remained an important seat of learning through medieval times, until St Andrews University was founded in 1413, the third oldest in the English speaking world. By 1495 there were universities in Glasgow and Aberdeen, and Scotland had more universities than England. Edinburgh came later but it never had a papal charter so it was not a real university. Strictly speaking it was only a 'town's college'. Glasgow will never let them forget!

This was a Golden Age in medieval Scotland. James IV was a popular and cultured Renaissance Prince who spoke five languages as well as Scots and Gaelic and took a deep personal interest in education, arts and science. Scots was now the language of the court and of government. It was a time of cultural achievement and national prestige.

Education came slower to the Highlands. Even lords like Menzies of Weem in Glen Lyon needed help to sign documents. A papal Bull of 1484 for the founding of Aberdeen University said it all. *In the northern or north-eastern part of the Kingdom there are certain places separated from the rest of the Kingdom by arms of the sea and very high mountains in which dwell men rude and ignorant of letters, and almost barbarous, so ignorant of letters that not only for preaching the Word, but also for administering the Sacraments of the Church proper men cannot be found.*[451] The occasional priest might teach a likely lad the basics of reading and writing but before the Reformation there was no parish system of education.

We have seen that one of the basic ideas of the Reformation was that everyone had to read the Bible for himself. That would require universal education.

The First Book of Discipline in 1561 pleaded *that your honours be most careful for the virtuous education and godly upbringing of the youth of this realm. - - - Every church* (should) *have a schoolmaster appointed, such a one as is able, at least, to teach grammar and the Latin tongue, if the town is of any reputation. If it is upland, where the people convene to doctrine but once in the week, then must either the reader or the minister there appointed, take care over the children and youth of the parish, to instruct them in their first rudiments, and especially in the catechism.*[452] Education was to be for all. The rich could provide education at their own expense and it was only necessary for the kirk to see that it was given under proper supervision. *The children of the poor must be supported and sustained on the charge of the church.*

The purpose of education was to prepare children *for the business of life and the purpose of eternity*. Education became a driving force of Scottish society, even if that would take many generations to reach places like Glen Lochay.

Killin had a school early in the seventeenth century and this may have been the first in the area.

1627 Killin Parish: *We haid ane school bot for laik of meanes it dissolved. It is necessarye.*

Kenmore Parish: *Thair is no schoole nor reider thair; nether has thair bein any provisoune heir-to-foir for thame.*[453]

In 1646 the Scottish Parliament passed an *Act for founding of schools in every parish.*

- *A school will be founded and a schoolmaster appointed with the advice of the presbytery.*
- *To this end, the heritors* (the landowners of the parish) *will provide:*
  - *A suitable house for the school.*
  - *An annual stipend for the schoolmaster, of at least 100 merks.*
  - *A new tax on land to pay for these.*[454]

Schools started in most parishes of West Perthshire between 1649 and 1654. Killin probably got a school again about that time, though the early Kirk Session records are lost so we do not know exactly when. [455]

In 1701, £2-6-8 of the rent of Tullich and Dalgirdy went to the schoolmaster's stipend.[456]

In 1709 *John Campbell in Dalgirdy is wryter and witness* of bonds.[457] He was the first person we know of in Dalgirdy who could read and write and that was unusual for a tenant farmer at that time. He had presumably gone to school in Killin. In 1725 Duncan McMartin could only initial his Tack of Dalgirdy.[458] Even in 1776, only Patrick McVean could sign out of the three tenants.[459]

By the 1790s *The parish schoolmaster here* (Killin) *has a salary of £10 Sterling from the heritors, which, with school dues and some perquisites as session-clerk, makes his living a little better than £20 Sterling annually. He has also a house and garden, and has ordinarily about 70 scholars, several of whom learn Latin, Greek and French with him. There are three other schoolmasters in the parish, who teach only the reading of English and Gaelic with writing and arithmetic; and three other schoolmistresses for teaching sewing and knitting of stockings.*[460]

By the end of the 18th century there were at least ten schools in Breadalbane - - - achieved through the cooperation of the Church, the local Kirk Sessions, a succession of generous and progressive landlords, and the Society for Propagating Christian Knowledge. The teachers in those 'Charity' schools were young *lads who had been educated at parish schools and who had been recommended to the directors of the SPCK as suitable. - - - There is no doubt that many of the teachers were poorly qualified and that they were miserably paid. They taught in houses that had been hastily and roughly built: the conditions both for themselves and the children were extremely trying.*[461]

Things improved by 1845. *The parish* (of Killin) *is well supplied with schools, viz. 1 parochial; 3 Society for Propagating Christian Knowledge; 2 supported by the Marchioness and taught by females; 2 adventure schools. In the parish school, besides the ordinary branches, Greek, Latin, mathematics and bookkeeping are efficiently taught. In March the number in attendance at all the schools was 435, being one in four of the population. The parish school is endowed with the maximum salary, with a commodious house and garden. The Society's teachers have from £15 to £17 with a free house, croft and cow's grass. Lady Breadalbane's schools are also endowed. The teacher at Killin receives £20 with a free house, garden and fuel. In this school about 50 girls and 10 boys receive their education gratis. The girls in addition to the usual branches are also taught sewing and knitting. There is also a dame school in the village, where very young children attend, and are taught the rudiments of English and Gaelic with knitting, and we are not sure the venerable teacher might lay claim to the honour of having invented the infant school system; she has a free house from the Marchioness. Nearly all children are at school. Gaelic is still used in home and church, but most people understand and speak more or less English. All the children above six years can read, and nearly all in Gaelic and English. Among the aged, especially the females, there are many who cannot write, but of the young, both boys and girls, almost all learn writing and arithmetic. The expense of education may average for the whole year about 10s. Nearly all the people, even the poorest, make an effort to give their children the benefits of education.*[462]

Killin School had been built in 1800 with additions in 1838. It had walls of stone and lime, a wooden floor and a timber and slate roof. There was one large schoolroom and two small classrooms. The schoolmaster had a six-room house attached to the school.[463]

Killin now had a well-established school, the envy of any small village at that time. Even if the minister's report in 1845 was wildly optimistic about the pupils' attendance and achievements!

That was all very well for Killin, but how about Glen Lochay? As early as 1716 the Presbytery of Dunkeld recognized the problem. *There is a need of a school at Glenlochay, which lies in the parishes of Kenmore, Killin and Weem, and several of the inhabitants six miles distant from any school* (i.e. Killin school), *and consisting of four hundred examinable persons, to be settled at Innischaorach, with fifteen pounds of salary for the encouragement of the schoolmaster.*[464] But there was no money to do anything at that time.

The minister of Weem, the Rev Archibald Campbell, was concerned about the continued lack of schooling in the detached portions of his parish. So when he died in 1740 he left money to fund schools at Crannich on Loch Tay side, Roro in Glen Lyon and Duncroisk in Glen Lochay. The Kirk Session records show how it worked.

Sunday Nov 15th 1742. Sermon at Roro. The people of Roro represented that their children had been badly off for some time past for want of a schoolmaster and as there was one John Kennedy just now in the country - - -. The minister upon trial found him pretty well qualified to teach a school - - he was therefore admitted as schoolmaster [465]

Sunday Jan 31st 1743. No sermon at Weem as the minister was preaching at Crannich. - - - John Murdoch Ground Officer in Crannich reported that they were badly off in this corner of the parish of Weem for want of a schoolmaster so there was one Alex Irvine who had good character for this business and as he conversed with him, he was willing to be schoolmaster among them. The Minister in order to bring this business to a right bearing enjoined John to speak to Achalader, the Earl of

Breadlabane's Factor, and procure an order from him to the Tenants to set about building a house for the master's scholars without delay. And Mr Campbell promised to speak to Achalader who was appointed sole trustee for the interest of six thousand Merks Scots mortified by the late Mr Archibald Campbell, Minister of Weem, and expressly ordered by him to be laid out for salaries to those schoolmasters viz. one to be fixed in Crannich, another in Roro, and the third in Duncrosk. And after conversing with Alex Irvine, he ordered him to set up his school immediately in regard John Murdoch promised to provide him with a house till the Schoolhouse would be built by the Tenants.[466]

I have not been able to find any such record for Duncroisk but it seems the first Glen Lochay School started about the same time. It would be a single-room bothy, like the bridge bothy in Dalgirdy, with dry-stone walls and a thatched roof. The schoolmaster would be a young man who could speak English and Gaelic and was able to read and write to some extent but had no other training. He would live in the school and have a small pendicle of land to help support himself.

There are three schools supported from a sum of 6000 merks Scots, mortified for that purpose by Mr Archibald Campbell - - - The interest of that sum only is employed - - - i.e. £5-11-1½ to each. This sum at the time it was first given was sufficient for supporting a lad to teach for seven months in the year, which at that time was all that was required as the people dispersed through the hills with their cattle in the month of May and the schools did not convene till after the harvest was finished.[467]

Clearly, these young men struggled to make a living.

1798. *Petition and offer of Patrick McDiarmid, tenant of Finglen, and James Dewar, schoolmaster in Wester Duncrosk in Glenlochy, for farm of Wester Duncrosk.*

That in regard that neither of the Petitioners - - - have a proper place of residence or accommodation for a family and being desirous at their advanced time of life to obtain a proper settlement, they beg leave to propose getting the farm of Wester Duncrosk equally between them.[468]

That remained the situation until 1858 when a new Glen

Lochay school was built on Dalgirdy land, ten minutes walk to the west of the cottage. This is now known as the 'Old Schoolhouse' and is a private house.

The original building was 24 feet long and 18 feet wide, with walls 9 feet high. It had a large single room with glazed windows and a fireplace. The Earl of Breadalbane supplied the land and materials free of charge. The tenants did the carriage and labouring, and may have paid the tradesmen. There was no legal title, so the building became the property of the estate and then after the *Education (Scotland) Act 1872* it passed to the School Board. Schooling was now meant to be compulsory for all children up to the age of thirteen.

The schoolhouse was - - - for the joint benefit of children of detached portions of the parishes of Killin, Kenmore and Weem.

At the time the School was built there was a large number of tenants in that part of Glenlochay (probably 12 or 14 besides cottars) and there was a duly appointed resident teacher, but now the whole of the different farms occupied by these tenants are in the hands of four families.

Since the passing of the Education Act 1872 the School has been kept open for the winter six months at the joint expense of Killin, Kenmore and Weem.[469]

Glen Lochay School Log started in 1874, shortly after the Act, and tells of the daily life of the school.[470] It shows that Acts of Parliament and official reports do not always give the full picture. Life up the glen could be very different from down in Killin. I should warn you that some of the comments about the pupils are not politically correct!

5th April 1874
HM Inspector's Report for Glenlochay Public School.
Teacher Mr John McNaughton (from Livingstone in the Lowlands).
Present 9 boys and 5 girls.
The Reading is creditable, the Handwriting very good, Grammar Geography and History very fair. The general intelligence of the scholars is well developed. They are deficient

however in Dictation and Arithmetic.

The schoolhouse floor is stone and the west wall very damp. There are no offices. The Master lives in the Schoolroom. His household furniture consists of a bed and two chests. He ought to live elsewhere.

22ⁿᵈ April 1874
Attendance very irregular this week owing to household affairs such as keeping house while parents are planting potatoes.

29ᵗʰ April 1874
The junior classes attend fairly regularly but the boys of any use for looking after lambs are absent of course they are above age.

15ᵗʰ October 1874
Attendance not so regular this week owing to potato lifting.

29ᵗʰ Jan 1875
A wearisome week. All the scholars with exception of one or two laid up either with fever or whooping cough and some days no scholar at all in attendance.

20ᵗʰ Dec 1875
John and Mary McDiarmid from Dalgirdy left school to go to Killin School. (They were aged eleven and nine years.)

3ʳᵈ Jan 1876
John Hamilton commenced the Latin rudiments today.

25ᵗʰ Jan 1876
Ebenezer Little left to herd the hogs for some weeks: puts him far behind his class.

16ᵗʰ Feb 1876
The McNabs in Class 3 are irregular in their attendance on account of stormy weather and long bad road coming six miles

through the glen.

Jan-Feb 1883
Attendance variable because of strong weather and snow.

18th May 1883
Only three scholars are present today. The remainder are assisting their parents with peats.

6th June 1884
Attendance still very poor. Two of the McNabs from the head of the glen have been attending of late about time for them as ignorant as the hills without three words of English.

5th Feb 1886
Owing to a heavy fall of snow which blocked the road the school was not opened on Tuesday.

15th Jan 1892
Two girls in First and Second Stage French read French together - - - with apparent pleasure.

23rd Dec 1892
Three boys attend regularly this week. Boy in Mathematics is very stiff at Euclid, fair at Algebra.

30th Dec 1892
Boy improves in mathematics and Latin

20th Jan 1893
Boy has dropped Mathematics – could not be made to understand Euclid.

28th Jan 1895
The boy D Ferguson does not seem to understand arithmetic at all. His younger brother is far ahead of him in that respect.
(Dan Ferguson, Dalgirdy, then aged 13. Younger brother James)

1st July 1896
Mr Jas Campbell, Tullich, Chairman (of the School Board), paid a visit to the school. Examined the children in Religious Knowledge and gave out several prizes.

22nd Nov 1896
Duncan and John Burns and James Ferguson (Dalgirdy) *do very good work.*

5th Dec 1896
Dan Ferguson (Dalgirdy, then aged 15) *came on Monday and is very far back. Impossible to make him understand his lessons.*

15th May 1897
Attendance poor just now. Most of the elder boys at peat making.

12th Dec 1900
Strong weather and little ones unable to come to school. Others attending well and progress satisfactory.

27th April 1900
School shut owing to all children having whooping cough.

1st Aug 1902 (Handwriting changes, possibly a new teacher.)
Standard Ex VI at compound interest, finished Plantagenet and Tudor lines (Sanderson's History) Geography of the world, over 3rd stage Domestic Economy, Grammar simple complex compound sentences parsing. Standard V Geography of Europe, Grammar simple sentences, parsing, History George III Simple proportion. Standard IV Geography of England, grammar simple sentences, parsing Arithmetic reduction. Standard III History Bruce and Mary, Arithmetic division with three figures, Geography of Scotland, Grammar finding subject and predicate, telling parts of speech. Standard II Arithmetic multiplication with

one figure, notation and numeration up to 100,000, Grammar nouns and verbs, Geographical terms and their meanings. Standard I Notation and numeration up to 100,000. Grammar nouns. All have poetry. Standard Ex VI 'Lady of the Lake' and 'Mary Queen of Scots'. Standard V 'The leak in the dike'. Standard IV, III, II, I 'the Battle of Blenheim' 'British Birds Nests' etc.

Bible Knowledge – Story of Moses, Joseph and the Life of Jesus, Shorter Catechism. Nature Knowledge, etc.

17th June 1904
Hugh and Lizzie McLelland from Badour put in an appearance on Tuesday. They have not been in school since August the result is they are very backward.

10th Aug 1906
Two little boys in infant class make good progress though one is much hampered in his progress on account of defective English.

5th April 1907
Eight attend well this week. Two who have been absent since October on account of distance and strong weather have fallen behind with the work.

10th June 1907
HM Inspector's Report
As most of the pupils on entering this school speak and understand only Gaelic their instruction is beset with serious difficulties at the onset. In spite of this, however, the appearance made by the school is distinctly satisfactory and compares very well with that made by many others in more favourable circumstances.

The senior pupils show a laudable inclination to read good literature in their spare time at home. This deserves encouragement and as the difficulty of obtaining suitable books in such an outlying district is very great the managers are advised to place a few suitable volumes in this school.

7th Jan 1908
Received small library from School Board this week.

26th June 1908
Today we received a library with maps and pointers etc. from James Coates Esquire, Ferguslie House, Paisley. This is a great source of delight to both young and old.

11th Sept 1908
Opened school on Tuesday this week. No pupils Tuesday, Wednes-day or Thursday but one little girl attended today.

2nd Nov 1908
Visited school and found one pupil present. Evidently the Scarlet Fever being at Tullich and now Chicken Pox having broken out in the glen.
(The school had several visits each year from the headmaster of Killin School and from the Chairman of the School Management Committee.)

17th Feb 1909
Visited school. Found everything in very good order. Discipline excellent. Registers well kept.

24th June 1910
Attendance irregular due to sheep clipping.

22nd Sept 1911
Several children *are at the grouse drives.*

1st Dec 1911
Owing to the pheasant drives the attendance is rather irregular.

31st May 1912
Wednesday being the day of the annual medical inspection in Killin was held here as a holiday for those who did not need to

attend.

21st Jan 1913
School opened on 7th January but the next week being exceedingly stormy no one was able to come to school.

10-27th Oct 1913
Miss Campbell having resigned, school closed.

20th Nov 1914
School reopened on 16th inst. Miss Susan Forbes teacher. Four pupils present.

2nd Dec 1918
Owing to an epidemic of Influenza among the children the school has been closed from 13th November to 2nd December.
(This was the great flu pandemic after WWI.)

7th Jan 1920
Roll of seven. The girl who left to go to Killin School after the qualifying exam is back here again and intends being here till she leaves school.

27th Feb 1920
The boy from outside the three mile limit came on Wednesday. Very far back having been practically off school for six months.

5th Mar 1920
Letter from XXX's father saying that the swing bridge had been swept away.[471]

8th Oct 1920
A tinker woman has put her boy aged six to school for a week or two, Can't make him do anything he is told. Does not seem to understand the simplest English. No more can I understand his dialect.

15th Oct 1920
Dr Stewart medically inspected the school and found all but one free from any defect.
(This appears to be the start of school medical and dental services.)

22nd Dec 1920
The Compulsory Officer paid the school a visit but did nothing as far as XXX is concerned.

14th Jan 1921
The Committee have arranged to have the father before them to ascertain why he neglects to educate his son.
(These last two entries appear to be the first real effort to enforce school attendance. During the rest of the 1920s, attendance was 85-90% and one attendance of 75% was noted to be the lowest of the year.)

27th May 1921
XXX is leaving at the term.

24th June 1921
Rev McGregor visited the school this week and examined the children in their Religious Knowledge. He was highly satisfied especially with the way they could repeat the Shorter Catechism.

9th Sept 1921
Attendance rather irregular owing to boys attending grouse shooting.

7th Oct 1921
Boys under fourteen not allowed to attend grouse drive.

9th Dec 1921
On Tuesday had to send the pupils home at dinnertime as the river was rising rapidly and would cut them off from their homes.

20th Jan 1922
Owing to a severe snow storm no school could be held. The
pupils were not able to come out in the deep snow.

2nd June 1922
Two new pupils – one eight past but never at school before
owing to weak legs.

26th Oct 1923
Two boys off lifting potatoes. The weather is very depressing.
Some days the school is very dark. (No electricity in those days!)

5th Sept 1924
Opened with role of ten. One boy has not yet come back
applying for an exemption for the shooting season.

26th Sept 1924
The boy YYY did not get exemption but has not been to
school yet.

10th Oct 1924
YYY says attending school in Fortingall. (Fortingall was 20
miles away, over in Glen Lyon. So believe that one if you will!)

24th Oct 1924
One of pupils attended Killin School to meet the dentist and
got three teeth pulled. Absent three days.

19th Mar 1926
The dentist found most of the pupils required treatment but
the parents did not give consent.

24th Sept 1926
Half ton of coal and 5 carts firewood put in cellar.

17th Dec 1926
Oil sent for lamps.

28th Jan 1927
A hurricane on 28th blew slates off roof, tree near school fell across road, children delayed in getting home as motor conveying them could not get past till the tree was removed. Impossible for children on other side of river to get to school as river rose rapidly. Worst gale on record for many years.
(This is the first mention of school transport.)

6th June 1930
The two ZZZ are delicate children and their bad attendance has hindered their progress, which has been slower than it would otherwise have been.

28th Apr 1931
I visited this school today and found it in very moderate repair. This school has no lavatories; this should be attended to at once.

1st May 1931
Master of Works visited school to see what repairs were necessary.

4th Sept 1931
School reopened. A new floor was laid during the vacation. Repainted.

1st & 11th Nov 1932
Clerk to the Education Board and representatives of the School Management Committee visited regarding proposals for alterations to the building

30th June 1933 HM Inspector's Report
This small school is carefully taught.
Most of the children make a creditable appearance.
The office provision is unsatisfactory, there being only one place for boys and girls.

3rd Oct 1933

Members of the Education Committee visited the school today and conferred with the parents regarding the proposed closure of the school. After hearing their views the Committee agreed to report that arrangements should be made for transferring the children to Killin School.

20th Oct 1933

It has been decided that this school should be closed and the children conveyed to Killin. This takes effect today. All stationery stock is being taken to the Clerk at Killin. Text Book stock sent to Supplies Dept. Perth while the cleaning stores on hand are left in cupboard and inventory of same taken to Office of Works Dept. Perth.

Glen Lochay School closed on 20 October 1933 and an era ended.

The last nine children went to Killin School. They ranged in age from six to thirteen and included James Campbell from Tullich and Jim Wright whom we saw had links to Dalgirdy.

It is a remarkable story. My grandfather was the dominie of a rural school like this and I have a hazy memory of sitting in his class when I was four years of age, so I have some idea what it was like.

For nearly two hundred years a series of young teachers struggled to bring education to this lonely Highland glen. The buildings were primitive and the resources few. They were professionally isolated, with little support, and most only stayed for a year or two. Their living conditions were as bad as those of the peasants they lived with.

They only had a handful of pupils, but with a wide range of age and ability and needs the teacher must meet. It was a struggle to get many to come to school at all, with constant pressure to help at home and on the farm. You get a strong impression that some were happy to use any excuse to stay away. It must have been an uphill battle that would drive the faint-hearted to despair.

Yet for all the difficulties, most pupils got a basic education and left school able to read and write and to speak English and Gaelic. A few made a start on Mathematics and French and Latin before going on to the Secondary School in Killin. And there was always a place for the *lad o' pairts* – a boy from a humble background who showed promise and wanted to better himself. Two of the Campbell boys from Tullich started in Glen Lochay School in the early 1900s and went on to become doctors.

Education was the key to the future.

20. THE RE-INVENTION OF SCOTLAND

Land of mountain and myth

Scotland hit an all-time low around 1700.

We had just suffered the worst of the Little Ice Age with seven failed harvests in a row. People starved to death, the birth rate halved, and the population fell 10%.

There was social turmoil. Thousands of desperate people left home and wandered the country in search of food and work. Lawlessness was rife.

The economy collapsed. By 1707 the Scottish pound was only worth one-twelfth of an English pound.

Scotland's last desperate gamble was to invest in its own colony in Panama. But the Darien scheme was badly planned and badly run, and we were too weak to compete with the big boys in the Empire game. The scheme collapsed and Scotland lost a quarter of its liquid capital. The country was bankrupt.

It makes our present recession look tame in comparison.

At the same time there was a political crisis.

When Queen Elizabeth died in 1603, James VI of Scotland was her closest heir and became James I of England. But the Union of the Crowns meant just that – James was king of both countries but it was not in any other sense a 'United Kingdom'. The Scots and the English were two different peoples with long-standing hostility and suspicion between them. We each had our own parliament, church, legal system and identity. James did his best to merge the kingdoms but faced strong resistance from both sides and made little progress. True union would need to be worked out painfully, step by step, over the next hundred years.

James and his Court moved to London and Edinburgh became a backwater. As usual in this situation, the Stuarts became Anglicized. Scotland now had an absentee king. Many of the Scottish elite looked to the centre of power and soon became more British than Scottish. To make matters worse, James's heirs were bad kings. Religious strife, political upheaval and Civil War split the country. Then, in 1688, the English threw the Stuarts out and the new kings of Great Britain had no link to Scotland. Many Scots felt marginalized.

Scotland was simply too weak, politically and economically, to compete on the world stage.

By 1707 the only solution was full union with England. Scotland depended on trade with England and the Union gave us equal access to the English market and the colonies. We also got capital investment and compensation for the losses of Darien. In return, England got a united British parliament and agreement on the royal succession. The other important concession was that the Scottish kirk and legal system stayed independent and that would prove vital to preserving the Scottish identity.

Critics scorned that Scotland *was bought and sold for English gold.*[472] In one sense that is true because the Union was indeed all about money. And of course there were powerful men – on all sides – who looked after their own interests and got power and wealth in the deal. So what is new? That is politics and just as true today. It may be that many ordinary Scots were instinctively against the Union, but their over-riding interest was to improve their own financial straits. *It's the economy, stupid.* Again, what's new? Harsh economic reality left the Scots little choice.

But this did leave the door open for the myth that *we wus betrayed!* Like Germany after WWI, that myth let us hide from uncomfortable truths. And the myth still lingers on.

The Jacobites have a hallowed place in Scottish culture and everyone knows about *Bonnie Prince Charlie,* yet it is difficult to know just how strong the movement really was. The bare bones are simple. It was an attempt to restore the Stuart kings to the thrones of Scotland and England, with two main Risings in 1715 and 1745. But there were also strands of anti-Union, anti-

English, pro-Catholic and party politics. It certainly got most support in parts of the Highlands with their clan structure, loyalty to a Scottish king and deep-rooted suspicion of Lowland and English governments.

The Risings never had much support in the Lowlands or England or any real chance of success. In your dreams, laddie! Many Scots, like the Campbells of Breadalbane, were hard-headed enough to choose the winning side.

The Jacobite dream died with two thousand Highlanders at Culloden on 16 April 1746. This was the last civil war in Britain, the last pitched battle on British soil, and the last heroic Highland charge against the disciplined firepower of the British army. It was all over in an hour and it was a massacre.

The aftermath was devastating for the Highlands. The Duke of Cumberland, King George II's son, took a harsh revenge on what he saw as treason and went down in history as *Butcher Cumberland*. His forces cut down fleeing Jacobites and slew the wounded. They rounded up suspects and many were executed, died in captivity or deported. They burned houses and drove off cattle, with echoes of the old *devastatio*. The lands of the defeated clan chiefs were forfeit to the Crown.

It was a clear victory for the state but a shameful episode. No British regiment has Culloden on its battle honours.

Once the sound and fury settled, the government pacified the Highlands with roads and garrisons and law and order. It passed Disarming Acts *for the more effectual disarming of the Highlands in Scotland and for more effectually securing the Peace of the said Highlands.*

But it also set out to destroy Gaelic culture. The Acts limited the power of the Highland chiefs and outlawed the wearing of 'Highland Clothes'. *No Man or Boy, within that part of Great Britain called Scotland, other than such as shall be employed as Officers and Soldiers in His Majesty's Forces, shall, on any Pretence whatsoever, wear or put on the Clothes commonly called Highland Clothes, that is to say the Plaid, Philebeg or little Kilt, Trews, Shoulder Belts, or any Part whatsoever of what peculiarly belongs to the Highland Garb; and that no Tartan, or party-coloured Plaid or Stuff shall be used for Great Coats, or for Upper Coats.*[473] The penalty was six months imprisonment for a first offence and seven years transportation on a second conviction.

The Society for the Propagation of Christian Knowledge took a more subtle approach. The SPCK was set up by a group of Lowland gentry who wanted to address the level of illiteracy, ignorance and superstition in the Highlands and make the Highlanders more godly and industrious. Their solution was to set up schools to provide reading, writing, arithmetic and religious instruction. The SPCK was soon one of the main providers of schooling in the Highlands and at its peak had 189 schools and 13,000 pupils. It set out to Anglicize the next generation and banned the use of Gaelic in its schools. I spoke to one old man not long ago who remembered being rapped over the knuckles at school when he failed to speak English.

The government had one more stroke of genius. What do you do with barbarians in your midst? How do you civilize them without waiting for the next generation to grow up? At the time of Culloden there was still a deep divide between Highlands and Lowlands. Most Brits, including Lowland Scots, thought of the Highlanders as barbarians to be feared and despised. Ten years later the British Army began to raise Highland regiments. William Pitt, the Prime Minister, would later claim the credit. *I sought for merit wherever it was to be found. It is my boast that I was the first minister who looked for it, and found it, in the mountains of the North. I called it forth, and drew into your service a hardy and intrepid race of men.*[474]

To the Highlanders, it was the best job opportunity open at the time and a chance to join the winning side.

The government and the army were more cold-blooded. James Wolf had fought at Culloden as a junior officer and a few years later wrote to a friend. *I should imagine that two or three independent Highland companies might be of use. They are hardy, intrepid, accustomed to a rough country, and no great mischief if they fall. How can you better employ a secret enemy than by making his end conducive to the common good?*[475] Ten years later, his Highlanders led him to victory on the Heights of Abraham at Quebec and won Canada for the British Empire.

Within a decade, the Highlanders went from bogeymen to heroes of the British Empire. They were now *The Fighting Scots* and *Scotland the Brave*. The very qualities that used to be condemned were now to be admired.

Sir John Sinclair, who compiled the first Statistical Account of Scotland in 1791, caught the mood to perfection. The Highlander - - - *has felt from his early youth all the privations to which he can be exposed in almost any circumstances of war. He has been accustomed to scanty fare, to rude and often wet clothing, to cold and damp houses, to sleep often in the open air or in the most uncomfortable beds, to cross dangerous rivers, to march a number of miles without stopping and with but little nourishment, and to be perpetually exposed to the attacks of a stormy atmosphere. A warrior thus trained suffers no inconvenience from what others would consider to be the greatest possible hardships, and has an evident superiority over the native of a delicious climate, bred to every indulgence of food, dress and habitation and who is unaccustomed to marching and fatigue.*[476]

The Highland regiments were in some of the most intense fighting at Waterloo. As Wellington said, *I don't know what effect these men will have on the enemy, but by God they terrify me.*[477]

They were *the thin red line* at Balaclava in the Crimean War. The 93rd Highland Regiment were all that stood between a Russian cavalry charge and the British camp. They did not have enough men to form up four deep or in the traditional square, so Sir Colin Campbell – no relation - broke the rules and formed them up two deep. '*There is no retreat from here, men. You must die where you stand.*' Legend says that his aide replied: *Aye, Sir Colin. If needs be, we'll do just that.* The 93rd fired three volleys and the charge faltered. The Russians might still have overcome the line but their commander thought this thin screen could only be a diversion so he withdrew. *The thin red line* became a figure of speech.

That tradition continued into the twentieth century. In WWI, Scotland lost nearly 150,000 men, one in ten of all the young men in the country. That was 3.1% of the total population compared with England's 2.2%, which may not seem very different but meant that Scotland had an extra 45,000 dead. Killin lost 28 men.

By the mid-eighteenth century, Scotland was starting to reap the commercial and economic benefits of the Union. Scots found jobs running the colonies and the Empire, and some made fortunes in the process. Others played major roles in founding the new nations of America, Canada, Australia and New Zealand.

Scotland was also recovering intellectually. The holy trinity of the Scottish Kirk, schools and legal system was vital in preserving a distinct Scottish identity, even as the Kirk became more moderate and anglophile.

The Scottish Enlightenment is one of the most unexpected episodes in our history. Despite some claims, Scots did **not** *invent the modern world,*[478] but they did punch way above their weight. David Hume was one of the leading philosophers of his and any other age. Adam Smith was the father of economics. James Hutton in geology, Joseph Black in chemistry, James Watt's steam engine. Scots law. Medical education. The list goes on and on. Never before or since was there such a galaxy of international talent working within Scotland. Though it is striking that they were nearly all middle-class Lowlanders with nary a Highlander amongst them.

The real surprise is that this intellectual frenzy bloomed so soon after the low point of 1707. Perhaps it was that very social upheaval and crisis of identity that forced Scots to rethink their place in the world. This was a national effort to *improve the common weal.* As we saw in agriculture but on a much broader scale, the emphasis was on *improvement* and the common good or well-being. The result was a flowering of original thought about man and his place in society that led to today's social sciences. Scotland could hold her head up high again.

Rabbie Burns, our national bard, set the Enlightenment to verse. He began life as an Ayrshire farmer and was an early Romantic who glorified Nature and opposed the march of 'reason' and 'progress'. His poems could be earthy and dealt with every aspect of life from love and the lassies, to drinking and the church. But he also had more serious thoughts about the state of man and society. After his death, his poems helped to inspire liberalism and socialism. He became an icon of the Scottish diaspora and is still celebrated worldwide in the annual Burn's Supper on 25 January. Even in communist Russia! Burns still seems a good example of what Scots are all about.

A man's a man for a' that

Is there for honest Poverty
That hings his head, and a' that;
The coward slave, we pass him by,
We dare be poor for a' that!
For a' that, an' a' that.
Our toils obscure, and a' that,
The rank is but the guinea's stamp,
The Man's the gowd for a' that.

What though on hamely fare we dine,
Wear hodden grey, and a that;　　　　(*hodden:* homespun
Gie fools their silks, and knaves their wine;　　woollen cloth)
A Man's a Man for a' that:
For a' that, and a' that,
Their tinsel show, and a' that;
The honest man, though e'er sae poor,
Is king o' men for a' that.

Ye see yon birkie, ca'd a lord,　　(*birkie:* smart young fellow)
Wha struts, an' stares, an' a' that;
Though hundreds worship at his word,
He's but a coof for a' that　　(*coof:* fool, dull-witted fellow)
For a' that, an' a' that,
His riband, star, and a' that:
The man o' independent mind
He looks and laughs at a' that.

A prince can mak a belted knight,
A marquis, duke, an' a' that;
But an honest man's aboon his might,
Guid faith, he mauna fa' that!   (*maunna:* must)
For a' that, an' a' that,
Their dignities and a' that;
The pith o' sense, and pride o' worth,
Are higher rank than a' that.

Then let us pray that come it may,
As come it will for a' that,
That Sense and Worth, o'er a' the earth,
Shall bear the gree, an' a' that.   (*gree:* degree, social rank)
For a' that, and a' that,
It's coming yet for a' that,
That Man to Man, the world o'er,
Shall brothers be for a' that.

The Industrial Revolution gave us a more practical boost. Coal mining, iron foundries and expertise in heavy engineering made Scotland *The Workshop of the World.* At its peak, Clydeside built more ships than the rest of the world put together. A quarter of the world's railway engines were made in works around Glasgow. Scottish engineers kept the world going. Even the Starship Enterprise had its *Scotty.*

Meantime, the myth grew stronger.

Some ancient Celtic literature would help to re-create our national identity, so could there be a Celtic Homer to proclaim our Gaelic heritage? How about a Scottish rival to Shakespeare? We needed an epic, melancholic and sublime, primitive but not savage, but not too civilized either. Like Homer, but in Gaelic. Sadly, there was very little old Scottish or Gaelic literature.

Then James MacPherson, a young schoolmaster from Ruthven near Kingussie, struck gold in 1759. Out in the wilds of the Highlands and Islands, he discovered fragments of the epic poems of Celtic Scotland. There was more to follow. In 1761 he published *Fingal,* an epic poem in six books written by Ossian son of Fingal.

It begins: *Cuthullin sat by Tura's wall, by the tree of the rustling sound. His spear leaned against the rock. His shield lay on the grass by his side. Amid his thoughts of mighty Cairbar, a hero slain by the chief in war; the scout of ocean comes, Moran the son of Fithil! "Arise," said the youth, "Cuthullin, arise. - - -"* [479]

It was all the fondest Scottish heart could desire. This was the stuff of legend from out of the mists of time. In MacPherson's own words, the poem was *truly epic*. It was *beautiful in simplicity but grand in the sublime*. Above all, it was a heroic tale about the noblest of noble savages. No crude forbears here, but high-minded, sensitive and chivalrous heroes. And MacPherson had translated it into rhythmic, biblical prose.

Fingal was a triumph in Edinburgh, London and across Europe. It was fodder to the Romantic Movement. But it also cast a whole new light on the literature, history and morals of ancient Scotland. Scotland could stand proud alongside ancient Greece.

Alas, *Fingal* was a forgery. At first it fooled nearly everyone, even David Hume. Only a few, like the worldly Samuel Johnson, were more sceptical. Hume soon saw the error of his ways and would not now believe it *though fifty bare-arsed Highlanders should swear on it*. MacPherson never did produce the Gaelic original of his 'translation' and in later life refused to discuss Ossian. The literary debate raged on, though *in Scotland their authenticity was never called in question. - - - The consenting silence of the whole country was, to every unprejudiced person, the strongest proof.* [480]

Yet whatever the evidence, Ossian lived on in legend. Even non-Celtic Lowlanders were converted. English critics might remain heretics but European Romantics were bowled over. Fingal was the prototype of the noble savage whose culture was being trampled under by the march of 'progress'. Even Napoleon was an Ossian fan, though that does seem a bit of a paradox.

Tales of the magical giant Fingal still abound across the Highlands. Some say the name Killin comes from *Cil Fhinn* or

'Cell of Fingal'. Fingal's stone behind the park in Killin marks his burial place.[481]

After the Disarming Acts were repealed in 1782, there was a revival of interest in Gaelic culture. The first Highland Society was formed in London, of all places. The Highland Society of Scotland began in Edinburgh in 1784 with broad aims. *The improvement of the Highlands and Islands of Scotland and the conditions of their inhabitants, an enquiry into the means of their improvement by establishing towns and villages – facilitating communications by roads and bridges – advancing agriculture – extending fisheries – introducing useful trades and manufactures, and the preservation of the language, poetry and music of the Highlands.*[482] By 1834 it became the Royal Agricultural Society of Scotland, which best reflects its origins and focus. Today's Gaelic Societies came much later with a much more limited goal. They simply wanted *to promote the Gaelic language and culture, and to cultivate the language, poetry and music of the Scottish Highlands.* [483]

No one did more to re-invent Scotland than Sir Walter Scott. *Scott-land* became a one word London joke. He had several strings to his bow.

Scott's *The Lady of the Lake* is Scotland's true epic poem.[484] The plot is based on the real historical struggle between King James V and the powerful Douglas family. But the poem is pure romance, with noble heroes, fair maidens, tragedy and triumph. It sold 25,000 copies within eight months of publication in 1810 and made Scott's reputation across the world.

Scott set *The Lady of the Lake* on Loch Katrine in the Trossachs, just south of Breadalbane. Overnight, he transformed dark, forbidding wilderness into magnificent mountain scenery. Painters like Horatio McCulloch made the mountains even grander and more spectacular. The Trossachs became a mecca for tourists. Scott did not invent tourism but he did unleash it on the Highlands.

To digress for a moment, the *Hymn to the Virgin* in *The Lady of the Lake* inspired Ave Maria.

Ave Maria! Maiden mild!
Listen to a maiden's prayer!
Thou canst hear though from the wild,
Thou canst save amid despair.
Safe may we sleep beneath thy care,
though banished, outcast, and reviled –
Maiden, hear a maiden's prayer!
Mother, hear a suppliant child!

The Lady of the Lake also provided the inspiration for the US Presidential Anthem.
Hail to the chief who in triumph advances - - -
Soldier, rest! thy warfare o'er,
Sleep the sleep that knows not breaking,
Dream of battled fields no more,
Days of danger, nights of waking - - -
Americans, of course, made up their own verses though they rarely sing them today. But Scott's title survives.

Scott invented the historical novel. *Waverley* was set in the Rising of 1745 but Scott recast the Jacobites as a noble, lost cause. He created an old-fashioned, charming and seductive vision of Scotland with all threat removed. There was a great cast of players: magnificent Highland scenery, ancient castles, dashing heroes, evil villains, a choice of dark and fair damsels, lost loves and self-sacrifice to duty. Scott made the Highlands and the Highlander irresistibly romantic – like young Lochinvar, *so faithful in love and dauntless in war.*[485]

Scott also invented our modern idea of Highland Dress. Despite what many people chose to believe, this was not the ancient dress of Scotland. Early travellers describe a long shirt and a plaid. Celtic weavers used local plants to dye their cloth, and some of this was striped or occasionally checked, but the overall effect was usually brown or russet. Only the better off could afford garments woven in brighter colours.

The first mention of 'tartan' was in 1538 when James V bought *three ells of Helan Tartans* for his queen. In the seventeenth century, a belt round the waist made the 'belted plaid' but it was not until the 1720s that it was called the 'kilt'. And it was only in the 1730s that the modern *philibeg* or 'short kilt' was invented. The lower part was now a separate garment, held up by a belt round the waist and with sewn pleats. This was a much more practical garment for daily life and work, but it was invented by an Englishman for his Scottish workers!

By the time of Culloden, many Highlanders wore a variety of 'tartan' checks and stripes but there were no fixed patterns or anything like the clan tartans we know today.[486]

Even while the kilt was banned at home, the Highland regiments made the kilt standard wear and developed the idea of each regiment having its own tartan. The Black Watch got the first 'government tartan' and other regiments added bands or checks of different colours. As the fame of Highland soldiers grew, the tartan kilt became the dress of heroes - *the ladies from hell*.

There had been various forms of bagpipes throughout Europe for more than a thousand years. They were well established in the Highlands by the mid-sixteenth century, when the MacCrimmon family of pipers wrote the first *piobroch*. But it was the Highland regiments who made the 'Great Highland Bagpipe' famous. If you have ever faced them at close quarters, you know that they are without equal as instruments of war. The skirl o' the pipes led the Highlanders into battle and struck terror in their foes. It was not only on parade and at the Edinburgh Military Tattoo. Pipers went over the top in the trenches of WWI and played on the Normandy beaches in WWII.

The climax came when Scott stage-managed King George IV's visit to Scotland in 1822. What an opportunity to invent a splendid pageant in which ancient Scotland would be reborn! Somehow, he persuaded the portly and unpopular Hanoverian king that he was not only a Stuart prince but also a Highlander. Scott and his cronies created a special outfit for the king in his very own bright red tartan that is still known as Royal Stewart. The kilt was belted as tight as possible round the royal waist with the aid of a whalebone corset. The outfit was festooned with gold buckles and Scottish gems and hung with gold chains, dirk, sword and pistols. The elderly king wore his usual red wig, rouge and face powder, and was crowned with a Glengarry bonnet and eagle feathers. And to round it off, a pair of pink tights to keep the royal bum warm! So the king appeared to a bemused Edinburgh society who must have struggled to keep their faces straight. God alone knows what a real Highlander in Glen Lochay would have made of it. But we can guess.

Scott invited all the clan chiefs and their followers to the Gathering. Only five turned up but one of them was the Earl of Breadalbane!

In preparation for the visit, Scott also encouraged the clans to *sort out their tartans*. The firm of William Wilson & Son of Bannockburn already supplied the Army and had the idea of regimental tartans. With the Highland Society of Edinburgh, they soon made up a catalogue of 'authentic' tartans for each clan. Scotland grew more tartan by the minute. An industry was born. Today, whatever your name and whether it is Highland or Lowland or even English or American, there is a tartan for you.

Perhaps that episode sums it up. Scott-land.

Yet Scott knew exactly what he was doing. It was all so fantastical that it dispelled reality and short-circuited criticism. Everyone had to play the game, for by this stage the image *is* the truth and all that counts is impact. *Ken ye not weel that 'tis aw a fable?*

Scott replaced the divide between Highlands and Lowlands with a romantic view of Scotland, far removed from the bleak industrial towns of the Lowlands or the problems of land use in the Highlands. He portrayed magnificent Highland scenery and air-brushed out any damp reality. He created a synthetic Scotsman, more Highland than Lowland, with misty roots in an ancient Celtic past. He re-branded Scotland and marketed it to the world, and his vision has coloured the world's perception ever since. He was the greatest spin-doctor Scotland ever had.

The final accolade came with the Royal Seal of Approval.

Queen Victoria fell in love with the Highlands and Prince Albert built her a fairy tale castle at Balmoral, which she called *our own dear paradise*. The Royal Family have used it as a holiday home ever since. Some cottage!

The Highlands became a playground for the rich and powerful – the *huntin, shootin, fishing set.*

Then the Scottish diaspora exported Celtic culture and myth around the globe. Perhaps three or four million Scots have emigrated over the past three hundred years, but few peoples have kept such strong emotional roots to their native land. There are now thirty to forty million people around the world who claim Scottish descent. There are almost as many Scottish Americans in the US as there are Scots in Scotland. Scottish Canadians are the third largest ethnic group in Canada. Half a million Scots went to Australia. Twenty per cent of the settlers in New Zealand came from Scotland.

In real life, most people who left the Highlands moved to towns in the Lowlands or in England. Most emigrants left from the Lowlands. Only a few thousands were direct victims of the worst of the Clearances.

But roots are more about myth than reality, and the myths are all about the Highland scenery, people and culture. And now they had new myths to add about the Clearances.

The trouble is that Scott was too successful. He cast a spell and the world fell in love with his image of Scotland. *Scotland is not a place; it is a state of mind.*[487] Scott-land superseded history. Scott neutered Scotland and created a vacuum in Scottish consciousness – in love with an imaginary past and immune to the future. His vision was so powerful that it was hard to escape. It was a blessing, a crutch and a curse, all rolled into one.

Even today there are some dreamers – and politicians - who ply that myth. Yet the rest of us cannot live in dreamland. Scotland must overcome that image if it is going to move on.

It may help if we remember that Scott did the same for medieval England. He coined the term 'Wars of the Roses'. He created the modern version of Robin Hood as *King of outlaws and prince of good fellows.* He invented the story about Sir Walter Raleigh laying down his cloak for Elizabeth I.

Scott was *as slippery as a baggie* (minnow) *up a Border burn.* He was a real Scotchman.

And, anyway, the real story of Dalgirdy is more fascinating than any myth. Whatever Scott said, Glen Lochay had to get on with the real world.

21. THE HYDRO
Power from the glens

The Industrial Revolution hit Glen Lochay, with a bang, in 1953 when the Hydro came to Breadalbane. 'The Scheme' had a lasting impact on the glen, for better and worse, and still gives rise to heated local feelings.

Scotland has 85% of Britain's hydro-power. The first small public supply was at Loch Ness, way back in 1890. But it was only after WWII that the electricity industry was nationalized and the North of Scotland Hydro Electric Board began large-scale work. Over twenty years, the Board built schemes across the Highlands that still supply 12% of Scotland's electricity.

The Breadalbane Hydro Electric Scheme covers 200 square miles of West Perthshire. The Killin Section has a catchment of 47 square miles across Glens Dochart, Lochay and Lyon. High rain-fall makes up for the small area. It has three dams and three power stations and produces 196 million units of electricity a year, which is enough to power 50,000 homes.

There were mixed feelings about the coming of the Hydro. Many landowners wanted to keep their estates as they were. Then, as now, there were fears about the impact on tourism. There were even fears this might be the start of industry moving into the Highlands, which might end the Highland way of life.

On the other hand, it brought progress and opportunity. It tapped the natural resources of the area and brought electricity to every house in Killin and Glen Lochay.

Captain Stroyan of Boreland fought hard to protect the glen in the face of compulsory purchase. He got the Lochay power station set back into the hillside and built of local stone. The pipeline coming down to the power station was hidden in the trees and buried above and below the treeline. Compare that with the pipe across the glen at Kennock, an eyesore because *no one bothered*. He also managed to save the Allt Ghaordiadh and

Allt Lebhain, which are two of the largest burns to remain 'un-captured'. Lucky for Dalgirdy!

The Scheme brought an abrupt end to the peace and solitude of Killin and the surrounding glens. Suddenly, for a few years, the area became a major construction site.

The Killin Section is ingenious because it works between the three glens and re-uses the same water several times.

Most of the burns have small concrete dams that feed water into the pipe system. These intakes are quite unobtrusive, except that there is often little flow left in the burns below them. The first branch gathers water from the burns on the north side of Glen Dochart and brings it through a tunnel under the mountain to Glen Lochay, opposite Dalgirdy. It then runs underground along the hillside to Kennock, where it joins a branch coming down the glen. These two branches gather water from the whole of the south side of upper Glen Lochay. A 6½-foot diameter pipe then carries the water down the hillside, across the glen and back up the other side, like a huge, upside-down siphon. Another branch collects the north side of the glen above Kennock. All of this water goes through a tunnel under the mountain to the Lubreoch dam in Glen Lyon. This is a massive buttress dam, 1740 feet long and 130 feet high, that raised the level of Loch Lyon by 77 feet. It forms the main storage reservoir in the scheme and supplies water to the Lubreoch power station that sits beneath the dam.

Water coming out of that power station flows three miles down the River Lyon to the Stronuich dam. This is a smaller dam that simply forms a head-pond. Beside it, the Cashlie power station gets water through a tunnel from another dam high in the hills above Glen Lyon. Water coming out of Cashlie also goes into the head-pond.

From the head-pond, water comes through a 4½-mile long, 13-foot diameter, concrete-lined tunnel under Meall Ghaordie back to Glen Lochay. It comes out on the hillside above the Lochay power station with an operating head of 592 feet. This is the largest power station in the Breadalbane Scheme and can produce 47 megawatts. At last, with all its energy used, the water discharges into the River Lochay in the lower glen.

At first, the Lochay power station was the control centre for the other stations. Since 1989 the entire scheme has been under remote control from an operations centre in Perth and the power stations are unmanned.

Electricity from the power stations goes by overhead lines to the Killin switching station at the foot of Glen Lochay and from there feeds into the Highland Grid.

The Scheme was a massive civil engineering project. As well as the main dams and power stations, they had to build hundreds of water intakes, 14½ miles of tunnels and 7 miles of pipe aqueducts. They had to improve the road up Glen Lochay, and build a new Hill Road from Kenknock across to Glen Lyon, 18 miles of access roads and dozens of bridges.

Access for the whole Killin Section was via Glen Lochay, which is still better than the long way round and up Glen Lyon. Before then, the only road up Glen Lochay was the narrow, twisting, up-and-down road on the north side of the glen from the Bridge of Lochay Tollhouse. The section through the Coilig was particularly difficult. So before the Hydro could start construction they had to improve the road.

Their first step was to build two miles of new road on the flat ground up the south side of Glen Lochay. They linked this to the old road by a new bridge over the river, where the Lochay power station stands today. During that phase, only light traffic was allowed on the old north road past Boreland Lodge. When the new south road was ready, all construction traffic had to go that way. That meant a lot of pressure to complete it on schedule in six months.

Then they upgraded the old Glen Lochay road from the power station to above Kenknock. Most of it follows the line of the old road, except for a minor re-alignment at Dalgirdy. They blasted better access through the Coilig. They repaired the old bridges at Duncroisk, Allt Lebhain and Kenknock and built new concrete bridges on top of them. You can still see the old bridges if you climb down beneath. They built a couple of new concrete bridges, one of which was at Dalgirdy. We have already seen that the old Dalgirdy bridge is the only one that remains in its original state because the new road and bridge took a more direct line. This lost the corner of the Bridge bothy and ten yards from Dalgirdy cottage front garden.

They replaced the old wooden bridge across the Lochay at Innischoarach with a new concrete bridge. You can still see the old postholes in the rock beside the new bridge. They also built a new bridge over the Lochay at Kenknock. These led to new access roads that shepherds, stalkers and hillwalkers still use to get on to the hills.

The Hill Road ran from Kenknock across the Lairig nan Lunn to Glen Lyon. This was five miles of completely new road across bare hillside up to fifteen hundred feet and they had to work in the most awful weather conditions. It follows the line first drawn way back in 1811 and was a major construction project in itself. Telford would have been proud!

When the Scheme finished, the Local Authority took over the Glen Lochay road. But the Hill Road is still a private road owned jointly by Scottish Hydro and the local estate. It was padlocked until the 1980s but then opened to the public. Since the estate changed hands a few years ago there have been further problems with access.

The dams in the Breadalbane Scheme provide a graphic record of the speed of engineering advances at that time. Stronuich is a 'solid gravity dam'. This is the simplest kind of dam, built of rock and concrete and simply relying on its weight to hold it in place. Lubreoch is a 'massive buttress type dam'. Buttresses made it stronger and meant that it took less rock and concrete, just like a steel girder is stronger than the same amount of steel in a solid bar. The first buttress dam in 1950, the Lawers dam in 1956, and the Lubreoch dam in 1958 show how quickly design improved. By Lubreoch, better buttress design and pre-cast arch rings made construction simpler and faster. Adding power station ash to the concrete mix used less cement. Overall, they cut unit costs by 60% from the old solid gravity dam.

The tunnels were a vital part of the scheme. The *average* speed of tunnel driving was three-quarters of a mile per month and at one point they set a world record of 557 feet in seven days. They completed the tunnels nine months ahead of schedule.

The Lochay Pipeline was built by the North British Locomotive Company in Glasgow because it was one of the few companies able to build such large pipe at that time. Boyhood memories linger of large sections of pipe crawling through Killin on trailers.

The Scheme brought much-needed jobs and a great economic boost to the area in post-war times. Local hotels, shops and services never had it so good. There was not an empty house or bed in the village. It also brought a small number of permanent jobs.

At its height, the Scheme employed between two and three thousand men. Hydro contracts said that *preference shall be given to the employment of Scotsmen.* In practice, men came from all over because a skilled man could make £35 a week at a time when local estate workers only got £3-4. But there was rapid turnover. Some men only came for a week and left as soon as they were issued with their new rubber boots. There were a lot of wild Irish, former prisoners of war and 'DPs' – displaced persons left over from the war. Many of them could only sign their name with a cross. Poles and eastern Europeans became known as 'Tunnel Tigers' because of the risks they took to earn big bonuses. One foreman put a squad of Irish on the day shift and Poles on the night shift so they would compete against each other.

It was hard and dangerous work and there was scant attention to site safety. Blasting was risky and it was easy to misjudge how much dynamite to use. Many a time 'just a pop' sent large chunks of rock flying through the air and into someone's roof. Poor air conditions in the tunnels caused chest problems. There are no full accident statistics but the Hydro itself admits that one camp of 1,000 men had 22 deaths in a year. That is the benefit of modern Health & Safety, for all that we complain about it today.

When you drive up the glen today it is difficult to imagine how busy it was. The men worked 12-hour shifts and work went on 24 hours a day, 7 days a week, 52 weeks a year. Goods trains brought a constant stream of material and supplies into Killin and convoys of lorries ferried it up the glens. They needed steel, gravel, sand and cement. They dug new quarries in the hills and moved thousands of tons of rock to the sites. There were bulldozers, diggers, dumpers, mobile cranes, earth-moving and drilling machinery. Buses moved the men from camps to sites and back again. Engineers and surveyors rushed around in Land Rovers. It was so busy they needed traffic rules on the single-track road, with loaded lorries and uphill traffic getting the right of way, though you did not argue the toss with a big lorry! Floodlights lit up the camps and worksites at night. The noise was never-ending, with engines, machinery and blasting. Work continued rain or shine, snow or ice, gale or storm. In winter, snowploughs kept the roads open so that work could go on. The sheep must have stood bemused by it all.

Engineers and their families lived in and around the village of Killin. The men lived in camps of up to a thousand men at Duncroisk and Kenknock. These were like WWII military camps with pre-fabricated Nissan huts, a few of which still stand at Duncroisk. They were a hive of activity. They had dormitories, kitchens, dining and common rooms, a beer licence and even a hospital. They had their own water supply and sewage systems, though they were not up to modern standards and in summer the stench could be awful. They were tough places to live with basic food and accommodation and few facilities. Doctor Mairi's over-riding memory of the camps is *mud, mud and more mud.*

There was little transport so the men had to make their own entertainment. And they were a rough lot who believed that if they worked hard they should also play hard. They had nothing to spend their money on, so they drank and gambled and fights were common. It was like the Wild West all over again. Police and doctors kept busy.

One incident catches the spirit of the times. For some crazy reason, one of the local estate owners brought his ocean-going yacht up to Loch Lyon so that he could steam up and down. In a loch only two miles long! Within a week, some Irish navvies 'borrowed' the yacht. There must have been great hilarity as the local gillies chased them up and down the loch in wee boats with outboard motors. They could not board the yacht but there was no escape and when the navvies eventually ran dry they had to surrender. The gillies gave them a choice - either the police or imprisonment in the laird's wine cellar – without the wine! They did not want the police, so they spent a week on bread and water in the cellar. And presumably lost a week's wages. Ian Stewart swears it is true!

It was reminiscent of the Klondike during the gold rush.

But the social life of the village got a boost like it never had before. There were dances on Friday nights and cinema shows in the village hall on Saturdays. The pubs were always full of men in their hydro uniform of donkey jackets and turned-down rubber boots. The village had never seen so much money. And Judy Bayley still gets a big grin on her face when she says it was paradise for a young girl with so many single men around!

Some locals objected to the noise of the 'Schemies' disturbing the peace. And sometimes they had cause. One night a drunken party wheeled their pal up and down the Main Street in a pram, wearing only a nappy and drinking his whisky from a baby's bottle.

But most of the old-timers remember it as a time of fun and laughter. Many incomers married local girls and some are still here today. And there were so many pregnancies in Glen Lyon that it became known as the 'Glen Sickness'.

By its very nature, the Hydro had a great and lasting impact on the River Lochay. It takes water from the upper Lochay, diverts it through to Glen Lyon, and then sends even more water back through to the lower Lochay. The Board will not release any official figures, but most of the locals agree that the flow of water in the upper Lochay is only about one-third or one-half what it was before. That makes it one of the most heavily extracted rivers in Scotland. Only the River Garry is worse, and you can see its empty bed as you drive north on the A9.

However, during summer drought the Hydro limit the amount of water they extract. And even when the turbines are not running they release 'compensation water' into the lower Lochay, so the Hydro does try to maintain a minimum natural flow. June 2010 was the driest summer in living memory and the water in the Lochay was the lowest I have ever seen it. Yet the entire Killin Section was closed down for maintenance and we couldn't blame them. So it is probably true that the Hydro does not have much impact during drought conditions. At the other extreme, when the river is in spate the Hydro only has the capacity to take about 5% of the flow. So the main impact is on the *average* flow, particularly during the salmon run.

The official Hydro story is that before the Scheme, salmon could not pass the Falls of Lochay at the Coilig, so there were no salmon in the upper glen. Locals swear there were. They even quote Duncan ban Macintyre's *Song to the misty corrie. - - - In the rugged gully is a white-bellied salmon that cometh from the ocean of stormy wave.* Judge Stroyan takes a more careful, judicial view. He accepts that a few salmon may have managed to get up, but says that the Lochay was *not a sporting river.*

Whatever, as part of the Scheme, the Hydro agreed to open up the River Lochay to make up for the loss of spawning grounds on the River Lyon. They built a fish lift at the Falls of Lochay, which is an ingenious shaft that works like a canal lock. Fish swim in a door at the bottom. Then the door shuts and the shaft fills up with water. The fish rise with the water and swim out a second door at the top into the upper river. Then the top door closes, the bottom door opens, and the shaft empties. And so the cycle repeats. The Hydro also built three fish ladders - below Tullich, just above Dalgirdy and at Kenknock. These are sets of small pools with the water pouring down small steps between them that the fish can easily jump. In the 1980s, there were further efforts to 'seed' the gravel beds in the upper river with salmon eggs.

Today the fish counter at the lift records 100-250 salmon going up the river each year. Despite that, there is no record of any salmon caught in the upper Lochay between 1994 and 2007. At least, not legally! Though there was a tale a few years ago that someone ran over an otter crossing the road with a salmon it had just caught. He swears it is true! And that his son insisted they give otter and salmon a proper burial!!

When the Scheme ended, Glen Lochay tried to return to normal but it would never be the same again. The road to the upper glen was now much improved, giving the locals better access to the wider world and making it easier for the world to come into the glen. But attitudes also changed. Years of living in a construction site made everyone aware of the outside world and its progress like nothing else could. No one could pretend they lived in their own little world any more.

Like it or not, the Hydro propelled the upper glen into the twentieth century.

22. REBUILDING THE COTTAGE

My own wee but 'n ben

Way back in the early 1780s, Duncan McVean Junior *built a good house with stone and lime and made a good room in one end with a chimney therein.*[488] We do not have any more detail from that time. So it was only when we came to rebuild Dalgirdy that we could really see what he had done.

He built the cottage on well-drained moraine, high above the burn. It is a good site that catches the sun, though it is more exposed to the west wind than the old *baile*. The front corner sits on a rock outcrop that appears in the corner of the living room inside. So it really is *built upon rock*.

Despite what Duncan said, he actually built the walls dry-stone of rough local schist. There is no damp-proof course but the stone is non-absorbent so there has never been any problem with rising damp. He only used lime mortar to point the outside of the walls and caulked the inside with a mixture of clay and straw. He left the end walls un-pointed inside the sheds on either end, so air could filter in through the shed on the west end, along the length of the front and back walls, and out the east end. This kept the whole structure free of damp, even when it lay empty. So although the walls seems primitive, they are really quite sophisticated.

The walls were three to four feet thick and because they were built of uncut stone they are quite uneven, which adds greatly to the character. That adds up to an amazing sixty tons of rock! The walls were low and the ceiling less than six feet high. You had to duck your head at the front door, though people were probably shorter in earlier times. The back wall was set into the hillside, so the floor was lower than the ground behind.

This was a cruck house, with the roof supported on two

wooden arches or crucks. Each arch was made of three oak boughs nine to ten inches in diameter, with crude joints pinned together by large wooden pegs. It was all hand-worked and you can see the adze marks. The bases of the crucks were set into the wall about eighteen inches up from the ground to save them from damp, which was standard practice in West Perthshire. The wood now has a beautiful ebony sheen from centuries of smoke.

There was no sawn wood in the roof. Three long fir trunks rested on the gable ends and the crucks to form the ridge. Two-inch diameter branches sloped from the ridge down to the back and front walls. Then there was a layer of turf. The thatch was more than three feet of heather and reeds and bracken. At some later stage, corrugated iron sheeting was added on top of the thatch, but we cannot find any record of when. The earliest 'tin roofs' in this area were in the 1890s. On the other hand, the National Trust reckons that Moirlanich in lower Glen Lochay only got its corrugated iron in 1930. So all we can say is that it was sometime between these dates.

There were two rooms inside – a 'but and ben'. The 'but' is on the right as you go in. It was only 11½ X 12 feet but this was the living room, kitchen and social centre of the house. It had a fireplace and chimney on the end wall, the stonework of which looks original. The fireplace was an enormous hole in the wall, about three feet wide, three feet high and two feet deep. There must have been some kind of stone or grate arrangement for the fire, but no trace remained. But there was still a metal bar projecting from the back wall to hang a pot on. The chimney was simply a tapered hole up the wall, so large you could stand up in it. There was no flue so it did not draw well and, depending on the wind, more smoke came into the room than up the chimney.

By the time we got the cottage, the inside of the walls was roughly pointed with plaster and painted over but we do not know if this was original or added later.

The 'ben' on the left was 10 X 12 feet. When we got the cottage, it had a wooden floor with the joists resting on the bare earth. The walls were lined with wood, made of planks nailed to a simple frame. That was probably the 'good' room where the tenant and his wife slept and entertained their social equals.

The rooms were divided by two wooden partitions about five feet apart. The front door opened into a small hallway that also gave access up to the roof. The small room at the back was only about 5 X 6 feet and opened off the living room. This was originally a 'box bed' that would give at least some privacy.

Again by the time we got the cottage, there was a ceiling made of a few light rafters covered with wooden boards. The space above was less than 30 inches high, with an inch of dirt from the roof. So, at best, it gave little storage space.

All the wooden walls were papered with newspaper and the oldest we found was from 1866, so these walls and ceilings date from at least that time. We do not know whether they were original, but Duncan did say that he had *a good room* so he must have had some kind of partitions.

The two rooms each had a window two feet wide by three feet high with eight small panes of glass. The windows were well-made of hard wood and set back in the thick walls so they were sheltered and it is possible they had lasted more than two hundred years. The box-room at the back had a window two feet high by fifteen inches wide. There was no sign of any window frame, so it may just have been blocked off.

There was a large shed built on to the west end that might have been used for a few animals and for storage. There was a smaller shed on the east end. The stonework looked as if these were both original build, though they now had corrugated iron roofs. Yet the first Ordnance Survey map of 1864 does not seem to show the sheds, so we cannot be sure.[489]

Look back for a moment. The Factor inspected the farms in Glen Lochay in December 1807.

I had the pleasure of spending two nights with the tenants in the upper part of the Glen. That is in the farms of Dalgirdie and Kenknock. I observed while with them that their situations were easy and comfortable, their farm cottages are snug and cosy.[490]

This was luxury compared with anything that went before yet it is hard for us to imagine a family living here with nine children. The 'but' would be pretty full with ten or more crowded round the fire. And they must have slept everywhere! The parents would sleep in the 'ben' with the younger children. They might have made some effort to separate the older boys and girls, so the girls might be in the box bed and the boys on the kitchen floor. Or younger men might slide into the loft space. But even then there must have been three or four in a bed. One way to keep warm on a cold winter's night!

How our perceptions change with time! By 1965 the County Sanitary Department reported that Dalgirdy was *unfit for human habitation.*

DESCRIPTION AND SITUATION: This is a detached single storey stone built cottage with corrugated iron roof, situated on the north side of the Killin/Glenlochay road, at a point approximately 7 miles north-west of Killin.

DEFECTS:

EXTERIOR:

No gutters or downpipes provided; stonework of walls open-jointed; no apparent damp-proof course; no sub-floor ventilators provided.

INTERIOR:

Vestibule: Walls damp

Living Room: Lighting poor (window small); ceiling low; walls damp; wood floor off-level; internal woodwork rotted

Bedroom: Lighting poor (window small); ceiling low; walls damp; wood floor off-level; internal woodwork rotted.

Box room: Lighting poor (window small); ceiling low; walls damp; wood lined walls rotted and holed; window missing.

GENERAL:

There is no bath, wash-hand basin, toilet facilities, cooking facilities, larder or clothes washing facilities provided and the cupboard accommodation is inadequate. Water supply would be obtained from a burn 15 yards distant. There are no mains gas or electricity provided.

SUMMARY:

In respect therefore of the poor lighting, low ceilings and dampness, together with the above mentioned defects and the lack of such adequate and suitably located accommodation and fittings as are necessary to enable the house satisfactorily to fulfil its functions, I am of the opinion that the house known as Dalgirdy, in the Parish of Killin, and at present vacant, is unfit for human habitation and is not capable of being rendered so fit at reasonable expense.[491]

So Perth County Council issued a Demolition Order. Fortunately for us, that was never carried out and the farm went on using the cottage as a store and shelter for the sheep. By the time we got Dalgirdy, it was about to be re-classified as an 'Agricultural Building'. If it had, it would have gone to wreck and ruin. Thirty years ago there was a cottage very like it beside the road over Glen Ogle. Today it is derelict and the roof has fallen in.

We got Dalgirdy in spring 1982. I tried to suggest it would be romantic to keep it as it was but my womenfolk – a wife and three daughters (even the dog is a bitch) – made it clear in no uncertain terms that was not an option. I still have a photo of them washing in the burn but I am not allowed to show it. They were all for character but wanted all mod cons too. So it was rebuild or divorce.

It took three summers and two winters, and the work fell neatly into these blocks. The great advantage was that we did not need to live in it while the work went on. We did it at weekends while I was doing a busy, full-time job. Although we wanted it finished as soon as we could, there was no deadline. And we could pay for it bit-by-bit out of income.

The first summer we stabilized the walls. While we were working, we 'camped out' in the cottage. It really was still snug and cosy with a fire roaring in the grate and the yellow light of an oil lamp. We slept in the two rooms, in sleeping bags and inflatable mattresses on the floor. We got water from the burn and had a gas camping stove in the kitchen. We even had a chemical toilet in the box-room.

Before we could do anything, we had to build a proper runway so that we could get vehicles up to the building. Fortunately, it was only about twenty yards from the road. There was a shallow ditch at the side of the road that we had to pipe and fill in. The local builder had cheap tunnel spoil and dumped a lorry load right where we wanted it, so it was just a matter of spreading it with barrow, shovel and rake, and over the next weeks our car rolled it flat.

The hillside rose about two feet up the back wall and we had to improve the drainage, so we dug it out by hand. We put in a field drain as deep as we could and ran it out to both ends. Then we laid slabs to make a path along the back.

The original lime pointing was crumbling and full of gaps. So we picked out every crack between the stones with a small pick-hammer. It was a tedious, dusty job that the whole family shared. I did not know anything about 'conservation' at that time, so we simply re-pointed it with a strong cement mix. But we did begin to learn about plasticizers and bonding agents to make the cement workable and help it stick to the stone. With the kind of stone and build that we had, it all worked well. Looking back, I am sure historic purists would be horrified!

We stripped out the rotten wooden floor and lining and had a bonfire. We dug out the loose earth and debris and levelled it off. And we dug about a ton of sheep shit out of the big shed. Then we got a big cement mixer truck to bring a load of concrete. It was able to drive up our new runway, stick its cement chute in the front door, and deposit the concrete straight into the house where we needed it. The rest went into the big shed. We used large, heavy-duty polythene sheets for a damp course. The whole family had great fun trampling the concrete down in rubber boots and we smoothed it off as best we could before beating a hasty retreat. But when we went up the next weekend it was all dried out and we had proper concrete floors.

We made a solid new front door and doors for the sheds.

We replaced broken glass and made shutters, but we were able to save the original windows. And we made a new window for the box-room.

The building was weather-tight and secure for the winter. We had two good sheds that we could use as stores and even to bivvy in. All was ready to start real building work next spring. And we left it unfenced on the open hillside so that the sheep would continue to cut the grass for us.

The first winter was planning.

You cannot just build where and what you want in Scotland. There are Planning Laws and Building Regulations and the Local Authority has a Planning Department to enforce them. So the first step was to get a copy of the Regulations and spend hours trying to understand them. Then find out about the Planning Department in Stirling and how it worked.

The immediate problem was that the planning staff could not give advice but only rulings. It took a while to find the way round this. What they could do was advise you what ruling they were likely to make on a proposal, though of course you could not quote them or hold them to it! So I would plan what I wanted to do and ask if that was likely to be acceptable. And if they said no, they might even explain why not, and that might lead to a discussion of the interpretation (never loopholes!) of that law or regulation. I spent a lot of time that winter buying pints of beer in the local pub after the Department closed at 5p.m.

There was no way that we 'townies' would ever get planning permission to build a holiday house in a place like Glen Lochay. Never. And there was no appeal. So, forget it.

But there is often more than one way to skin a cat. The critical point was that Dalgirdy was still on the Local Authority's list as a house, even if it was uninhabitable. If it had been downgraded to an Agricultural Building we could not have changed it back to a house without planning permission. If it had become a Listed Building of historic interest then we could not have changed it in any way but only preserved it as a museum. But if we were simply bringing an existing house up to habitable standard that would not need planning permission. Bingo!

So we could 'renovate' the building, provided it was more or less the same size and shape and appearance. We could not extend or enlarge it. So we should keep the original walls, which we wanted to do anyway. We could completely replace the roof and even gain a few extra inches in height. We could not build windows out of the roof, but we could put in flat windows because they did not need planning permission. Inside, there were few restrictions. So we could just about demolish and rebuild the cottage, so long as we did not use these words and the end result matched the original.

The Building Regulations were much more straightforward. They were simply about building standards that made a house fit for human habitation. There would be no judgement on our plans. Provided we stuck to the Regulations, we would get a Building Warrant without question.

The old Demolition Order showed the main problems. The ceiling was too low, the windows too small, and the lighting insufficient for modern standards. So we raised the ceiling to seven feet six inches. We wanted to keep the small front windows because they were a part of the character of the cottage and large modern windows would ruin its appearance. It took a while to think of the answer. The key point was that the new ceiling was about 18 inches above the top of the old back wall. So we could put long, flat windows into the roof to let more light into the rooms from behind. These were at the back, so did not change the appearance of the building from the front. And we already knew that flat roof windows did not need planning permission.

We even managed to squeeze in two small attic bedrooms. The old loft was very low but the original roof timbers and thatch were very thick. Even after we raised the ceiling, the new attic was five foot nine inches high at the peak. The sizes did not meet the Regulations to be habitable rooms but if we called them storage spaces that would be OK!

Then it was just a matter of measurement and looking up the tables in the Regulations. For example, a 12½-foot span needs eight-by-two inch joists with eighteen-inch spacing. We got a student architect to draw up professional plans and put them into the Planning Department with the small fee. And, lo and behold, we had our Building Warrant!

The other thing we must not forget was £500,000 personal injury insurance to cover everyone working on the site. Oh, and I got my tetanus boosters up to date.

The second summer we rebuilt the roof.

First we had to demolish the old roof. Great fun! We wanted to start as early in the season as possible, so we planned it for Easter weekend and we were lucky with the weather. It was unskilled but heavy work that needed a lot of hands, so we hired a group of Boy Scouts and gave a donation to their funds. My old Scout Troop still had one of the Hydro huts down at Duncroisk and that made a good base for us all to stay.

The corrugated iron roofing slid off in two great halves. We got photos of the old thatched roof as it must have looked in its early days. Then we pulled off great forkfuls and rakings of thatch and turf, that seemed to be more dirt and dust than straw. We had great piles of it all around and it burned with clouds of smoke drifting down the glen. Just like it must have been when Montrose's army burned Dalgirdy in 1645.

And then the back wall came tumbling down. Remember these were dry-stone walls and only our cement pointing held the outside face. The problem is that such walls depend on the roof resting on them to weigh them down and lock the stones in place. Take off the roof and the walls begin to crumble.

Then the skies opened and the rain poured down. Soon, our good concrete floor was an inch deep in filthy, sooty water and we looked up at the bare arch of the cruck against a deep purple sky. That was the only time in the whole project that I came close to despair. What had we done? What had we taken on? Were we mad?

So I went on an Agricultural Department course to learn

how to build dry-stone dykes. And I must confess that I cheated a bit and used some cement at key bits. But the critical thing with a dry-stone wall is that strength and stability depend on how you position the stones and you never rely on the cement.

We spent another weekend 'capping' the front and back walls to carry the weight of the new roof. We gathered large flat stones two or three feet across, heaved them up to head height and cemented them in place across the top of the walls. It was now sound enough to walk along the wall. Up to this point it was rough work and we had done it all ourselves but the next stage was critical.

Next weekend we hired two local bricklayers for a day and they built proper brick wall-heads. The lines and levels had to be just right because that set the base for the whole roof. And although I could do a little brick work, this had to be perfect.

Another problem was that the old woodwork was riddled with wet rot, dry rot and woodworm. Think of a wood disease and we had it. Obviously we did not want this to infect the new roof, so we had to scrub down and sterilize all the stone. And if we wanted to preserve the crucks, they needed special treatment. So we got on protective clothing and used ten gallons of special chemical paste to coat the crucks half an inch thick. That would soak into the wood for more than a year before we could clean it off and apply new varnish.

The new roof was skilled joinery work, way beyond my ability. But my pal Bill was a self-employed joiner who had trained in the days of traditional house building. No cheap pre-fabricated trusses here but proper joists and rafters, built to last. He was happy to take on the job, paid a rate for each weekend's work. But he was not willing to take on the ordering and supplies. Especially not fifty-five miles away, miles from anywhere, where we must be sure that we had everything we needed. So I had to do the organizing and I am proud to say that we only once ran out of the right size of nails.

We bought all our wood and materials from a supplier I had been at school with. He delivered it right on site and we stored the large beams under polythene sheets and everything else in the big shed. Any extras that we needed, we brought up in the car. I remember one weekend we had to bring more wood tied on the roof rack and sticking out front and back with red rags on the ends to warn other road users. There were four of us in the car and all our supplies for two days. We even took out the front seat to make room for a diesel generator. The car was weighed down on its springs and leaning over to one side. We had to slow down when turning right in case we toppled over!

Bill and I had a funny relationship but it worked well and we never once fell out.

Early on the Saturday morning I would collect Bill and two teenage 'volunteers' and drive up to Killin. We rented the Scout hut and slept there, and I brought the food and did the cooking. As employer, I would agree with Bill what we were going to do that weekend. Once we started work, however, Bill was the boss. I was his assistant and had to do exactly what I was told, while the two boys worked as labourers. We would work until evening. Then down to the Scout hut, cook dinner, a well-earned beer, and fall into our sleeping bags. Next morning Bill and the boys stayed in their sleeping bags while I fried sausage, bacon and eggs and got the coffee going. But we usually managed to get started work before 9a.m. and did a full day's work until late afternoon. At the end of the day our roles reversed. Now Bill asked me, as employer, if everything was OK and I paid the wages. Then I drove everyone back home to Glasgow. Tired, dirty, unshaven and deeply satisfied.

The first weekend, Bill spent ages measuring the wall-heads and we held our breath until he said they were OK. That weekend we got organized and laid the joists. The next weekend, we erected most of the rafters and the main ridge. Suddenly, you could see the shape of the roof and it looked like a building, even if was still just a skeleton. No more doubts that we would be able to complete the job.

It took several more weekends to build the roof and make it waterproof with roofing felt. We built in Velux windows for the attics and homemade roof windows for the main rooms. The local builder's son came for a day to do the tiling. I spent a day building up the gable walls to meet the roof.

Then all that was left to do was the roof trim and the gutters. The down-pipes were a sight. Some looked like a dog's hind leg with three or four bends to wind down and around the stones. Then drains at each end of the cottage to lead the water down to the roadside ditch and the burn.

The shell of the building was complete and weather-tight. From the outside it looked like a new cottage.

In autumn, Sandra and the family came to inspect it and admire our work. I should mention that they had never seen the cottage between the old roof coming off and the new roof being complete. Maybe just as well! There is an old Scots saying that men and weans should not see a job half-done, but in this case it was the womenfolk.

The second winter was plumbing. I had never done any plumbing so I went to an evening class for apprentice plumbers at the local Technical College. But first I had an interview. It was like a music hall charade. Why did I want to learn plumbing? I explained. Was that the only reason? Yes. Did I have another job? A surgeon! Surely that was a good job? Plumbers did not really earn more than surgeons! It dawned on me that they were simply protecting their professional interests and did not want to train any cowboy plumbers. I managed to convince them.

The guys on the course were great, once they got over the early jokes at my expense. I got several plumbing books – there was no Internet in these days – and had soon read more about plumbing than most of them. For plumbing is a practical trade. Apprentices learn their skills from an experienced tradesman and by doing the job, not reading about it.

But they were kind and tolerant, teaching me the practical skills I needed. I spent a couple of months planning everything and the teacher checked it out. Then each week I would buy a bag of plumbing goodies and take them into the class. One week it was a sink, with taps and connections; the next a toilet, cistern and all the works. And the guys would show me how the bits fitted together and correct my mistakes.

The third summer was internal fittings and services. I had never realized that the shell of a building is only half the job. Fitting out takes just as much work and costs as much again.

Bill and the boys came back for a few weekends to fit the internal walls. These were simple wooden frames covered by sheets of plasterboard. We lined the outer walls with strap and plasterboard, leaving the air to circulate behind, though some bits were at rather odd angles to get round large stones. We lined the attic too, with fibreglass insulation behind the plasterboard. That was the one big mistake I made in all my ordering. I worked out how many rolls of fibreglass we needed but did not realize they came in packs of three, so we had insulation everywhere until it was bursting out the seams! Then we had a plasterer for a day to skim the surface and fill in the cracks.

We put down floor tiles for ease of cleaning and maintenance. In a tiny country cottage, that is vital. We saved beautiful, 100-year-old, solid teak doors that were being thrown out from my old hospital. Bill built an outer front door from one inch flooring planks on a four-by-two frame, and funny little doors for the attics. We used flat-pack units for the kitchen. Last of all, we applied the wood trims that made all the difference to the final appearance.

So much for the structure of the building, but what about services?

There is no mains water or sewage in Glen Lochay, so we had to build our own private water supply and sewage system. That was only possible because we had the Allt Ghaordaidh next to the cottage and it came down a steep hillside behind us.

One hundred and ninety yards up the hill was enough to give our water supply a head of 120 feet. I phoned the professor of engineering who looked up his tables and said that we needed a one-inch bore pipe. Modern Alkathene pipes are easy to work, do not corrode, and come with a wide range of fittings.

For sewage, we needed a septic tank that would break down the waste before it went into the burn. And the Local Authority checked the burn had enough flow to take it, even in drought conditions. Good job the Hydro had not taken it! There was a shallow gully behind the cottage that ran down to the burn and was an ideal site for the tank. The only problem was that the ground was solid rock and there was not enough depth for a pre-fabricated septic tank. So back to the reference library to get plans for a homemade tank.

We hired the Scouts again for a work squad, and planned another early start to the season. This time we were not so lucky. Like so many years before, it snowed at Easter. But at least this time the cottage really was fully weather-tight, with a fire blazing away and a constant supply of tea and coffee to heat us up. There were fifteen of us, with picks and shovels and back-breaking labour. We hired a diesel generator and a small jackhammer that pounded away non-stop the whole weekend.

By the end of the weekend we had a trench all 190 yards up the hillside to the water intake. In places it was only about a foot deep rather than the ideal three feet to protect the pipe from frost, but the rock beat us. Now we really appreciated what the old subsistence farmers were up against! We had a better trench from the back of the cottage to the gully for the main drain. That one had to be just right, even though it took hours of work to cut through solid rock. We also had to lever out a couple of big rocks that must have weighed a quarter of a ton each.

Once again we hired two bricklayers for a day to build the septic tank. But we sealed the tank with a waterproof cement mix and did the minor brickwork for the manholes. We made our own water intake with a large plastic pipe into the burn, an oil drum as a header tank, and a muslin filter. Then we laid the drains and led the main outlet into the centre of the burn beneath a large, wedged stone. It would be the following year before I hid the septic tank with an eight-foot high dry-stone dyke.

There were still days of plumbing work inside the house. We did it all with old-fashioned compression joints, that are more expensive but easier to dismantle and replace. The whole system was centred on the bathroom and we left the pipes exposed for ease of checking and maintenance. Because the cottage would lie empty in the winter, we had to be able to drain the system completely so all the pipes sloped down to four drain points. We ran hot and cold water pipes to the bathroom fixtures and the kitchen. There was a toilet, sink and shower for the bathroom. We also needed a ceramic filter for the drinking water and a heater for hot water.

But we still had no power, and at that time we could not afford to bring in electricity. The answer was gas. We built a small gas shed on the back of the cottage with two large red gas cylinders – the kind you see at road works. This is propane, which works down to -20°C. There was an automatic change-over valve so the supply continued when one cylinder ran dry. Gas piping is just like other plumbing, except that it is thinner and uses special gas-proof connections. It comes in flexible coils that are easy to lead round corners and through tight spaces, just like electric cables. So all we had to do was lead it to a cooker, a water heater, and gas lamps in all the rooms. Gaslight is not as bright as electric light but it is a yellow, romantic light that seemed very much in keeping.

I got my plumbing teacher to come and help the day we let the water in. It was just as well! Half my joints leaked, but that was when the compression joints paid off because they were easy to re-do, properly this time. He did smoke tests on the drains. And I would never have risked the gas without his professional approval.

The final step was for the Local Authority to test our water supply and that took three attempts before the filter system worked properly. There were too many sheep on the hillside, adding their E-coli to the burn. But, to make up for that, the mineral content of the water was almost the same as Scotch. I have been testing it carefully for thirty years now and I am slowly coming to the conclusion that it is just right for adding to my single malt. And that kills off the E-coli anyway!

Then we got our Habitation Certificate and Dalgirdy was re-classified as a house. Except, of course, that also meant we had to start paying local taxes.

We had our family holiday in Dalgirdy that summer. We

spent the first few days decorating. It was lovely weather and Sandra pasted wallpaper on a table outside the front door where the only problem was that the local cattle kept coming to lick the paste. The kids had great fun, even if the wee one got more paint on herself than on the shed door she was supposed to be painting. A final coat of bright white stone paint and Breadalbane Red woodwork, and Dalgirdy looked a picture cottage on the hillside.

We went home to Glasgow for a few days to clean up. Then we put away our work clothes, packed our holiday gear, and came back up to Dalgirdy for our first real holiday there. No more building work!

It took three summers and two winters. We did most of the work ourselves, with family and friends, and our own hands. We employed a total of 23 tradesmen days – 14 joiner days, 4 bricklayer days, 1 plasterer, 1 tiler and 1 plumber. Altogether, it cost £11,850 – about £90,000 in today's money.

It was all great fun and worth every bruised thumb, ache and blister. Very few people today have the satisfaction of being able to say *I built my own house.*

23. RED DEER, KITES AND SALMON

Scotland's Natural Heritage

On a frosty autumn morning, the sun rises late over Loch Tay and begins to dispel the low-lying mist in the glen. The stags are roaring in the high corries and the sound carries miles in the still air. It is one of the most evocative sounds in the Highland glens. It is the rutting season.

The Monarch of the Glens announces his presence. The strongest and most dominant stags fight to gather a harem of hinds and make sure it is their genes that are carried on to the next generation. They must service each hind as she comes into season for a few short hours and be on constant guard that no competitor gets a chance. They have no rest. By the end of the rut they are exhausted and have lost a third of their body weight.

Some deer have a most unusual pregnancy. The foetus develops so far but stops over the worst of the winter before it begins to grow again. Then many of the calves in a herd are born about the same time in June when the weather is kind and there is plenty of sweet new grass. It is a miracle of biological timing to fit the seasons.

Very young fawns lie perfectly still on the hill all day while their mothers are feeding a mile away. Their spotted coat is such good camouflage that you almost trip over them before you spot them. Then, when they are a little older, a few hinds may look after a 'nursery' of 15-20 fawns. But before the height of summer the fawns are running with their mothers and can go up the hill and disappear over the skyline in minutes.

Men have always hunted the deer. The first hunter-gatherers came to Scotland in pursuit of deer. Medieval kings laid claim to the deer in the Forest of Mamlorn at the head of

Glen Lochay. The Victorian *huntin, shootin, fishin set* helped to regenerate the Highlands. Deer stalking is now an important part of the rural economy and is worth over £100 million a year. It provides more than three hundred full-time and as many as two thousand part-time jobs. [492]

Stalking is an historic field sport, steeped in ancient lore and tradition. But in the absence of natural predators like wolves and bears it is also essential to control deer numbers, remove weak and sickly animals, and maintain a healthy population.

Most of the commercial stag shooting takes place between August and October. You need to be reasonably fit and well clad but everything else is provided. Breakfast of porridge and cream, a short journey in a 4X4, and the stalker leads you into the hills on a nineteenth century stalkers path. Some estates still use the traditional ponies, but after an hour you leave them to wait. Now you must go more carefully.

Stalkers are followers of the wind, for that determines where the deer will be each day. The stalker knows the likely spots and you use terrain and wind to keep you hidden while you make your approach. You can never be sure what you will find but that is the nature of the hunt.

Once the stalker spots a likely target, you must move with great stealth as you try to get within a hundred yards for a good shot. You crawl on your belly through heather and wet bog, but getting soaked and muddy helps your camouflage and is part of the game. And if the wind changes, you retreat and move over the shoulder of the hill to try a different approach.

The stalker selects and points out the target. He sets up the rifle and you finally get it in your hands. 'Take your time. Shoot when ready.' Your heart beats fast. You hold your breath and gently squeeze the trigger. The stag stumbles and crashes to the ground. 'Good shot! Well done!' You are so excited that you almost pee your pants.

Now for the hard work, but the stalker does most of it. He 'grallochs' the deer and spills its blood and guts on the heather for the carrion to enjoy. If this is your first deer, it is tradition to smear the blood on your face. This pays homage to the spirit of the deer and is a right of passage into adult life. The smell and feel of it will stay with you for the rest of your days and you wear it with pride, even if townies will never understand. The carcass is lighter now and together you drag it down the hill to meet the ponies.

Walking back to the lodge with the sun low in the sky and a deep primeval sense of satisfaction, you feel closer to the land than you ever have before. Is this how our ancestors felt? The kill is the climax but much of the skill and pleasure is in the hunt and the field craft. But it is more than hunting; it is about managing this land with its flora and fauna.

A well-earned dinner and then you share an evening full of stories at the fire. It is a special experience and one that will live in your memory for the rest of your life.

The ultimate *Macnab Challenge* is to bag a stag, a brace of grouse, and a salmon all on the same day. A young lad on a neighbouring estate really did manage it last year.

Scotland has the best hillwalking in the world and Meall nan Tarmachan is the best ridge in the Southern Highlands.[493]

You can drive up to fifteen hundred feet and that gets you straight on to the high hills. It is an early start on a bright April morning and the dew is heavy on the ground. The snow is gone early this year, the ground is hard and dry, and the going is easy. The National Trust for Scotland has built a good footpath up the mountain, which has healed the erosion of over-use and blends into the landscape. They have also enclosed the east side of the mountain in a fence to keep out the sheep and deer and allow the natural vegetation to regenerate. But it is still an hour or more of hard walking that loosens up your muscles and you discard outer garments as you warm up. As you gain height, you look down on the Hydro dam but the reservoir is half empty this year with the low spring rainfall.

Then suddenly, after a final steep climb, you are on the summit of Meall nan Tarmachan. It is a Munro, one of 283 Scottish mountains over three thousand feet. You are on top of the world. It is wall-to-wall sunshine with not a cloud in sight, though there is enough breeze to give a slight wind chill.

The air is crystal clear and you can see for miles. Ben Lomond lies to the southwest. Serried ranks of peaks to the north lead to the bulk of Ben Nevis on the horizon. I have climbed them all and the sight brings back many happy memories of good days. Below, you look down on Loch Tay and the village of Killin.

Ahead lies a marvellous high-level ridge over three more peaks with only a few hundred feet drop between. Today, there is a good path worn by thousands of feet. The start is easy, down a long broad slope to a tiny lochan. Many years ago, I made a high-level camp beside it but had a terrible job finding it in low cloud and broken ground, before there was any path. Then a sharp climb up to a block of rock that is the summit of Meall Garb, before an airy hundred yards of knife-edge ridge with the ground dropping away steeply on both sides. There is even a short rock scramble off the west end, though you can by-pass that if you know the way over the north face.

The next section of path meanders up and down and round and about over lumps and bumps to reach the summit cone of Beinn nan Eachan. Looking back, you can now see tiny figures on each of the other tops. To the west, you look down the full length of upper Glen Lochay, and if you know where to look you can make out the white dot of Dalgirdy. A small gaggle of geese fly below on their way back to Iceland for the summer, cackling as they go. There are no ptarmigan now, but meadow pipits and wheatears have moved back up the hill with the approaching spring. Ravens croak harshly as they soar along the cliffs. If you are really lucky you might even see the flash of a peregrine falcon crossing the ridge ahead. And a small herd of deer browse a mile out on the north ridge, keeping a wary eye on you and your dog. A simple cheese sandwich, some chocolate and ice-cold water from the last burn taste like a banquet.

The final peak is Creag na Caillich. Here the path winds round the top of the cliffs, on the very edge, with an eight hundred foot drop below. You seem to be looking straight down on Killin. You need a good head for heights, though there is another way round if you decide that discretion is the better part of valour! The way off is easy, down the west ridge and round below the cliffs. Here, you pass within a hundred yards of the Neolithic stone axe factory, though most walkers do not even know it is there.

The day ends with an hour's walk back along the Hydro road to the car. Because it follows the line of the catchment pipe it is more or less flat and the going is easy. The hard exercise is over. You can relax and enjoy the rhythm of your legs. As you move along the hillside, you have ever-changing views of Loch Tay. You look up in turn to each of the peaks you crossed and see occasional figures high above, who still have far to go but hours of pleasure ahead.

Then down to the local pub for a few pints of beer – for purely medicinal purposes, to replace fluid and electrolytes lost in sweat – with the warm after-glow of sun and wind on your face. And home to a long soak in a hot bath, a ravenous meal, and fall asleep in front of the fire.

Why do we do it? After all, we end up back where we started with nothing to show for all that effort. *Because it is there* is only part of the story.[494] *Because I can* gets a bit closer. There is the sheer bodily pleasure and satisfaction of a day's hard physical exertion and the feel of well-used muscles. It gets our endorphins flowing. But we are also privileged to have access to a very special place. There is a freedom in the air of the high tops, free from the cares of everyday life below. We are closer to Nature; experience her beauty in all its moods, more aware of her raw power and the fragility of life. You can *feel* why early peoples believed that gods and spirits lived in these high places. *Nearer my God to thee.* It puts us in our place in the grand scheme of things. *What is man that thou art mindful of him?* But perhaps that is all too philosophical. Perhaps it simply makes you feel good to be alive.

When hillwalking became more popular in the 1960s, some

landowners were worried that we would disturb the deer and especially their breeding. The number of hillwalkers has increased ten-fold since that time and on a good summer weekend there are tens of thousands of people on the Scottish hills. That has certainly moved the deer away from the more popular areas, but they usually only move a mile or two and they still have plenty of space. There are now more than 300,000 red deer in Scotland, double the number in 1965.

Since 2003 we have had a statutory Right of Access to the hills in Scotland.[495] Most reasonable estates make walkers welcome and are happy to offer advice on suitable routes. In popular areas there is a hill-phone service. Estates leave a recorded phone message with information about where they will be stalking that day and suggestions for alternative routes.

In return, hillwalkers must show consideration for those who live and work on the land and depend on stalking for their livelihood. We can reduce disturbance by:

• Checking with the estate or hill-phone when planning our day's route.

• Keeping to established tracks.

• Keeping to the main ridges and not cutting down corries as this disturbs the deer less.

• Following the Countryside Code:
   - Taking responsibility for our own actions.
   - Respecting the rights of others.
   - Caring for the environment.

With goodwill and consideration on both sides, the mountains are big enough for deer, stalking and hillwalkers to share.

The red kite is an icon of the conservation movement.

It is an elegant and graceful bird. If you hired a top designer and gave him an unlimited budget, he could not do better. It is a slender bird of prey, larger than a buzzard, with long wings and a forked tail. It has a chestnut red body with dark streaks, an orange-red tail and a pale, streaked head. In flight, its underside has a distinctive pattern of reddish-brown, dark and light grey areas. The wings are long and slender, with a sharp angle and obvious dark flight feathers.

Its wingspan is 5½ feet but it only weighs two or three pounds, so it is incredibly agile. It soars effortlessly in the sky, holding its wings almost motionless, steering by constant movements of its tail and fine adjustments to its flight feathers. It is often seen singly or in pairs, hunting the hills and glens for food. Larger gatherings occur at feeding stations where they provide spectacular aerial displays.

In medieval times red kites were common throughout Britain, even in towns where they scavenged for refuse. By Victorian times they were hunted to extinction.

Red kites were re-introduced to Scotland in 1989, first in the Black Isle and then in several other areas. One of these is at Ardgaty, just south of Breadalbane.[496] The bird hide is open to the public and you can see as many as thirty birds at the feeding station. But the birds roam free and occasionally come up to Glen Lochay. Today there are about 120 pairs nesting in Scotland and in winter there may be as many as 350 birds. The number is slowly increasing but the main limitation is still illegal poisoning.

The successful re-introduction of the red kite is only one example of conservation. It is not only possible to conserve but also to restore some of the wildlife we have lost. Red kites, golden eagles, sea eagles, ospreys. Beaver, wildcat, pine marten, red squirrel. Native woodlands.

Scotland's stunning seas and coasts, mountains and moorlands support a wealth of wildlife. Wildlife tourism is now well established and plays a vital part in Scotland's rural economy. More than a million trips each year have the main aim of viewing wildlife. This brings in £65 million to Scotland's economy and supports over 2700 full-time jobs.[497]

Salmon, trout and Arctic char came to Scotland soon after the Ice Age and they are all still here today. Atlantic salmon are the king of fish and the Tay is one of the best salmon fishing rivers in the world.

Salmon eggs begin life in gravel beds and clean, unpolluted water high up in the River Lochay. They hatch in spring when the water temperature rises. At first they stay under the gravel, feeding off the yolk sac. After four to six weeks, again depending on temperature, the young fish or fry emerge. They develop typical spots of colour down their sides and grow quickly as they feed off tiny water organisms. By the time they are one year old they are known as parr and feed on small insects. They remain in fresh water for up to four years.

In the spring of their third or fourth year they become more streamlined and turn a distinctive silver colour as they begin to adapt for life in salt water. In late spring they head out to sea in shoals.

Adult salmon stay at sea for the next one to four years. They travel great distances to the rich feeding grounds in cold northern waters where they feed on sand eels, krill and herring. In their first year at sea, fish swim to the Faroe Islands, but older fish go to sub-arctic water near Greenland. The average size of an adult fish after two years at sea is 28-30 inches and 8-12 pounds but it then increases rapidly with age.

Adult salmon head back to the river where they were born, navigating thousands of miles by unerring instinct. They 'hold' in the loch or deep pools until the water conditions are right to travel upstream. Then the salmon run is one of wonders of the natural world as fish after fish jumps up the foaming falls. The record jump is twelve feet high. Once they get to the upper reaches, the female scrapes a hollow in the gravel where she lays up to 7,000 eggs and males fight to fertilize them. The eggs then take more than a year to hatch before the life cycle starts all over again.

The adults do not eat much on the journey home, either at sea or going up the river. By the time they lay their eggs they are thin and exhausted, and few survive to go back to sea and do it all again.

The traditional opening of the salmon season on the Tay is

at Kenmore in the middle of January each year. Anglers travel from all over Scotland and the UK. They gather in the morning in front of the Kenmore Hotel where a local dignitary conducts the opening ceremony. The fishermen then line up behind the Atholl Pipe Band, fishing gear to arms, and parade the short distance to the river. They take up positions on both banks and the final parts of the ceremony take place on the Tay itself. A representative from Dewar's World of Whisky offers a toast to the river and the river is blessed. The dignitary is rowed out to the middle of the stream and makes the first caste. Then, with the cry 'Tight Lines!' all anglers make their first cast of the new season.

It is a great fishing festival. The MacTaggart Kenmore Trophy and a gallon of whisky go to the angler who lands the largest salmon on opening day.

The record for a salmon in the UK was a massive 64 pounds, caught on the Tay by Miss Georgina Ballantyne on 7 October 1922. That was the talk of gentlemen's clubs around the world and helped to promote women's angling. Sadly for male superiority, we now know that female pheromones may actually attract the largest specimens! But very few fish today exceed 40 pounds. Fisherman's tales of 60-pound fish are probably exactly that – especially about the one that got away!

The joy of fishing: it can be sublime or drive you insane. On a good day you become one with the peace and tranquillity of the river, the play of light on the river, the natural life on its banks. A rod in your hands has a magical calming effect on the stress of modern life.

You set up your gear and make your first cast, full of hope and expectation, but of course nothing happens. Patience is a virtue and anglers know all about patience. You cast again with a perfect lob that places the lure exactly where you want it. You wind it in slowly and can see in your mind's eye the lure swimming across just above the bottom, waggling away and sending out positive vibrations to attract the fish. You wait for the first gentle nudge. Your line gets caught up in rocks or trees and you change your lure and cast again. And again. And again.

River salmon are the ultimate test of the fly fisherman. Local lore about the moods of this river, its pools and salmon lies, the best lures and tackle, can only be gained by years of experience and close observation. The skill of the cast is in the 4 S's: the size of the fly; the sink of the fly beneath the surface; reeling it in at the ideal speed; and the swing of the fly to make it appear alive.

A bite! The take is strong rather than violent but you know immediately that it is a good fish. The fish makes a couple of surging runs and you have to move along the bank before you slowly draw it in. As it comes closer to the bank it seems to get stronger and you realize it is bigger than you thought. A quick thrash and it cuts the line as easily as if its mouth is made of iron! That is your last bite of the day.

Another day. A terrific tug, the rod bends almost double and your heart is in your mouth. The line screams out and the fight is on! He runs down the pool and across the torrent until you are nearly out of line but then he makes a mistake by stopping to rest. Slowly, you draw him back to the quieter water on your side. He runs again, heading for the sea as fast as he can, but somehow you manage to slow him down and bring him to a stop. Once more, quietly and gently, you draw him in and await his further pleasure. You do not have long to wait. He heads upstream, jigs and throws himself out of the water several times and you are sure you will lose him. Your legs are trembling, your arms are tiring, your mouth is dry, and you don't know what to do next. Then you slip on a greasy stone but somehow hang on to the rod. Slowly, over what seems like hours, you draw him in, again and again. Somehow, the hook holds. At last, he tires. You draw him into the shallow water close to the bank, showing the silver of his belly. So near and yet so far! You only have one pair of hands and you need them both to hang on to the rod like grim death in case he makes a last desperate effort. But fortunately your friends have gathered round to watch your fight so help is at hand to net him and bring him ashore.

If it is a big one, you make sure you weigh it on accredited scales and have a witness. And put it on YouTube!

To preserve stocks and allow fish to spawn, most Scottish rivers now have a 'catch and release' policy. Two-thirds of all salmon caught on the Tay last year were released to continue upstream.

There are more than three million anglers in the UK. Salmon and trout angling is worth more than £100 million pounds a year to the Scottish economy and supports around 2,800 jobs.[498]

Meantime, most salmon for the table now come from fish farms. Scotland is the largest producer of farmed salmon in the EU. There are some 250 fish farms in Scotland, providing 1,000 jobs and producing 150,000 tons of salmon each year. That is worth more than £500 million at farm-gate prices and accounts for one-third of Scotland's food exports.[499]

Red deer, kites and salmon: Land, sea and air. *All creatures great and small; the Lord God made them all.*

Scotland's natural heritage is a valuable national asset. Nature-based tourism includes all visits that are wholly or partly related to the landscape, wildlife and natural beauty. That may be simply enjoying the scenery, walking, adventure activities, field sports or wildlife watching. Scottish Natural Heritage estimates it is worth £1.4 billion a year, 40% of all tourism spending in Scotland. It supports 39,000 full-time equivalent jobs.[500]

But it is much more than that. Our natural heritage is a priceless part of Scotland and what it means to be Scottish.

EPILOGUE

Nae man can tether time nor tide[501]

It is late autumn and the cottage season will soon be coming to an end. The nights are drawing in and there is a nip in the air. Grasses, plants and trees are preparing for winter and the hills are ablaze in russet, yellow, bronze and gold. It is the season of mellow fruitfulness but with early hints of harder days ahead. It will soon be time to close up the cottage for the winter. Sitting by the fire with a final dram of good malt whisky, it is a time to reflect on what has been and what is yet to be. I gaze into the flames and think back over this story of Dalgirdy.

Dalgirdy was never important. There were no kings or castles or great battles here. No one ever heard of the people who lived here.

But Dalgirdy represents many thousands of other small places and little people who made Scotland. It was swept along on the great tides of Scottish history and played its part, even if it only had bit parts and was often helpless flotsam on the tide. We were but foot soldiers on the moors of time. Yet without foot soldiers there would be no lords or kings and we fought and won, and bled and died, just like those whose names went down in history. Kings and governments may have grand designs, but what really matters is the impact on ordinary people's lives.

So, Dalgirdy offers a window onto the history of Scotland and her people. Real people; real lives.

Today, Dalgirdy is ours. We 'own' it in the legal terms of today. But in a different sense we belong to Dalgirdy just as much as it belongs to us. It is part of who and what we are, just as we make it what it is.

And we are only one link in the long chain of people who have lived and loved and worked here. We are its custodians for our brief moment in its long history. I wonder what future generations will say of us and our time here. I hope they judge us kindly.

The future is not mine to tell, yet I cannot help but wonder.

The future of Dalgirdy will depend most of all on the people who are here, for people make places. But just as in the past, its future will also depend on wider changes in its world.

We cannot live in the past – and we would not want to. We cannot live in some myth or Dreamland either. We have to live in the real world and that world is changing and Scotland must change with it. Just like Dalgirdy. Our sights and our dreams must be on the future rather than the past, in the real world as it is rather than as we might wish it to be.

So, what kind of society do we want to be and what kind of life do we want to have? And how do we bring that to pass? Whether Scotland remains part of the UK or becomes an independent country – and I am not taking sides on that political debate – we face challenges ahead.

The Highlands have almost all the best wild land left in Britain. That is a precious and irreplaceable asset. It is our most spectacular landscape with rich and abundant wild life. It draws people to enjoy its solitude, beauty and adventure, to nourish body, mind and spirit. It is the land we love. It is a place to live, to work and play.

We do not own this heritage but hold it in trust, handed down to us from past generations. So we have a responsibility to care for it, improve it where we can, and pass it on in good condition to future generations. But that immediately raises further questions. What do we want this land to be – and for? Can we all agree? How do we deliver these goals? What will it cost and how do we pay for it?[502]

The challenges are great but challenges also mean opportunities that depend on what we make of them. We have faced and overcome many challenges before in our tumultuous history, and we can do it again. It will not always be easy but nothing worthwhile ever is. We must have *the will to do, the soul to dare.*[503]

Scottish is a state of mind: fiercely proud of our ancient heritage but outward looking too in this big, wide, beautiful world. Yet wherever we may be in the world, Scotland will always be our homeland. And this land that we call ours will aye be here while the sands of time shall run, or at least till the next Ice Age wipes the schist clean again or the rocks melt wi' the sun.

> *For these are our mountains, this is our glen.*
> *This land that begat us shall see us again.*

AUTHOR'S NOTE

Dalgirdy is real and so are the facts but I have also tried to tell the story. It is a blend of history, field archaeology, estate records, literature, legend and trying to imagine what it was really like. I hope you can see which is which. The historical facts are as accurate as I could make them but I left out a lot of 'ifs' and 'buts' and 'maybes'. With apologies to academic historians, I have over-simplified to pick out the main threads of the story and weave the big picture. But even more important, I wanted to get under the skin of history, to imagine how it would *feel* if we were transported back to these times. Sitting in the remains of the Iron Age homestead on a glorious summer evening or a wet winter day, 2000-year-old ghosts can still send shivers down your spine. I hope this kaleidoscope gives a taste of what life was really like in Dalgirdy.

Gathering the evidence was much like doing family history and many of the methods and the sources are the same. The great advantage is that Dalgirdy provides a solid anchor. So even when the thread breaks you can pick it up again.

I have used a lot of original quotes because they give a genuine flavour of the times in a way that my words never could. The Sources are there for those who want them but unobtrusive for those who simply want to enjoy the story. The quotes are verbatim, printed *in italics,* though they are obviously selected to make a point and many are abridged - - - to pick out key bits. Some of the undated quotes are out of strict chronological order where that would have confused the storyline to no good purpose.

I am particularly grateful to the National Archives of Scotland (now part of the National Records of Scotland) for permission to use so much of their material. They have the most marvellous collection of old records and in this day and age it is simply amazing that we not only have access to the originals but it is free. It is truly awesome to hold a 240-year-old letter handwritten by one of the people in this story. That brings history alive. Thank you to the staff of the Historical Search Room for many happy days.

I am also grateful to Perth & Kinross Council Archive for permission to reproduce Highways material in Chapter 14 and Stirling Council Archive for extracts of the Glen Lochay School Log in Chapter 19. Sir Roderick Campbell of Barcaldine, John Donald Publishers, Edinburgh University Press, the family of Sir Alexander Gray, and Professor Christopher Smout gave kind permission to reproduce material as cited.

The list of Sources includes some more general background material. For anyone who wants to read more, I would strongly recommend two books. *In Famed Breadalbane* by the Rev WA Gillies is the classic reference book on the area. It was not only the starting point for all of my research but inspired me to it. Fortunately, it has now been republished under the Northern Books from Famedram imprint and is still in print. TC Smout's *History of the Scottish People 1560-1830* is another gem. Anyone who wants to feel what history was like for ordinary people cannot do better.

See www.highlandroots.net for more.

Special thanks to my wife Sandra who put up with the trials and tribulations of my research and writing over the past three years, though it did help to keep me out of her hair when I retired. She also painted the book cover.

Three people are experts on particular aspects of this story and deserve particular thanks. Judge Angus Stroyan owns Boreland Estate and knows Glen Lochay from his youth. Finlay Macaskill farms Tullich and knows Dalgirdy and the glen, man and boy. Dugie MacInnes has spent twenty years studying the archaeology of Glen Lochay and also introduced me to the estate records. All three showed immense patience with my endless questions. This book would not exist without you.

Professor Christopher Smout CBE, Emeritus Professor of

Scottish History at the University of St Andrews, spent many patient hours checking the manuscript and correcting the worst of my historical clangers. I am deeply grateful for his tolerance and kindness to an amateur historian. The errors that remain are entirely my own.

Many other people helped. Thank you to Gina and Willie Angus, George Bickerton, Ken Chew, Carol Ferguson, Gillean Ford, Jimmy Gauld, Dr Craig Haggart, Dr Mairi McColl, John McGivern, the late James Macnab of Macnab, Trevor Shaw, John Sinclair, Ian Stewart, Dr David Syme and Roger Twigg.

I am also grateful to the following, in no particular order: Killin Heritage Society; AK Bell Library, Perth; Perth & Kinross Council Archives; Perth Museum; Stirling Council Archives; National Library of Scotland, Map Section; National Museum of Scotland; Mitchell Library, Glasgow; William Patrick Library, East Dunbartonshire; National Museum of Rural Life; Highland Folk Museum; Royal College of Surgeons of Edinburgh; Royal College of Physicians & Surgeons of Glasgow; Glasgow University Library; Scottish and Southern Energy.

None of these people or institutions bear any responsibility for the use I have made of the material.

I hope you have enjoyed Dalgirdy as much as I do.

SOURCES

Chapter 1 Dalgirdy
1 Exchequer Rolls of Scotland Vol VIII p336
2 GD50/116 pages 127-8
3 Dwelly online Gaelic dictionary.
www.cairnwater.co.uk/gaelicdictionary/index.aspx?Language=en
4 Cunliffe B The Ancient Celts. Oxford University Press 1997.
5 Old Statistical Account of Scotland p460
6 Dorothy Wordsworth Recollections of a tour made in Scotland AD
1803. Edmonton & Douglas; Edinburgh 1874 (2nd Edition)
7 Gillies Page xvi
8 Sir Walter Scott The Fair Maid of Perth.
9 Now part of the National Records of Scotland, Edinburgh
http://www.nas.gov.uk/onlineCatalogue/
Breadalbane Estate Records Reference GD112

General background:
Gillies WA In Famed Breadalbane. The Munro Press, Perth 1938
Reprinted by Northern Books, Famedram Publishers: Ellon,
Aberdeenshire 1980

Chapter 2 The Land
10 Dictionary of the Scots language. http://www.dsl.ac.uk/index.html
11 Robertson J General View of the Agriculture in the County of Perth.
Perth 1799 Page 21 http://books.google.co.uk/books
12 Tay Western Catchments Area Project
www.salmon-fishing-scotland.com/twcp.pdf
13 Tacitus. The Agricola. Page 12. The Oxford Translation revised, with
notes. With an introduction by Edward Brooks, Jr. Philadelphia, D
McKay c1897 http://www.gutenberg.org/cache/epub/7524/pg7524.html
14 Omand D (Ed) The Perthshire Book. Birlinn; Edinburgh 1999. Parry
ML Climatic change, agriculture and settlement. Dawson; Folkstone 1978
15 Dodgshon RA The Little Ice Age in the Scottish Highlands and Islands:
documenting its human impact. Scot Geog J 2005; 121(4):321-337
Cullen KJ et al King William's Ill Years: new evidence on the impact of
scarcity and harvest failure during the crisis of the 1690s on Tayside.
Scottish Historical Review 2006;85(2):250-276
16 http://en.wikipedia.org/wiki/The_Scream
17 Third stanza of the poem 'Scotland' by Sir Alexander Gray (1882-
1968). By kind permission of the family of Sir Alexander Gray.

General background:
Kempe N Wrightham M (Eds) Hostile habitats: Scotland's mountain environment. Scottish Mountaineering Trust, Edinburgh 2006.
McKirdy A, Gordon J, Crofts R Land of mountain and flood: the geology and landforms of Scotland. Birlinn Ltd: Edinburgh 2007
Tay Western Catchments Area Project Final Report. Scottish Native Woods; Perthshire 2010. www.salmon-fishing-scotland.com/twcp.pdf

Chapter 3 Early Peoples

18 Donnelly M Excavations at Ben Lawers Nature Trail. In Ben Lawers Historic Landscape Project The Pilot Season 1996 GUARD Report 290.2 Section 6.3 pages 31-41
19 Butter R Kilmartin: an introduction and guide. Kilmartin House Trust: Kilmartin, Argyll 1999.
20 Edmonds M et al Survey and excavation at Creag na Caillich, Killin, Perthshire. *Proc Soc Antiq Scot,* 122 (1992), 77-112 (http://ads.ahds.ac.uk/catalogue/adsdata/PSAS_2002/pdf/vol_122/122_07 7_112.pdf)
21 The National Museum of Scotland, Basement, Early People Gallery, Case No. J2.
22 Proceedings Society of Antiquaries of Scotland 1881-82, Vol XVI P27.
23 www.crannog.co.uk
24 http://www.pkht.org.uk/Projects/Black-Spout-Homestead-Pitlochry/
25 Dugie MacInnes Personal communication
26 MacInnes D 2008 Dalgirdy: an archeological field survey in Glen Lochay. ACFA Occas Paper #76
27 Radford CAR Peebleshire: an inventory of the ancient monuments. RCAHMS: Edinburgh 1967
28 Reynolds PJ Iron Age Farm: the Butser Experiment. Colonnade Books, London 1979
29 Simmons V In Koch. JT (Ed) Celtic Culture: A Historical Encyclopedia. 2006 p1615.
30 Auel JM The Clan of the Cave Bear. Hodder & Stoughtan , London 1980
31 http://en.wikipedia.org/wiki/Roundhouse_(dwelling)
32 Cunliffe B The Ancient Celts. Oxford University Press 1997.
Armit I Celtic Scotland. Historic Scotland: Edinburgh 2005.
http://en.wikipedia.org/wiki/Celtic_languages
33 Tacitus. The Agricola. p25 The Oxford Translation revised.

General background:
Moffat A Before Scotland. Thames & Hudson, London 2005

Prior F Britain BC Life in Britain and Ireland before the Romans. Harper Perennial: Hammersmith, London 2004

Chapter 4 The Wolf and the Eagle

34 The Book of Highland Minstrely 1846
35 Bowie W The Black Book of Taymouth p356 Constable, Edinburgh 1855 http://archive.org/details/blackbookoftaymo00inneuoft

Chapter 5 The Romans

36 Tacitus. The Agricola. Page 25. The Oxford Translation revised.
37 Fraser JE the Roman conquest of Scotland: The battle of Mons Graupius AD 84. The History Press; Stroud, Gloucester. 2008 www.romanscotland.org.uk/pages/campaigns/mons_graupius/contents.asp
38 Tacitus The Agricola Page 30. The Oxford Translation revised.
39 Tacitus The Agricola Page 33. The Oxford Translation revised.
40 Herodian History of the Empire Book III.14
41 Herodian History of the Empire Book III.14
42 Ammianus http://www.vortigernstudies.org.uk/artsou/ammian.htm

General background:
Goldsworthy A The Complete Roman Army. Thames & Hudson, London 2003. http://en.wikipedia.org/wiki/Roman_legion
http://en.wikipedia.org/wiki/Roman_military_personal_equipment.
Keppie L. The legacy of Rome: Scotland's Roman remains. John Donald, Edinburgh. Third Edition 2004.

Chapter 6 The Birth of a Nation

43 Isidore of Seville Early 7th century Etymologiae Book XIX Part 23 No. 7
44 Butter R Kilmartin: an introduction and guide. Kilmartin House Trust: Kilmartin, Argyll 1999.
45 Foster p111
46 Gilbert JM Hunting and hunting preserves in medieval Scotland. John Donald, Edinburgh 1979
47 www.duffus.com/Articles/senchus_fer_n_alban.htm
48 Bernard Cornwell writes historic fiction, but he vividly evokes the horror and brutality of battle in the shield wall.
49 Anglo Saxon Chronicle http://omacl.org/Anglo/part2.html
50 Historia Regum Anglorum – Transl by Rev Joseph Stevenson 1855 http://www.ebooksread.com/authors-eng/joseph-stevenson/the-church-historians-of-england--pre-reformation-period-volume-3-p2-vet/page-5-the-church-historians-of-england--pre-reformation-period-volume-3-p2-vet.shtml

51 www.mostly-medieval.com/explore/chapters.htm
52 Robert Burns 1793
53 Declaration of Arbroath 1320

General background:
Foster SM Picts, Gaels and Scots: Early Historic Scotland. Historic
Scotland, Edinburgh 1996.
Driscoll ST Alba: the Gaelic Kingdom of Scotland AD 800-1124. Birlinn
with Historic Scotland, Edinburgh 2002.
Aitchison N The Picts and the Scots at War. Sutton Publishing,
Gloucester 2003
http://en.wikipedia.org/wiki/Edward_I_of_England

Chapter 7 The Early church
54 http://www.philipcoppens.com/glenlyon.html
55 Bede 731AD Ecclesiastical History of the English People
56 Watson WJ The place names of Breadalbane. Transactions of the
Gaelic Soc of Inverness 1927-28;34:248-279
57 MacInnes D 2003 Tullich Farm: an archaeological field study in Glen
Lochay. Assoc. Chartered Field Archeologists Report No 36. Stirling
Council 2003
58 Adomnan Life of St Columba
59 Bede 731AD Ecclesiastical History of the English People
60 Robertson TS 1898 Notes on Saint Fillan's Priory and Churchyard
Proc Soc Antiq Scot Vol XXXII p121-4
61 There is a full description of St Fillan's relics and legends in Gillies p64.
62 Bower's Scotichronicon. Quoted in Grant A Independence and
nationhood 1306-1469 Edinburgh University Press, Edinburgh 1984 p109
63 Old Perthshire Folktale. Recounted by the late Ella Walker A village
history – Killin http://www.killin.co.uk/kn/issues/kihist.pdf
64 Black Book of Taymouth p373
65 Dr Mairi McColl, personal communication

Chapter 8 The Lairds of Glenorchy
66 Yeoman P Stirling Castle. Official Souvenir Guide. Historic Scotland,
Edinburgh 2011.
67 See Gillies for a detailed history of the Campbells of Glen Orchy
68 GD112/1/5
69 Exchequer Rolls of Scotland Vol VI p49
70 ER Vol VI p49
71 ER Vol V p481
72 Black Book of Taymouth Preface pii

73 GD112/1/47
74 ER Vol IX p10 & p573
75 Boardman S The Campbells 1250-1513, John Donald, Edinburgh 2006 p334 By kind permission of Birlinn.
76 Campbell A. A history of Clan Campbell. Edinburgh University Press, Edinburgh 2002 Vol 1 From Origins to Flodden p167 By kind permission of Edinburgh University Press
77 GD50/7 p23
78 GD112/1/47
79 Gillies p360
80 GD50/116 pages 127-8
81 Gillies p119
82 Register of the Privy Seal of Scotland Vol 2 p.320 No.2152
83 Personal communication, Dr Louise Yeoman.
84 Gillies p121
85 GD112/76/28
86 GD50/7 p24
87 Black Book of Taymouth p22
88 Amelia Georgiana Murray MacGregor. History of the Clan Gregor. William Brown: Edinburgh 1898 pages 86 & 481 The Chartulary 1 of the ClanGregor Sept 2 1527.
http://www.archive.org/details/historyofclangre01macguoft
89 Gillies p365
90 See 47 above
91 King James VI. 29 July 1587 GD112/1/389
92 Act of Privy Council April 3rd 1603.
93 Black Book of Taymouth p346

General background:
Gillies WA In Famed Breadalbane.
www.electricscotland.com/history/nation/breadalbane.htm

Chapter 9 Peasant Life

94 John of Fordun's Chronicle of the Scottish Nation 1380s.
http://www.archive.org/details/johnoffordunschr00fordrich
95 Grant IF Highland Folk Ways. Routledge & Kegan Paul, London 1961. And http://www.am*baile*.org.uk/en/
96 Samuel Johnson. A Journey to the Western Isles of Scotland 1773
97 James Boswell The Journal of a Tour to the Hebrides with Samuel Johnson 1773
98 GD112/17/11 p270
99 Samuel Johnson. A Journey to the Western Isles of Scotland 1773

100 Jean Froissant 1385 In Dickinson & Donaldson Early Travellers in Scotland. Edinburgh: David Douglas 1891 Vol II p10
101 Black Book of Taymouth p418
102 http://www.constitution.org/eng/conpur058.htm
103 Black Book of Taymouth p394
104 GD50/116 p 279-80 & 285
105 GD50/116 p315
106 GD50/116 p244 Gillies p147
107 Smout p144 & 225
108 Black Book of Taymouth p379
109 Cullen et al. King William's Ill Years: new evidence on the impact of scarcity and harvest failure during the crisis of the 1690s on Tayside. Scottish Historical Review 2006;85(2):250-276
110 Black Book of Taymouth p379
111 GD 112/21/224/A
112 Adomnan Life of St Columba
113 Ziegler P The Black Death. Collins, Glasgow 1969
Jillings K Scotland's Black Death. Tempus: Stroud, Gloucester. 2007
114 John of Fordun. Chronicle of the Scottish Nation
http://www.archive.org/details/johnoffordunschr00fordrich
115 Bocaccio The Decameron
http://www.fordham.edu/halsall/source/boccacio2.html
116 GD112/1/561
117 Old Statistical Account for the Parish of Killin 1791
118 Aeneus Sylvius 1435. In Early Travellers in Scotland. Vol II p2-3
119 Don Pedro de Ayala 1498 In Early Travellers in Scotland. Vol II p3-6
120 James Boswell The Journal of a Tour to the Hebrides with Samuel Johnson 1773
121 Samuel Johnson. A Journey to the Western Isles of Scotland 1773

General background:
Smout TC A History of the Scottish People 1560 - 1830. Fontana Press, London 1969

Chapter 10 Subsistence Farming
122 MacInnes & Wood 2004. MacInnes 2008
123 GD112/11/1/4/26
124 GD112/16/13/1/2
125 www.nls.uk/maps/roy
126 MacInnes & Wood 2004
127 Early Travellers in Scotland p254
128 Robertson p303

129 Robertson p308
130 GD112/15/370/74
131 GD112/16/13/1/6
132 Harrison JG Ben Lawers: A Report for RCAMS 2003 p134
133 Old Statistical Account p472
134 Robertson 1799 p206
135 Thomas Morer 1715 In Early Travellers in Scotland Vol II p266
136 MacInnes 2008
137 Grant p101
138 Robertson 1799 p61
139 Robertson p61 & 71
140 GD112/17/2 p30v
141 Black Book of Taymouth p352-363
142 GD112/17/5
143 Baron Baillie Court Book 1623. Black Book of Taymouth p364
144 Grant p129
145 Robertson 1799 p349-350
146 GD112/17/12 p88
147 Dugie MacInnes, personal communication
148 Grant p199
149 Robertson 1799 p352-4
150 Grant p201
151 GD50/15/1
152 GD112/10/1/4/75
153 Robertson 1799 p60

General background:
Bil A The Shieling 1600-1840: The Case of the Central Scottish Highlands. John Donald, Edinburgh 1990
Grant IF 1961 Highland Folk Ways. Routledge & Kegan Paul, London
Harrison JG Ben Lawers: A Report for RCAMS 2003
MacInnes D, Wood JS An archaeological field survey of Dalgirdy in Tullich. Assoc of Certified Field Archaeologists. Occasional Paper No. 68. 2004
MacInnes D Dalgirdy: an archaeological field survey in Glen Lochay. Assoc of Certified Field Archaeologists. Occasional Paper No. 76. 2008
Robertson J General View of the Agriculture in the County of Perth. Perth 1799 http://books.google.co.uk/books

Chapter 11 The Scottish Kirk
154 Reid H Reformation: the dangerous birth of the modern world. Saint Andrew Press, Edinburgh 2009

155 Smout p45 By kind permission of Professor TC Smout.
156 www.electricscotland.com/history/america/fur_trappers.htm
157 http://www.swrb.com/newslett/actualNLs/bod_ch03.htm
158 Gillies p265-6
159 Quoted in Gillies p265
160 Gillies p284
161 Quoted in Gillies p319
162 Old Parish Records, Perthshire 361/1-3 Box 415
163 Quoted in Gillies p 302
164 National Archives of Scotland CH2/1246/6. The earlier records
before 1771 are lost.
165 CH2/1246/6 P83
166 CH2/1246/6 p181
167 CH2/1246/6 P173
168 CH2/1246/6 P355
169 CH2/1246/6 P507
170 CII2/1246/6 P521
171 CH2/1246/6 P540
172 OPR Killin
173 CH2/1246/6 P546
174 CH2/1246/7 P16
175 CH2/1246/8 p190
176 CH2/1246/7 P59
177 CH2/1246/7 P201
178 CH2/1246/7 P217-8
179 CH2/1246/9 P23
180 CH2/1246/9 P24
181 CH2/1246/9 Killin Kirk Session Cash Book P41
182 McLachlan G Improving the common weal. Edinburgh University
Press, Edinburgh 1987
183 Perth & Kinross Council Archives
184 http://en.wikipedia.org/wiki/Disruption_of_1843
185 CH3/1242/2 p31-2
186 CH3/1242/2 p71

General background:
Gillies WA In Famed Breadalbane. The Munro Press, Perth 1938
Reid H Reformation: the dangerous birth of the modern world. Saint
Andrew Press, Edinburgh 2009

Chapter 12 The Earls of Breadalbane
187 Prophecy by the Lady of Lawers

188 Once again, see Gillies for a detailed history of the Earls of Breadalbane
189 Lord Macaulay The History of England Vol 4 Chap XVIII http://www.gutenberg.org
190 MacKy Memoirs of the Secret Service. Nichols & sons, London 1733 p119 http://archive.org/details/memoirssecretse00mackoog
191 Gillies p172
192 Gillies p182
193 GD112/17/11 p96
194 GD112/15/442/48
195 Black Book of Taymouth p367
196 Gillies p209
197 Gillies p212
198 Queen Victoria The Journal of our Life in the Highlands
199 Gillies p229
200 Hogarth C The Killin Branch Railway. Stirling District Libraries, 1993
201 http://www.rampantscotland.com/poetry/blpoems_crofter.htm
202 Quoted in Gillies p251

General background:
Gillies WA In Famed Breadalbane. The Munro Press, Perth 1938
http://www.electricscotland.com/history/nation/breadalbane.htm

Chapter 13 Law and order
203 GD50/124 No. 83
204 John of Fordun's Chronicle of the Scottish Nation 1380s.
205 A *Memorandum concerning the Highlands* 1746 GD112/47/1(5-9)
206*Basilikon Doron* His Majesties Instructions To His Dearest Sonne http://www.stoics.com/basilikon_doron.html
207 1587, c. 59, Acts of the Parliaments of Scotland, Record edition, vol. iii, p 461. Also Register of the Privy Council, vol. iv. pp. liii.-lv, 781 *et seq.*
208 Harrison JG Ben Lawers: A Report for RCAMS 2003 Chap 3. Also www.happywarrior.org.genealogy/Baronies.htm#Introduction
209 Black Book of Taymouth p 376
210 GD112/17
211 Harrison 2003 Chapter 3. GD112/17/5 f.1-5; GD112/17/9 f.72r
212 GD112/17/2 p97
213 GD112/17/2 p160v
214 GD112/17/4 p27
215 GD112/17/4 p96b
216 GD112/17/4 p179b
217 GD112/17/5

218 GD112/17/6 p150b
219 GD112/17/6 p410
220 GD112/17/8 Page 31
221 GD112/17/8 Pages 47-49
222 GD112/17/11 p113
223 GD112/17/11 p174
224 GD112/17/11 p225
225 GD112/17/11 p294
226 GD112/17/11 p303
227 GD112/17/11 p328
228 GD112/17/11 p367
230 GD112/17/11 p399
231 GD112/17/11 P 502-503
232 GD112/17/12 p50
234 GD112/17/12 p71
235 General Wade's Report on the Highlands 1724
http://www.electricscotland.com/webclans/geog/chapter8.htm
236 Wade 1724
237 Haldane ARB The drove roads of Scotland. David & Charles 1973 p112
238 Haldane p80
239 Old Statistical Account 1791
240 GD112/39/275/15
241 GD112/39/275/16
242 GD112/39/275/16
243 http://en.wikipedia.org/wiki/42nd_Regiment_of_Foot
244 E777/244 Report by John Campbell of Barcaldine, Factor upon the Annexed Estate of Perth, Of the Barony of Lix.
245 Gillies p204
246 GD112/52/214/1-2 & 4-5
247 GD112/15/475/38
248 GD112/16/7/3/8 Undated
249 http://hansard.millbanksystems.com/commons/1846/aug/07/flogging-in-the-army
General background:
Smout TC A History of the Scottish People 1560 - 1830. Fontana Press, London 1969

Chapter 14 Roads and bridges
250 Haldane ARB The drove roads of Scotland. David & Charles 1973

251 Montrose's Despatch to the King 1644 Quoted in Napier M The life and times of Montrose p299. Oliver & Boyd, Edinburgh 1840 http://books.google.co.uk/
252 Robertson 1799 p92 Grant 1961 Highland Folk Ways. p281-3
253 Black Book of Taymouth p67
254 GD112/17/8 p59
255 GD112/15/281/11
256 GD112/47/23/15
257 Memorandum by the 2nd Earl of Breadalbane GD112/47/1/5
258 www.pkht.org.uk
259 Penant T A Tour in Scotland 1769 http://archive.org/details/atourinscotland03penngoog
260 GD112/9/41 p203-4
261 GD112/9/5/10/2
262 GD112/15/221/4
263 GD112/15/212/4
264 GD112/15/221/2
265 GD112/15/221/5
266 GD112/15/221/7
267 The Statistical Account of Scotland 1791. Vol XII p480
268 GD112/12/5/2/16
269 First Edition Ordnance Survey 6 inches to 1 mile map www.nls.uk/maps
270 Perth & Kinross Council Archives CC1/2/40 p28 Minute Book of the Weem District Statute Labour Road Trustees. By kind permission of Perth & Kinross Council Archives.
271 Finlay Macaskill Personal communication
272 Thomas Telford 1757-1834 An Eskdale Tribute. LG Leuscher 2007
273 Commission for Highland Roads & Bridges, 5th Report, 1811, p 42-3
274 Perth & Kinross Council Archives CC1/2/1/4 Minutes of Perthshire Highway Commissioners
275 Haldane p81
276 Perth & Kinross Council Archives CC1/2/1/8, CC1/2/3/2 Perth Trustees under Roads & Bridges.
277 Perth & Kinross Council Archives CC1/2/3/2
278 Perth & Kinross Council Archives CC1/2/3/2
279 Perth & Kinross Council Archives PCC/R/1930 (Roads Dept) Breadalbane Scheme.

Chapter 15 Improvement
280 Herman A The Scottish Enlightenment: the Scots' invention of the modern world. Fourth Estate, London 2001

281 Harrison JG Ben Lawers: A Report for RCAMS 2003
282 Haldane ARB The drove roads of Scotland. David & Charles 1973
283 GD112/17/1/10/11, GD112/17/9
284 CH2/1246/8 Communion roll
285 GD112/74/888/14
286 GD112/17/8 p23
287 Robertson 1799 p31, 286
288 Finlay Macaskill Personal communication
289 Robertson 1799 p165
290 E777/244 Report by John Campbell of Barcaldine, Factor upon the Annexed Estate of Perth, Of the Barony of Lix.
291 GD112/16/13/1/9
292 Robertson 1799 p349
293 Robertson 1799 P172 & 174
294 RHP973/1 McArthur M (Ed) The survey of Lochtayside 1769. Publications of the Scottish History Society, Third Series, 27 (1936)
295 GD112/11/1/1/30
296 Robertson 1799 page xiii
297 Robertson 1799 p409
298 Rainsford-Hannay F Dry Stone Walling. Faber, London 1976
299 GD112/11/6/3/35
300 GD112/15/417/30 & 39
301 GD112/15/438/28; GD112/15/442/42a; GD112/15/442/48; GD112/15/442/49
302 Though the final abolition of runrig on the estate was not until 1789. GD112/11/2//1/21/2
303 GD112/14/13/8/1
304 Robertson 1799
305 Finlay Macaskill Personal communication
306 Robertson 1799 p324
307 GD112/9/54
308 Robertson 1799 p180-1
309 GD112/11/6/4/95
310 Robertson 1799 p304
311 Robertson 1799 p309
312 GD112/16/13/1/2; GD112/16/13/1/2; GD112/16/13/1/9
313 GD112/16/7/3/24
314 Robertson 1799 p410
315 GD112/16/4/2/22-3
316 GD112/14/13/2/41
317 GD112/11/6/4/59
318 GD112/16/13/4/9

319 Smout p323
320 GD112/10/2/5/16

General background:
Harrison JG Ben Lawers: A Report for RCAMS 2003
Robertson J General View of the Agriculture in the County of Perth.
Perth 1799 http://books.google.co.uk/books

Chapter 16 Dalgirdy People
321 Register of the Privy Seal of Scotland Vol 2 p.320 No.2152, Gillies
p360
322 GD112/17/2 p160v
323 Old Parish Register of baptisms, Killin
324 Glen Lochay Residents. Dugald MacInnes, Personal communication.
325 GD112/11/6/3/35
326 GD112/11/6/3/35
327 Known descendants of Donald McVean of Glen Lochay
http://www.bobbiev.net/mcvean3.html
328 GD112/11/6/2/31
329 GD112/11/5/1/65
330 GD112/11/6/2/31
331 Known descendants of Donald McVean of Glen Lochay. By Albert
McVean 1976. http://www.bobbiev.net/mcvean3.html
332 GD112/11/6/2/31
333 GD112/11/5/2/32
334 GD112/11/7/3/35
335 CH2/1246/6
336 GD112/16/7/5/25, OPR Killin
337 GD112/11/2/3/46
338 GD112/11/2/3/46
339 GD112/11/6/3/6
340 GD112/16/31
341 http://www.nls.uk/maps/joins/664.html
342 GD112/14/13/8
343 www.auchindrain.org.uk
344 GD112/11/6/2/31
345 GD112/11/6/4/56
346 GD112/11/1/4/26
347 GD112/11/1/4/26 GD112/11/3/4/37
348 GD112/16/13/7/6
349 GD112/16/13/7/3
350 GD112/11/5/2/32 GD112/11/6/2/31

351 GD112/11/5/2/5
352 GD112/11/5/2/32
353 GD112/11/6/3/6
354 GD112/11/7/3/35
355 GD112/16/7/3/8
356 GD112/16/4/2/16
357 GD112/11/5/2/5
358 GD112/11/6/4/56
359 Known descendants of Donald McVean
360 Known descendants of Donald McVean
361 GD112/14/13/2/41 & GD112/52/606/13
362 GD112/16/4/2/22
363 GD112/16/5/2/20X
364 GD112/16/4/4/5
365 GD112/16/4/4/8
366 1851 Census RD 360
367 1841 Census RD 360. First Edit 6 inch OS map www.nls.uk/maps
368 Information in this section is from successive Censuses: 1841-1851
Censuses RD 360, 1861-1891 Censuses RD 361
369 1888 Statutory Deaths 361/00 0008
370 1876 Statutory Deaths 361/00 0019
371 1871, '81 & '91 Censuses RD 361/ 1884-85 VR 113/31/351; 1883
Statutory Births 361/00 0024; 1868 Statutory Births 884/00 00501;
Personal communication, Mrs Carol Ferguson
372 1869 Ref: SC49/31/87 Perth Sheriff Court
373 1901 Census 361/00 006/00 0061; 1916 Statutory Deaths 361/00
00101; VR113/67/p629
374 Carol Ferguson personal communication.
375 http://www.risa.co.uk/sla/song.php?songid=22253
376 1939 Statutory Deaths 361/00 00031
377 Prentice daughter, personal communication 1984
378 Finlay Macaskill & Mrs Macaskill, personal communication
379 Finlay Macaskill & Mrs Macaskill, personal communication
380 John Sinclair, personal communication
381 Known descendants of Donald McVean
382 Gillies p197
383 Old Statistical Account, Parish of Killin
384 http://www.archive.org/stream/gaelicsongsofdun00maciuoft/
gaelicsongsofdun00maciuoft_djvu.txt
385 GD112/47/2/3

Chapter 17 Trade & Industry

386 Grant A Independence and Nationhood: Scotland 1306-1469 Edinburgh University Press 1984 p71
387 Black Book of Taymouth p365
388 MacInnes D Tullich Farm: an archeological field survey in Glen Lochay. ACFA Occas Paper No. 36 2003.
389 Atkinson J Late medieval bloomery sites: settlement and industry in the Scottish Highlands. In Govan S (Ed) Medieval or later rural settlement in Scotland: 10 years on. Historic Scotland, Edinburgh 2003 pp35-43 http://www.molrs.org.uk/downloads/confproc.pdf
390 Garnett T Observations on a tour through the Highlands and part of the Western Isles of Scotland. 1800
391 GD112/17/4 p107
392 GD112/17/2 p30
393 GD112/17/4 p109b
394 GD112/17/4 p203v
395 Johnstone A Wood JS Tirai, Glen Lochay, Killin. ACFA Occasional Paper No. 9. 1996
396 GD112/17/4 p32
397 Black Book of Taymouth p 390
398 Robertson J General View of the Agriculture in the County of Perth. Perth 1799 p396 http://books.google.co.uk/books
399 GD112/16/5/1/17
400 Penant T A Tour in Scotland 1769
401 Old Statistical Account Parish of Killin 1791
402 GD112/16/7/5/15
403 GD112/16/7/6/9
404 Old Statistical Account Parish of Killin 1791
405 GD112/16/7/5/15
406 Pennant A tour in Scotland 1769 p104
407 Harrison 2003, Gillies p187
408 Gillies p188
409 GD112/11/1/4/26
410 Gillean Ford, personal communication.
411 New Statistical Account, Parish of Killin
412 Hogarth C The Killin Branch Railway. Stirling District Libraries, 1993

Chapter 18 Medicine

413 Black Book of Taymouth p22
414 Origines Parochiales Scotiae Vol 2 p116
415 Geyer-Kordesch & MacDonald 1999 p79
416 CH2/1384/8 p77

417 GD112/18/12/7/14
418 1858 Medical Act (UK)
419 GD170/1030 By kind permission of Sir Roderick Campbell of Barcaldine
420 GD112/43/7
421 GD112/15/8/28
422 GD112/74/350/1-5
423 GD112/64/15
424 GD112/74/350/13-16
425 Paton H (Ed) The Clan Campbell From the *Campbell Collections* by Sir Duncan Campbell of Barcaldine & Glenure. Macniven & Wallace, Edinburgh. Volume I 1913 p243
426 GD112/15/401/73
427 GD112/15/409/87
428 Glasgow University Graduate Records
429 GD112/15/428/83
430 GD112/74/360
431 GD112/11/1/4/3
432 E788/11
433 E788/11
434 E788/11
435 First Statistical Account, Parish of Killin 1791
436 GD112/11/8/1/38 & GD/52/606/13
437 GD112/15/458
438 CH2/1246/6 P506
439 Gillies p292
440 Killin Kirk Session Minutes CH2/1246/8 p15
441 McLachlan G (Ed) Improving the common weal: aspects of Scottish Health Services 1900-1984 Edinburgh University Press, Edinburgh 1987 pp26, 167
442 1851 Census
443 GD112/11/10/11/6
444 Testament & Inventory: Dunblane Sheriff Court SC44/44/35
445 British Medical Journal 1890;2:1155
446 Glasgow Medical Journal 1942; 138:96
447 www.dewarcentenary.org.uk/wp
448 Dictionary of Scots language http://www.dsl.ac.uk/index.html
449 Dr Mairi McColl, personal communication.
450 Reports on the State of Certain Parishes in Scotland, 1627

General background:
Dingwall H A famous and flourishing society: the history of the Royal

College of Surgeons of Edinburgh 1505-2005. Edin Univ Press 2005.
Dingwall HM A History of Scottish Medicine. Edin Univ Press 2003
Geyer-Kordesch J, MacDonald F Physicians and surgeons in Glasgow.
Hambledon Press, London 1999

Chapter 19 Schools
451 Gillies p324
452 http://www.swrb.com/newslett/actualNLs/bod_ch03.htm
453 Reports on the State of Certain Parishes of Scotland
http://books.google.co.uk/books?id=gE0JAAAAQAAJ&pg=PA153&sourc
e=gbs_toc_r&cad=4#v=onepage&q&f=false
454 http://en.wikipedia.org/wiki/Education_Act_1646
455 Gillies p327
456 GD112/15/103/15
457 GD112/17/10
458 GD112/2/150/13
459 GD112/10/1/4/75
460 Old Statistical Account, Parish of Killin
461 Gillies p332
462 New Statistical Account, Parish of Killin
463 ED18/2341
464 Memorial to the Society for Propagating Christian Knowledge.
Quoted in Gillies p330
465 CH2/1384/1 p15
466 CH2/1384/1 p19
467 Old Statistical Account, Parish of Weem
468 GD112/11/6/4/82
469 HH38/19/23/2, 3 & 7
470 Stirling Council Archives PC3/17/6
471 In accordance with the Data Protection Act I have not identified
children after 1911.

General background:
http://en.wikipedia.org/wiki/History_of_education_in_Scotland

Chapter 20 The Re-invention of Scotland
472 Burns. A parcel of rogues in a nation
473 Disarming Act 1746
474 Pitt's speech in the House of Commons, 14 January 1766
475 Wolfe to Rickson, June 9, 1751, Banff, quoted in Beckles Wilson, *The Life and Letters of James Wolfe*. William Heineman: London 1909. p139
476 Sir John Sinclair Analysis of the Statistical Account of Scotland 1826

477 Disputed quote attributed to the Duke of Wellington.
http://en.wikiquote.org/wiki/Arthur_Wellesley,_1st_Duke_of_Wellington
478 Herman A The Scottish Enlightenment: The Scots' invention of the
modern world. Fourth Estate: London 2001
479 Fingal: an ancient epic poem. http://www.sacred-
texts.com/neu/ossian/oss24.htm
480 Blair H Critical Dissertation on the Poems of Ossian 1763.
481 Gillies p21
482 www.rhass.org.uk/information/thesocietysfoundation
483 http://gsi.org.uk/history/
484 http://www.walterscott.lib.ed.ac.uk/works/poetry/lady.html
485 Scott The Ballad of Lochinvar, in Marmion.
486 See Trevor-Roper Chap 7 for a more detailed account.
487 Cliff Hanley

General background
Trevor-Roper H The invention of Scotland: myth and history. Yale
University Press: New Haven 2008
Kelly S Scott-land: the man who invented a nation. Polygon; Edinburgh
2011

Chapter 21 The Hydro
General background:
Ford GM Tunnellers, Tango Dancers and Team Mates. Jamieson &
Munro 2000. Distributed by Stirling Council Library.
Hydro-Electric. Looking at Southern Hydro Group: a guide to HE power.
Payne PL The Hydro: A study of the development of the major hydro-
electric schemes undertaken by the North of Scotland Hydro-Electric
Board. Aberdeen University Press 1988
Scottish & Southern Energy. Power from the Glens.
Tay Western Catchments Area Project Final Report. Scottish Native
Woods; Perthshire 2010. http://www.scottishnativewoods.org.uk

Chapter 22 Rebuilding the Cottage
488 GD112/11/6/3/6
489 http://maps.nls.uk/counties/index.html#perthshire
490 GD112/16/4/6/50
491 Demolition Order issued by County Council of the County of Perth,
12 November 1965. Survey No. C77/12a

Chapter 23 Red deer, kites and salmon
492 www.deerstalkingscotland.co.uk

493 WH Murray Mountaineering in Scotland. Dent, London 1947. Reprinted Baton Wicks, London 1997. Scottish Mountaineering Club Hillwalkers' Guide The Munros.
494 George Mallory. Why climb Everest?
495 www.outdooraccess-scotland.com
496 http://argatyredkites.co.uk/index.php
497 The economic impact of wildlife tourism in Scotland. The Scottish Government. 2010
www.scotland.gov.uk/Resource/Doc/311951/0098489.pdf
498 The economic impact of game and coarse angling in Scotland. The Scottish Government 2004
www.scotland.gov.uk/Publications/2004/03/19079/34371
499 www.scotland.gov.uk/Topics/marine/Fish-Shellfish/FactsandFigures
500 http://www.snh.gov.uk/docs/B726802.pdf

Epilogue
501 Burns. Tam o' Shanter
502 Managing Change in Scotland's Landscapes Conference, Perth, 27 Nov 2012.
John Muir Trust www.johnmuirtrust.org
503 Scott. The Lady of the Lake